Colossians
Christos Singularis

by

Phillip A. Ross

ISBN: 978-0-9820385-5-0

Published by

Pilgrim Platform
149 E. Spring St., Marietta
Ohio, 45750
www.pilgrim-platform.org

Biblical quotations are from the *English Standard Version* (ESV), Standard Bible Society, unless otherwise cited. *AV* refers to the Authorized Version, also known as the King James Version. MKJB refers to the Modern King James Bible, Jay P. Green, Sovereign Grace Publishers, 1990.

Strong's refers to Strong's Exhaustive Concordance of the Bible, by James Strong, various editions.

Printed in the United States of America

For Eric & Cathey
in appreciation of their
patience and perseverance

TABLE OF CONTENTS

Foreword

The Apostle, Paul, wrote letters to seven churches in the Roman World. He discussed a wide range of issues, including theology, personal relations, family relations, being a church, living the Christian life and recognizing and avoiding heresy. He has made such a mark on Christianity that it is hard to conceive what Christendom would be without Paul's writings.

Our loving Father gave us a four dimensional view of Jesus and His teachings as a foundation for His new revelation in Christ. The Holy Spirit inspired Matthew, Mark, Luke and John to record the life and teachings of Jesus. God knew that we needed more than the Gospels, so the Holy Spirit anointed Peter, James, John, Jude, and especially Paul to help us build our lives on the foundation of Christ.

Colossians is often neglected, being overshadowed by the theology of Romans, the teaching of the body of Christ and the love chapter of Corinthians, the legal controversy in Galatians, the practicality in Ephesians, the perseverance in Philippians and the expectation of the Lord's Coming in Thessalonians. Nevertheless, the Holy Spirit had things to say to us through Paul's epistle to the Colossians. Paul wrote them this letter that in many ways carries the same message as his letters to the Galatians and Ephesians. He seeks to free the Colossians from the bondage to asceticism (Galatians) and instruct them in living the Christian life (Ephesians). He expected that the Colossians would share this letter with the Laodiceans, so they too could benefit from the truths of the Holy Spirit.

Paul did not plant the church, Epaphras, Paul's disciple did. Since, in a sense, Paul was their "grandfather" they had come to his attention. Colossae was situated in a fertile valley. It had an illustrious history as a center of trade, but by the First Century it had become overshadowed by the growth of Laodicea and Hierapolis. By the time of Paul's writing Colossae, while still a fertile area, had become just a waypoint on the trade route.

Antiochus IV Epiphanes, some three centuries before had banished thousands of Jews from Israel, transporting them into this region. In Paul's day there was a sizable population of ethnic Jews here. They had the spiritual foundation of the Old Testament Scriptures. It was both an hospitable place for preaching the Gospel of Christ the Messiah and a place where resistance to the teaching of the Messiah as a Suffering Servant and a sacrificial lamb could be anticipated. All in all, this was fertile ground not only for producing food, but also for the sprouting of the Gospel.

Rev. Ross highlights what Paul and the Holy Spirit wants them and us to know. Paul wrote to the Colossians, instructing them to pass the letter on to the Laodiceans. It is obvious that his words were intended to be shared, spread around. How could he have conceived that nearly two millennia later Paul's epistle would not only benefit the Colossians, the Laodiceans and perhaps other churches as well, but also believing Christians of this modern world.

Ross raises the standard of the uniqueness of Jesus the Christ, the Messiah in this work. He points out that this uniqueness, the "singularity of Christ," is enwrapped in the mind-boggling concept of the Trinity. Ross helps us struggle with this one-in-three and three-in-one contra human logic concept. Ross tells us, "The word singularity is defined as a trait marking a thing or person as distinct from others; a peculiarity."(pg. 12) Christ is unique in all the world, in all the cosmos.

Ross guides us through the reality that the Triune God was in the man, Jesus, "His wholeness became focused or localized in His humanity." (pg. 165) The uniqueness of God Himself a member of the Trinity of God the Father, God the Son and God the Holy Spirit (as children say) "squinching" Himself down to a human cell and growing in a virgin's womb, is beyond human reason. This is a singular occurrence that causes us to marvel.

This work again and again highlights the "singularity" of the Trinity. God is not only distinct in His unreasonable three-in-one person, but also in being fully man, Jesus acts in many ways distinct from humanity. He stands out as the distinct beacon of what humans should be—loving, compassionate, merciful, righteous, immovably standing on principle, declaring sin wherever He finds it, calling for absolute justice, and having no reluctance to call to account those in authority. The careful reader is astonished that the

Person who has compassion on the widow of Nain can cour-ageously describe the Pharisees as hypocrites. It is strange to us that Jesus can in one breath commend Peter for acknowledging Him as the Messiah, but in the next call Peter by the name of Satan. This is the singularity of Jesus the Son of God.

The Holy Spirit is a one-of-a-kind. He has ministered majestic-ally throughout human history and yet never points to Himself. He is fully God, and yet ever pointing away from Himself to the Father and to the Son. His ministries are unique. He is not the Father. He is not the Son. He is the Comforter, the Guide, the Teacher, and the Convincer. He is the power who conceived Jesus in the virgin's womb. He is the one who baptized Jesus in Himself at the river Jordan. This is the singularity of the Holy Spirit, the Spirit of God.

The Father is unique. He declares "I am the LORD, and there is none else, there is no God beside me: (Isaiah 45:5, KJV) He is unique because He created all things (except Himself) from noth-ing. He preexisted matter, time and space. He spoke Adam into being and created Eve. He revealed Himself to Noah and Moses. He led the Children of Israel out of bondage and through the wilder-ness. He manifested His shekinah glory in the Tabernacle. This is the singularity of God the Father.

Each Person of the Trinity is unique, distinctive, peculiar, and yet they are not unique to one another—they are One. Jesus was in the creation as was the Holy Spirit. The Father was in the son of man as was the Holy Spirit. The Son and the Father participated when the Holy Spirit communicated His messages and warnings to the prophets, They were there in the coming of the Holy Spirit at Pentecost, and are present as He guides people today to surrender to Christ and receive the blessing of salvation and eternal life.

In this context of the Singularity of the Trinity, Ross digs into Colossians. He excavates gems in the Greek exposing them to our minds. He opens up this Epistle, placing the truths Paul taught the Colossians into our hands. These lessons Ross highlights for us and shows us how we need to listen to Paul's instructions to Colossae. Further, he points out how we need to embrace these teachings and inculcate them into our own lives.

Ted Bradshaw, B.A., M.Div.
Shoreline, Washington
May 12, 2010

INTRODUCTION

The aloneness of the gospel has been a topic of interest and confusion for eons. It was Martin Luther (1483-1546) who coined the term "grace alone" in response to the arguments by a corrupt church that relied upon non-biblical sources to define the biblical gospel. Luther's concern was to return to the original biblical sources in order to recover the original biblical teachings.

The Reformers proclaimed five *Solas*: *Sola Scriptura* (Scripture Alone), *Solus Christus* (Christ Alone), *Sola Gratia* (Grace Alone), *Sola Fide* (Faith Alone) and *Soli Deo Gloria* (God's Glory Alone). The enemies of the Gospel have twisted these *solas* every which way, and have confused many people. For example, the emphasis upon *sola scriptura* does not mean that other books are off limits. And yet *solus Christus* (Christ alone) does mean that other mediators between man and God are not simply off limits, but that no other mediators actually exist. Each *sola* must be understood individually and holistically, within the context of Scripture.

SINGULARITY

Singularities, popularized by Ray Kurzweil[1] are all the rage. In mathematics a singularity is defined as "a point at which the derivative does not exist for a given function but every neighborhood of which contains points for which the derivative exists." Got it? It is the point at which math gets quirky, and normal analysis fails. It is the point on a graph which must exist mathematically, but cannot itself be known, defined or computed. It can only be inferred from neighboring points.

If it sounds confusing, it is because it is. But is it important? Yes

---

1 http://singularity.com; *The Singularity Is Near: When Humans Transcend Biology*, Ken Kurzweil, Viking Adult, 2005.

and no, depending on what you believe about the creation of the universe and how important you think creation is for understanding the world today. Another dictionary defines singularity as "a point of infinite density and infinitesimal volume, at which the descriptions of space and time become abnormal according to the theory of General Relativity. According to the big bang theory, a gravitational singularity existed at the beginning of the universe." According to the Theory of Evolution, everything came from a singularity at the beginning of time, which means that for the Theory of Evolution a singularity takes the place of God regarding the creation of the universe in the sense that this singularity is the source of the universe in the same way that for Christians God is the source of the universe.

The insight or speculation that a singularity may be Godlike comes from the doctrine of the Trinity, which posits that God is One yet Three. God holds unity and particularity together without damaging or diminishing either. It's not a hard-and-fast comparison, nor a fully-formed theory. It's just an idea that may be worth exploring. And that is some of what I will do in these pages.

In this study of Colossians I have taken the doctrine of the Trinity seriously and applied it broadly. This means that I have assumed it to be true of God, and therefore true of people because we are created in the image of God (Genesis 1:26). We are not trinitarian in the same way that God is, but in a similar way, in the way that the image of a thing is not identical to the thing, but is recognizably similar. God's trinitarian character is the "image" in which He created us because God's trinitarian character is the way that He has revealed Himself to us. It is the "image" of Him that we are to "see" in Scripture. And occasionally, the idea of God as singularity seems to find expression in Scripture.

The assumption of the immediate reality of the Trinity adds a depth and texture to the biblical text that is not available apart from it. Why? Because if God's character is trinitarian, then the characters of the Father, the Son and the Holy Spirit are also trinitarian. There is both unity and multiplicity, individuality and corporality, in the Godhead and in reality because of the divine role that God plays in reality. The God of Scripture is both one and three at the same time without losing any meaning or uniqueness. God is also Son and Spirit. The Son is also Father and Spirit. The Spirit is also Father and Son. God's identity is, then, both individual and corporate at the same time and without any loss of identity regarding the integrity of His wholeness or the individuals involved.

Many people find that the idea of the Trinity is impossible to understand or just a figment of imagination. Yet, many of those same people readily believe in black holes, even though there is no actual evidence for their existence. Black holes cannot be seen, they're black—dark. They are constructs of calculation or mathematical entities. They exist by implication regarding the surrounding space and neighboring objects. And yet scientists and astronomers swear that they are real.

Is it such a stretch to compare the reality and existence of God to the reality and existence of a singularity or black hole? Obviously, I don't think so. There are some interesting similarities, though the idea of such similarities does not suggest a plurality of Gods apart from the Trinity. No, the Trinity is absolutely unique and is probably related to the three dimensionality of space (length, width, height) and time (past, present future). Nor can it be denied or ignored that the Trinity is a unity of Persons, not forces, conditions or entities.

The central characteristic of a singularity that is Godlike is its simultaneous oneness and manyness, its simplicity as a single entity and its complexity as the locus of several entities. Like the Godhead, a singularity is both simple and complex, both one and many. I am not going beyond this most basic comparison. It is simply a thought, not a full-blown thesis. But it's interesting, and it may be useful for the reconsideration of the reality of God by mathematicians and scientists.

This book, however, is not about black holes or singularities. It is about Colossians. It is about God the Father, God the Son and God the Spirit. It doesn't hijack Colossians to justify the idea of God as a singularity. Rather, it suggests the complexity of God's singularity, the *Solas Christos Singularis* of God, as a way to understand the depth and texture of Paul's letter. This book is theology, not science. And yet, Scripture does suggest that theology and science are intimately related in that God is central to the world and everything in it.

PRESUPPOSITIONAL TRINITARIANISM

The Trinity is a difficult concept. I am applying the perspective that I believe the Bible teaches, which I am calling presuppositional trinitarianism, to all reality. So, while God's ultimate being as the

Trinity is absolutely unique, all of reality shares the characteristics of God's trinitarian being—not perfectly, but through a glass darkly. That means that we are trinitarian, and that everything in this world is trinitarian because everything issues out of God. The family relationship in the Trinity provides a kind of common DNA structure to everything that God has created.

The Trinity is absolutely unique to Christianity, and is why Christianity is the only true religion. The Trinity hasn't gotten much attention since the early church fathers mangled it in the press of Greek philosophy. The truth is that the Bible stands in opposition to Greek (and all other man-made) philosophies or categories of thought. This work is an effort to express what the Bible teaches in a way that stands apart from the categories of Greek thought, while being faithful to the trinitarian categories of Scripture. The Trinity is everywhere in Scripture.

Presuppositional trinitarianism is simply a matter of presupposing the reality and veracity of the Trinity as the foundation of all reality as a matter of faith. I am trying to read the book of nature and the Bible faithfully, by assuming the reality of the Trinity. I'm trying to read Scripture with the eyes of faithfulness to the Trinity.

This is not a novel approach, but is a very ancient approach that has been obscured by the overlays of Greek philosophy by the early church fathers. I have used this approach in my treatment of Corinthians, as well, and am assuming some familiarity with that work.[2] A few other writers are working in the same vein—Peter Leithart, Ralph Smith and R.J. Rushdoony's work, *The One And The Many: Studies In The Philosophy Of Order And Ultimacy* (Ross House Books, second edition, 2009).

COMPLETED EDITION

The publication of this book began early in the Twenty-First Century when Dr. Douglas Vickers[3] suggested that I publish my work with Wipf & Stock, one of the early publish-on-demand publishers that he had used. I was surprised and encouraged by his suggestion, but skeptical. So, I decided to print a small book to see how it went. That book was a study of Colossians titled *Nothing But*

---

2   *Arsy Varsy—Reclaiming the Gospel in First Corinthians* and *Varsy Arsy—Proclaiming the Gospel in Second Corinthians*, by Phillip A. Ross, Pilgrim Platform, Marietta, Ohio, 2008.
3   Professor Emeritus of Economics, University of Massachusetts, Amherst (1990s), has held positions with universities in the United States and Australia and has served with the National Bank of Australasia and Vauxhall Motors Ltd.

Christ—Another Look at Colossians (Wipf & Stock, Eugene, Oregon, 2001). My intention was only to see if they would actually publish me, and evaluate the quality of the product. They did, and it was fine. So, I began preparing other manuscripts for them. I have since moved on. The present volume is a reworking of that manuscript and the completion of the study of Colossians.

Though some scholars doubt that Paul wrote this letter, I don't. Some scholars doubt everything. That's what they are paid to do. Christians need to be very careful with scholarship. Too many people trust the scholars over the Bible, and that's a serious mistake. It's not that scholarship is bad, only that too much of it is godless.

Paul was combating error—again. People forget that Paul was always correcting people—Christians! If it weren't for people getting things wrong, Paul may not have written any letters. But as it was, the enemies of the gospel were hard at work in the early churches, twisting God's Word every which way they could. They still are. So, Paul wrote to straighten them out. Thank God he did.

My intention here has not been to read everything written on Colossians and then try to add something new or to make some unique point. This is not a scholarly book. It's an expanded sermon series that is intended to make the issues, concerns and truths of Paul's letter to the Colossians come to life, God willing.

Special thanks to those who have provided their comments, questions, perspectives and edits to this work: Paul Williams, Eric Brown, Elizabeth Johnson and Ted Bradshaw.

I am thankful for my wife, Stephanie, who undergirds my work, and my children, young men now, who have found their legs in Christ. All of my work is for them. I pray that they will find it increasingly helpful as they mature in Christ. And, as I have said before, I'm not asking them or anyone else to agree with me. Lord knows, I have my shortcomings and foibles. But what I am asking is that people engage my work. My hope is not to get everything right, though I value the effort. Rather, my hope is that people will think deeply about the gospel and engage it seriously.

My intention is to model ordinary faithfulness and to demonstrate how Scripture provides various corrections for ordinary Christians in the midst of our fallen world, and how faithfulness to the only, real, trinitarian God in Jesus Christ through the Holy Spirit impacts the faithful reading of Scripture. If Christians do not bring faithfulness in the trinitarian God to their reading of Scripture, they will miss the message of the trinitarian God, "for we walk by faith, not by sight" (2 Corinthians 5:7).

Christians are broken and renewed people. The acknowledgment and confession of our brokenness is essential to the process of renewal. And renewal is not possible apart from faith in Christ. Christians are people who have learned from their mistakes. I'm simply trying to help with that learning process by showing how relevant Scripture is to our contemporary situation.

Phillip A. Ross
Marietta, Ohio
April 2010

1

HEAVEN'S HOPE

*Paul, an apostle of Christ Jesus by the will of God, and
Timothy our brother, To the saints and faithful brothers in
Christ at Colossae: Grace to you and peace from God our
Father. We always thank God, the Father of our Lord Jesus
Christ, when we pray for you, since we heard of your faith
in Christ Jesus and of the love that you have for all the
saints, because of the hope laid up for you in heaven. Of this
you have heard before in the word of the truth, the gospel,
which has come to you, as indeed in the whole world it is
bearing fruit and growing—as it also does among you,
since the day you heard it and understood the grace of God
in truth, just as you learned it from Epaphras our beloved
fellow servant. He is a faithful minister of Christ on your
behalf and has made known to us your love in the Spirit.*
—Colossians 1:1-8 (ESV)

Caught between Greek culture and Jewish philosophy, the
church at Colossae was being pulled away from Christ by the
false teaching that spirits required veneration through asceticism and rituals involving food and special celebrations. Paul wrote
to teach them that salvation is found only in Christ. The Colossian
church had been started by Epaphras, who had ministered to Paul
while he was in prison at Rome. There Epaphras told Paul about a
strange teaching that threatened the health of the churches in the
Lycus Valley (Colossae).

We can benefit from Paul's teaching today because the church in
our day is also being pulled off course in many directions by many
forces, including asceticism, ritualism, and various errors of contemporary worship that have turned worship into performance and spectacle aimed, not at God, but at attracting unbelievers by appealing to

a false spirituality, much as it was in Paul's day. In fact, the church today is in a state of utter disarray and gospel confusion. Too many Christians and their churches have drifted away from the historic teachings of Christianity in a quest for novelty and an unbiblical spirituality. Unfortunately, this is not anything new, it has been going on for a very long time.

The contemporary problem is the almost complete disregard of theology by too many Christians and the failure to study the Bible, much less the historic Christian literature, and the lessons that are available to us. Christians have struggled with similar concerns from the very beginning of the church and we can learn from them. George Santayana has correctly observed that as long as people fail to learn from history, they are doomed to repeat it. But of all people, Christians should know better because God has provided Scripture to correct this particular error.

Apart from Christ, people can only run in the same ruts, and that is precisely the problem—people have abandoned God. People disregard God and His Bible. This is a problem that has always plagued God's people, Old Testament to New. The Old Testament prophets railed about it, but were unsuccessful at turning people back to the Lord apart from God Himself acting in history. And God's action usually brought painful lessons taught through various calamities, as evidenced in the various destructions of Jerusalem.[4]

Paul began by identifying himself as the author of this letter, and as an apostle of the Lord "by the will of God" (v. 1), according to his own testimony. Paul was converted and led, not by his own decision or will, but by the will of God. In fact, Paul had been converted against his own rebellious will. Prior to his Damascus Road conversion Paul had no desire to be a Christian. He had been adamantly opposed to Christ and at that time was fully committed to working against Christ. Yet the Lord converted him in a most dramatic way—contrary to Paul's own best judgment at the time. Indeed, Paul was an apostle *by the will of God*. This was a very poignant phrase for him to use.

---

4   The Temple was built in 970 – 930 B.C. Israel (the Ten Tribes) was crushed by the Assyrians in 722 – 720 B.C. during Isiah's time. Judah was destroyed by the Babylonians in 586 B.C. when they sacked the city, during Jeremiah's time. Construction of a new temple began in 537 B.C. After a hiatus, work resumed 520 B.C., with completion occurring in 516 B.C. and dedication in 515 B.C. Five centuries later, this Second Temple was renovated by Herod the Great in about 20 B.C., and was known as Herod's Temple. It was destroyed by the Romans in 70 A.D.

Paul mentioned Timothy as his brother in the faith. Though Paul had written the letter, it was sent (signed) by both Paul and Timothy. No doubt, Timothy must have had a role at Colossae. Otherwise Paul would not have mentioned him. Timothy's mention was a kind of endorsement. The point was that Paul and Timothy were working for the same cause or purpose.

Colossae was only ten miles from Laodicea and much of its history can be associated with Laodicea. Whether Colossae was affected by the lukewarm faith of the Laodiceans is unclear. But because the theology that Paul countered at Colossae was so aberrant, it is difficult to think that it wasn't caught up in the same or a similar spiritual disease that had plagued Laodicea. This kind of contagion is quite understandable. We observe in our own time that churches that have drastically changed their theological perspective today end up being lukewarm at best. Consider the Unitarian Controversy of the 1800s in New England or the decimation of Calvinism in most of the early American denominations.[5]

Paul wrote "to the saints and faithful brothers in Christ at Colossae" (v. 2). So, he must have believed that there were faithful Christians there. And of course, the Lord had not given up on neighboring Laodicea either. Even at the height of the Laodicean apostasy the Lord warned them, "As many as I love, I rebuke and chasten; therefore be zealous and repent" (Revelation 3:19). The church at Colossae was surely redeemable in spite of the problems that troubled the church there. Paul's mention of their faith (Colossians 1:4, 2:5) doesn't mean that they were all faithful. Many of them were faithful, but some weren't. Regardless, he wrote to address their problems.

Today Laodicea represents the epitome of faithlessness because of the Lord's threat to spit them out. Nonetheless, we should not neglect God's hope for repentance among such people. If God could so hope, then our hope should follow suit.[6] The Lord's purpose is always to redeem His people, and He will not fail to do so. Thus, it would behoove us to hope for the power of redemption in Christ.

---

5   See, for instance, *The Democratization of American Christianity*, Nathan Hatch, Yale University Press, 1989. Also see the various essays on Christian history at www.pilgrim-platform.org/history.htm.

6   Does God hope? Yes, but not like we usually do. God's hope is not tentative, but certain. He knows what will happen, and fully expects and anticipates it. This is how the hope of faithfulness works. God is faithful, and expects the fulfillment of His will without doubt about whether it will come to fruition. God's hope is certain, as ours should be.

Indeed, that hope is the engine of redemption because it fills God's people with the certainty and trustfulness of His promises.

Paul's usual greeting was then given in the name of God the Father and Christ the Son, with an emphasis that he and Timothy and the wider church as well were engaged in prayer and service for them. Paul's endorsement of Timothy was intended to solidify the fact that he and Timothy were on the same team. Notice that he told them that he was praying for them. He will go on to tell them exactly what he was praying for. That way, when it happened, they would rightly conclude that his prayers had been answered.

ENCOURAGING THE SAINTS

Paul wrote in order to address the problems in the church that had been reported to him. Paul never visited Colossae, but wrote to them on the basis of what he knew to be true among God's people elsewhere. Many churches faced similar problems because the Jews were adamant about putting an end to Christianity. Because Paul knew about the problems in the Colossian church, it is significant that he began his letter with encouragement. Those who had been holding the line against the apostasy were undoubtedly weary of the struggle. So, Paul bolstered them with encouragement, hoping that others who read his letter would also lend their encouragement to the embattled saints at Colossae.

We can all learn from Paul's method of encouragement. The way he went about encouraging the Colossians may surprise us. He didn't prop up their self-esteem by telling them how great they were. Rather, by telling them that he had boasted of their faithfulness to others he challenged them to meet and maintain the honor and quality of his boast. Paul used this method elsewhere (2 Corinthians 1:14) and must have found it useful.

Paul did not encourage the saints to bask in their accomplishments, or to hold on to any positions they had taken up against those who held to false doctrines. He simply bypassed their accomplishments, their struggles and any positions they held in opposition to the false apostles in their midst. Rather, Paul challenged them to live up to his boast, his expectations. Paul was aware that there had been false teaching in their midst, yet he didn't begin by chastising them for it. Rather, he encouraged them to rise above it by announcing his pleasure in the testimony of their faithfulness. He knew that the saints would rise above it because Christ would complete in them what He had begun. Here is a model for positive encouragement that we would be well served to learn.

Contrary to popular teaching in our schools and universities today, the difficulty with rewarding people's behavior by stroking their self-esteem is that the encouragement of self-esteem teaches people to be pleased with what they have already accomplished. Satisfaction with what had already been done is encouraged, and the challenge to drive for greater success is discouraged because the reward (a sense of self-satisfaction) is given for what has already been accomplished. Stroking self-esteem fuels the fires of pride and self-confidence. Not only does it blunt the challenge of ongoing self-improvement, but it easily leads to idolatry.

That was not Paul's method. Paul did not stroke their self-esteem. Rather, he encouraged the aspirations of his readers to excel by revealing his personal pleasure in the progress of their character development, not in their achievement. He attributed to them an excellence that they had yet to attain, and showed them his confidence that they would indeed accomplish everything he expected. Paul's encouragement did not allow them to rest on their laurels, but drew them forward to further achievement. When people you admire praise you on the development of your character and confidently boast that you will continue to meet their highest expectations, your admiration of them encourages you to live up to their expectations. The expectations that people we admire have for us fuel our own hope, and hope draws us forward into a better future.

Obviously, if their boast about you is too far fetched or too much out of character it will backfire. They have to know you well. And if their assessment of you is realistic, you will be more likely to trust their expectations for you.

The art of providing such encouragement is to allow your boast to lead your friend's character development but not be out of reach. To give the encouragement maximum effectiveness your boasting should center upon character qualities, not mere accomplishments. The danger of boasting about accomplishments is that the encouragement ends with its accomplishment. For instance, if I boast that you can high-jump six feet, once you jump it that encouragement is finished. But if I boast that you are a disciplined high jumper, my encouragement can serve for a lifetime.

PRAY FOR THEM

Paul spoke not only of the faithfulness of the Colossians, he told them that he had been praying for them. Prayer is an awesome weapon in God's arsenal. But to be properly used we must tell the people we are praying for that we are praying for them, and specifically what we are praying for. We need to tell people that we are praying for them in order to encourage them to look for the results of the prayer, in order to show them how it works.

By letting people know of your prayers for them you are testifying both to your own faithfulness and to the power of prayer. By encouraging them to look for the results of your prayers, you are inviting them to find proof of the reality of Christianity in their own experience. The proof of Christianity is really only found in one's own life. Such proof is the incontestable experience of God's work in one's own personal conversion. It is difficult to deny the Lord when you experience Him working in your own life.

Paul was very specific in both his prayers and his boast. The boast, he said, was not simply his own, but he added his voice to the reports of their faithfulness that he heard about. The boast was not simply one man's opinion, but was common knowledge in the community of faith, in part because of Paul's boasting. The Colossians were not simply encouraged to live up to Paul's expectations, but to the expectations of the greater faith community as well. By boasting about them Paul was holding them up to the faithful expectations of the larger faith community.

A lot of people are uncomfortable with the idea that others have expectations about them, but it's quite normal. Everyone has expectations about all kinds of things. It's not only *not* a bad thing, but it's unavoidable. Paul was employing the proper use of peer pressure by using it in the service of Jesus Christ. The goads of social conformity are powerful social forces that cannot be eliminated, denied or escaped. Americans tend to disavow the forces of social conformity by embracing the doctrine of rugged individualism. We are Americans and don't have to conform to anyone's standards, or so we think.

And yet, historically Americans are among the most socially conforming people in the world. We are the dupes of mass advertising, believing that we are unaffected by it, when in reality we are obsessed by the socially conformed appetites that are dictated by the covetous trends and profiteering of fashion and style. Americans, and the majority of the world at this point in history, are obsessed with fashion, style and novelty. Why? Because people don't know who they really are so they turn to these things to forge their identities. We live in the midst of an identity crisis evidenced by the current passion for personal authenticity and identity among the young.

Again Paul's method was not to honor social expectations by limiting his appeal to simple outward conformity. Rather, Paul first gave due honor and thanks to Jesus Christ because the expectations of faithfulness belong to Him. Paul did not encourage faithfulness for the sake of fitting into some kind of religious society, but for the sake of pleasing Jesus Christ. Jesus Christ expects the faithfulness of His people, and is pleased by it.

It is important to understand that in today's world Christ's expectations are not the same as those of the church. Churches should have the same expectations as the Lord, but too often don't. Unfortunately, the church's expectations often run counter to those of Christ! Paul did not simply call people to be like their Christian peers. Unfortunately, other Christians provide poor role models. Again, it shouldn't be that way, but too often it is. It was then and it is now. So, Paul called them to satisfy the expectations of Christ's faithfulness, biblical faithfulness, to stand apart and alone when necessary, apart even from those who claim Jesus Christ when their claims are not in line with His teaching.

Because Paul was mature in the faith, he also called Christians to use him as a role model, to imitate his behavior. "I urge you, then, be imitators of me" (1 Corinthians 4:16). "Be imitators of me, as I am of Christ" (1 Corinthians 11:1). Faithfulness involves the imitation of the real thing. "Therefore be imitators of God, as beloved children" (Ephesians 5:1). "Brothers, join in imitating me, and keep your eyes on those who walk according to the example you have in us" (Philippians 3:17).

One of the best ways that people learn is by imitation. Whether in music, sports or math, there is nothing more helpful than watch- ing an expert do it right. If a picture is worth a thousand words, a video is worth a million. So, having an expert who can show you the right way and work with you to learn it is simply priceless.

CONFORMITY

Social expectations and conformity are weapons of spiritual and cultural development. And where Christ does not dominate them Satan reeks havoc with them. Paul suggests that the faith that is already in the Colossians, the faith that he had heard about and encouraged, had its origin, not in social conformity, but in Heaven, in God's decree, in Christ. Paul harnessed the forces of social psychology to serve the purposes of Christ. He was not opposed to the power of peer pressure, social conformity, or the encouragement and imposition of personal and social expectations on others, but insisted that they must serve God, not man.

In days gone by churches used social conformity to help their members bond to the church community. We can see remnants of this practice in the clothing styles of Roman Catholic priests and nuns, and in Mennonite and Amish communities. It fact, this kind of conformity is still in use today, but it is not led by faithful churches. People, particularly children and youth, even young adults, continue to be driven to find personal identity through clothing styles. But today the church isn't dictating the styles, Wall Street is. The world of fashion is dominated by the most worldly people imaginable—and worse!

But Paul was not simply talking about clothes, style or fashion, but about character and morality, about belief and behavior. Social expectations about character and morality are real forces. Unfortunately, the "ins" and the "outs" have reversed places over the past hundred years or so. No area demonstrates this better than sexual mores. A hundred years ago sex was a taboo topic. We can argue the merits of our Elizabethan sexual heritage, but if marriage and families are a measure of value in this area, all measurements point to the social degradation of marriage and families. Where sexual activity outside of marriage used to be forbidden and socially discouraged, it is now acceptable, even popular, to be sexually active outside of marriage. Today, virginity and prudence will earn a scarlet letter. And the floozies will get a spot on Oprah.

Indeed, the forces of social conformity and expectation produce real effects in the world. And if they do not serve Christ, they will serve Satan. No one can escape the social pressures of conformity and expectation. They are part of our trinitarian character as human beings. Jesus called people *sheep* because these characteristics of conformity are common to everyone. We cannot escape them.

Consequently, if we do not dedicate them to Christ, if we do not use the forces of social conformity and expectation intentionally in service to Jesus Christ, they will destroy us. They will tear the church apart. And they will tear society apart, as they are presently doing.

But the issue is not whether or not to use them. They are in use already. As human beings, we cannot do otherwise than use them. We are always affected by what other people think, say and do because we are social beings. The social aspects of our being reflect the fact that we are created in God's trinitarian image. Our individual identities are intrinsically caught up in the identities of other people (social groups like families, friends, churches, neighborhoods, etc.) because we are created in the trinitarian image of God.

This is only to say that we are influenced by and adaptable to our environment, to our social conditions. The fact of this influence and adaptability is both our strength and our weakness as a species. When we are rightly influenced and adapted, we are strong, and when we are wrongly influenced and adapted, we are weak. The issue not *whether* to use the forces of social conformity and imitation, but *how* to best use them to Christ's advantage.

Paul was harnessing the forces of influence, encouragement and social conformity for Christ. We must see our peers as saints in the Lord, as people who are sanctified, set apart, for the Lord. We must be conformed to Christ's expectations, and expect other Christians to do the same—not to meet our standards, but to meet God's standards in Scripture in the light of Jesus Christ. We must impose the expectations of maturity and sanctification in Christ upon other Christians, and shame the world out of its childish and adolescent morality, its foolish attraction to Satan's novelties (Jeremiah 13:26, 17:13; Titus 2:8; Colossians 2:15; 1 Peter 3:16; etc).

The effort to inoculate ourselves and our children against the effectiveness of the forces of social conformity is futile. They are effective forces precisely because they produce an effect, because they work! The momentum of worldly conformity in the Twenty-First Century threatens to sweep away everything in its wake. Such forces play upon human nature itself, and they cannot be stripped of their effectiveness without changing human nature. And only God can change human nature!

So, we must commit ourselves to the dedicated use of social conformity to God's purposes. We must not abandon the forces of encouragement and discouragement, of peer pressure and social conformity to the values and aesthetics of Scripture, but engage them in the service of the gospel. We must not allow the world to use them to tear Christ's church apart by contaminating us and our churches with the corrosive acids of worldliness.

HOPE

Hope is the key to spiritual encouragement. Hope is not only the expectation of something good, but hope requires that the expectation be realistic. If what you hope for is impossible to achieve or to receive, your hope is not hope at all but a mere pipe dream, a figment of your imagination. To be real hope, the object of hope must be realizable, it must be possible. Hope for the impossible is not hope at all, but an idle dream, an imaginary phantasm.

Hope is the engine of faithfulness throughout the Scriptures. Peter said that Christians must always be ready to explain their hope to anyone who asks about it. Christian hope opposes the distress that people have about the end times. Christian hope is not the desire to escape the pain and difficulties of the tribulation. Christians are not to hope for the destruction of the world, nor to hope to escape the destruction of the world. Christianity is not about the destruction of the world. It's about redemption and renewal, not destruction. Our hope is that God's will for Christ will someday be a common human hope. Christian hope is always optimistic. Christianity is not a tragedy but a comedy,[7] not depressing but uplifting.

The ideas of truth, trust, faith and hope are practically interchangeable in the New Testament. They all involve a confident expectation of a positive and beneficial outcome. Hope is an attitude. Hope is a position to hold, and a posture to assume, especially in the face of difficulties. It's easy to hope when the sun is shinning, but it is essential to hope when the rain comes down and the waters come up. We are to practice in the sun so we can perform in the rain.

Paul told the Colossians that their hope had already been laid up in Heaven. The hope that they needed, the hope that Christ provides is a treasure that was already theirs. It was not a distant dream, but was theirs at that very moment by the power of Christ. Hope in Christ is a sure thing because God has guaranteed it.

So, how do we get hope? While Heaven is the ultimate source of genuine hope, its proximate source is "the word of the truth, the gospel" (v. 5). The power of the hope of Christ is the Word of God, the truth of God's Word, the truth of the gospel of Jesus Christ. We

---

7   See: *Deep Comedy: Trinity, Tragedy, & Hope In Western Literature*, by Peter J. Leithart, Canon Press, Moscow, Idaho 2006.

get it through exposure to it. We "catch" it. Paul also said that "faith comes by hearing, and hearing by the word of God" (Romans 10:17). The power and effectiveness of the Holy Spirit is a function of God's Word. The gospel is not contained in the words of Scripture like a bug in a box. Rather, God's Word is the gospel, like a bug with a bite. To "get it" at all is to get bitten, to get infected by the Holy Spirit, with the hope of Jesus Christ.

Paul went on to describe the dimensions of Christ's power and effectiveness. He said that faith is assured because Christ's presence and power are already working in the world to change hearts and minds. God's purpose is not merely to proclaim the gospel of Christ to the whole world, but to actually bring forth the fruit of repentance among believers, and to ultimately convert the whole earth.[8]

Paul testified to the power of the gospel because he had seen God's fruit. Paul had seen many people converted, himself included. He knew the power of God's will because he had been broken by it. He was himself the fruit of conversion and repentance. Not only would the Holy Roman Empire crumble before the forces of Jesus Christ, but the Old Testament system of sacrifices and priestly atonement would give way to Christ. What had stood for thousands of years would crumble to dust at the feet of Christ.

In essence Paul said, *This thing is big! Bigger than your hopes and dreams! Bigger than Rome! Bigger than Jerusalem! God will have His way. People will either be part of God's salvation in Christ, or they will be crushed beneath it. God is on the move and is already present in your lives!*

In addition, Paul said that Epaphras had been God's true representative among them. Paul described him as a "dear fellow servant and a faithful minister of Christ" (v. 3). Paul endorsed Epaphras in order to differentiate between the true and the false teaching that had plagued Colossae.

The Colossian church had been infected with a Greek-influenced form of Jewish philosophy that taught that Christians were still vulnerable to various Pagan forces. Some people thought that those spirits needed to be placated through the practice of devotion,

---

8 "God's history is universal history. He is growing all humanity into a Bride for His Son. (Of course, sad to say, some individuals within humanity—those who won't repent—are pruned away from this glorious destiny.)" *Crisis, Opportunity and the Christian Future*, James B. Jordan, Anathasius Press, Monore, Louisianna, 1994, 1998. 2004.

austerity or holiday celebrations (Colossians 2:16). The Jewish influence kept them tied to Old Testament traditions that had been fulfilled or changed by Christ. Paul endeavored to help them understand that Christ had done it all, that they needed nothing but Christ alone, that their acceptance of Christ was a function of their union with Christ.

It was not enough that Epaphras was God's representative who spoke the truth of the gospel. The false teachers had made the same claim. Saying that you speak on behalf of God is too easy. Counterfeit prophets had already gained a foothold in Colossae. No doubt, there were people in Colossae who said that God was speaking through them. What made the difference in Epaphras' case was the love of Christ.

It wasn't simply that Epaphras claimed to love the people of Colossae. Rather, Epaphras shared with Paul, not *his* love for them (though he surely loved them), but *their* love for the Lord. It wasn't their love for one another that held them together. It was Christ's love for them all, and their love for Christ that held them in communion. What motivated Epaphras was the love of the faithful Colossians for the Spirit of the Lord. In this testimony Paul saw that Epaphras was concerned for and motivated by their love of Christ. That couldn't be counterfeited! He wasn't motivated simply by his own love for Christ, but by the love of the saints for Christ. His motivation was the love of Christ that they held in common. He loved them because they loved Christ and he loved Christ. Christ was the common object of their love.

The love of Christ, the love and concern for God's Word and for God's people is the uncounterfeitable evidence of God's existence. And the primary place to see this evidence is in one's own self. Once you see it in yourself you can recognize it in others. But if you don't see it in yourself, you won't recognize it in others either. Faithful saints love Christ above all.

CB&O

Falling in love with God is a response to the absolute singularity of God, to His one-of-a-kindness. Real love always involves a passion for a particular person, a single, unique individual. For Christians that Person is Jesus Christ. The word *singularity* is defined as a trait marking a thing or person as distinct from others; a peculiarity. Christians are peculiarly related to God (Exodus 19:5, 1 Peter 2:9). Christians treasure God (Matthew 131:44). Christians love God alone in Christ alone through the Holy Spirit alone because God loves Christians alone in Christ alone through the Holy Spirit alone. *Christos Singularis!*

2

THAT YOU MAY

And so, from the day we heard, we have not ceased to pray
for you, asking that you may be filled with the knowledge of
his will in all spiritual wisdom and understanding, so as to
walk in a manner worthy of the Lord, fully pleasing to him,
bearing fruit in every good work and increasing in the
knowledge of God. May you be strengthened with all
power, according to his glorious might, for all endurance
and patience with joy, giving thanks to the Father, who has
qualified you to share in the inheritance of the saints in
light. —Colossians 1:9-12 (ESV)

Paul began with encouragement, not the kind of encouragement that puffs up self-esteem, but the kind that calls us beyond our self-concern. Paul encouraged the Colossians to
become all that God wanted them to be—not to be what they wanted
themselves to be, but to be what God wanted them to be, to love and
obey God's Word, to submit to Jesus Christ, and to obey His various
authorities (fathers, mothers, elders, civil authorities, etc.) through
His Holy Spirit.

Notice that even though Paul greatly appreciated the stories of
faithfulness that he had heard regarding the Colossians, and that he
assured them of his trust in their genuine faithfulness, he continued
to pray to God for their sanctification. He encouraged them precisely
because He did not want them to rest on their laurels, thinking themselves to have arrived at some sort of pinnacle of faithfulness. They
had begun well, but they were not finished. There was much more for
them to accomplish in Christ.

Here we find one of the spiritual errors of contemporary Christianity. Many Christians have come to think that they have somehow

arrived in the Promised Land of the gospel because they live in America and have the many benefits of modern politics, science and technology. We mistakenly think that God's purpose has been to provide political freedom and technological advance, not realizing that politics and technology are easily co-opted by Satan to distract God's people away from God's central concerns. And Satan has had much success in the Twentieth Century. "You shall know them by their fruits. Do men gather grapes from thorns, or figs from thistles" (Matthew 7:16)?

Look at the fruit of modern American politics and technology. Is it not the fruit of corruption? I am not saying that modern politics and technology are always necessarily bad, only that inasmuch as they are not dominated by the forces of Jesus Christ, they are too easily coopted by the forces of evil.

In the effort to understand them as value neutral in relationship to God and the Bible, we have given them over to the enemies of the gospel. Why is this the case? Because there is no such thing as value neutrality. The idea of objective neutrality is a falsehood that replaces biblical values with supposed objective values. But human beings are subjective beings who cannot escape their subjectivity. All human views and values are subjective. Only God has access to objectivity, and that means that God's view and values are necessarily biblical. Thus, any appeal to objectivity that is not biblical is an appeal to humanism in one form or another. It is an appeal to godlessness.

Were Paul writing today he would encourage Christians to maintain the faith and the freedom to worship that has been won at so great a cost, and to use politics, science and technology—the academy—in the service of Christ. Clearly, Paul encouraged his readers to continue to grow spiritually, to "take every thought captive to obey Christ" (2 Corinthians 10:5), and remind us of our duty to mature in the faith "so that we no longer may be infants, tossed to and fro and carried about by every wind of doctrine, in the dishonesty of men, in cunning craftiness, to the wiles of deceit" (Ephesians 4:14).

Specifically, Paul said that Christians are to pray for knowledge, wisdom and understanding (v. 9), to live honorably by practicing God's admonitions fruitfully—which means doing what is necessary to acquire and apply biblical knowledge wisdom and understanding in one's own life (v. 10), and to continue these things all one's life. These are the practices of spiritual maturity that contribute to the manifestation of God's will on earth.

Paul encouraged the Colossians because they had begun the walk of faith. He encouraged them to continue that walk. Paul assured the Colossians that he would continue to pray for them, that he would call down the power of the Holy Spirit to lead them into further growth and maturity. Paul directed his prayer specifically to their need for knowledge, wisdom, and spiritual understanding. Certainly they needed other things as well, but he began with knowledge, wisdom and understanding.

Know What?

But knowledge and understanding of what? It is important that we understand what Paul was praying for because, just as he prayed for them, he prayed for all Christians. Don't we need knowledge, wisdom and understanding, too? Faith's foundations—beyond God's grace and Christ's sacrifice—include the knowledge and understanding that result from or are produced by the grace of God. We might say that God's grace and Christ's sacrifice are the objective, historical foundations of salvation, and that our own knowledge and understanding are the subjective foundations of personal, spiritual growth in Christ. Knowledge and understanding must be personal, experiential and practical. But again we must ask —knowledge and understanding of what?

The question is mine, not Paul's. Fortunately, Paul provided the answer. I just want to call it to your attention. He said the "knowledge of (God's) will in all spiritual wisdom and understanding" (v. 9). Where will we find understanding and knowledge of God's will? In the Bible.[9] And where will we get spiritual understanding? Through personal regeneration by God's Holy Spirit who will guide our understanding of Scripture to insure that it is in line with the faith once delivered to the saints (Jude 1:3). It is the Holy Spirit who provides understanding, and He does so by leading, guiding and motivating His people to spiritual growth and sanctification through engagement with Scripture and the community of the saints.

Paul wrote in 1 Corinthians 2:11, "For who knows a person's thoughts except the spirit of that person, which is in him? So also no one comprehends the thoughts of God except the Spirit of God."

---

9   See *The Wisdom of Christ in the Book of Proverbs*, by Phillip A. Ross, Pilgrim Platform, 2006.

And in Hebrews 4:2, "For good news came to us just as to them, but the message they heard did not benefit them, because they were not united by faith with those who listened."

Spiritual understanding comes by faith, and faith by the Holy Spirit. We cannot correctly understand spiritual things without the presence of the Holy Spirit in our lives. And because the Spirit's presence is a mark of regeneration, spiritual understanding requires spiritual regeneration. Have you noticed that only the born-again understand what being born-again means? Those who are not born-again cannot understand it. It is experiential, not intellectual. Similarly, the word *fuchsia* is meaningless until you have seen the color—experienced it.

Am I saying that the born-again are a special class of people? I'm saying that God knows no other church than the church of the regenerate. That is God's purpose through Christ. And it's not that I am saying that Christians are a special group of people, but that God is saying it. This is the group that God intends to save. All of God's people are born-again people. All of God's people are *ekklēsia*, called out people, people called by Jesus Christ. Christians are different, but the difference is not a function of socio-economic class, nor should it result in any socio-economic class differences.

Those who have not been born-again are not actually Christian. While it is true that being a Christian is like being pregnant in that there are only two states: pregnant and not pregnant. But by the same token being pregnant does not guarantee that a baby will be born. Nor does a birth guarantee that a child will grow to be an adult. Does this mean that some regenerate people don't end up being saved? Perhaps. It is a complex and disputed issue. But the issue is not whether God will complete what He began. God saves all He intends to save. The issue is that people can fool themselves about their own salvation (Matthew 7:21).

We must factor into our considerations the realities of stoney ground Christians, where God's seed fell on stoney ground and began to grow, but had no depth of soil and dried up in the sun. (Mark 4:5-6). It was real seed, real growth and real failure. Just was with all human beings, there is more to life than being born. Similarly, those who have been born-again have yet to complete their adoption process. "And not only the creation, but we ourselves, who have the firstfruits of the Spirit, groan inwardly as we wait eagerly for adoption as sons, the redemption of our bodies" (Romans 8:23). I'm not saying this, Jesus and Paul are! Apart from this reality there is no purpose for perseverance.

Then again, because God will complete what He has begun (Philippians 1:6), those whom Christ has called will one day be fully Christian. And should someone's supposed Christianity fail to produce the fruit of repentance, belief and faithfulness in Christ, it can only be surmised that the original seed was not a Christian seed.

Christians are a *peculiar* people (1 Peter 2:9) according to the Authorized Version. The Greek word (*peripoiēsis*) refers to a people selected by God from the nations, from every ethnicity, to a people who are God's own possession. Paul, speaking to Titus about Christ said, "that he (Christ) might redeem us from all iniquity, and purify unto himself a peculiar people, zealous of good works" (Titus 2:14—Authorized Version). It's not that *some* of God's people are peculiar, meaning born-again and called-out of sin, but that *all* of them are.

RESPONSIBILITY

However, it's not that the born-again simply have a special status that makes them peculiar or markedly different from other people. What makes Christians peculiar is that they have a special relationship with Jesus Christ—and that relationship imposes upon them special opportunities and responsibilities. If you want the privileges of the status—the relationship—but not the burdens of the responsibility, you are fooling yourself about being born-again. Can people fool themselves about this? Absolutely! Consider those "Christians" the Lord rejected. "On that day many will say to me, 'Lord, Lord, did we not prophesy in your name, and cast out demons in your name, and do many mighty works in your name?' And then will I declare to them, 'I never knew you; depart from me, you workers of lawlessness.'" (Matthew 7:22-23).

Jesus came as a servant, and expects all of His people to be servants of God. Christians are to serve the Lord, to work for the accomplishment of God's will on earth as it is in heaven. We are to serve God, not one another—nor the lost. Of course, we are to help those who are lost to find the Lord and to abandon their old godless ways. But our service to them is not to encourage their lostness.

Jesus did not call His people to be the servants of the degenerate. Christians are not called to be servants of sin or of unrepentant sinners. Christians are not called to serve the good of society by satisfying the degenerate (or unregenerate) desires of men, even when they are clothed in respectability. Christians are not to be concerned for the greatest good of the greatest number. Jesus said that "the gate is narrow and the way is hard that leads to life, and those who find it are few" (Matthew 7:14), not many. We do, however, expect the sheer numbers of Christians to increase over time in such a way that eventually "every knee shall bow ... and every tongue shall confess to God" (Romans 14:11, Revelation 19:6).

This does not mean that all Christians are to be involved in social service, or that we must work exclusively with the poor. While there is nothing wrong with social service or working for the poor, Christians are primarily called to serve God in Christ Jesus. The issue is the focus, character and purpose of Christian service. Of course, Christ wants what is best for everyone.

The point I'm trying to make is that Christians are called to live in service to God, not to some definition of "the good of society" that is not clearly and historically established by God's Word. We are to be in service to Jesus Christ first, and only to His people as a byproduct of our service to Him. Furthermore, we are not to protect the wicked from the pain and consequences of their own sinful decisions and actions. We are to warn them by convincing them that the warning is not ours but God's—because it is! God Himself will teach His elect to renounce their sin and wickedness, and those who refuse to repent will burn in Hell to the glory of God's sovereignty, to the honor and integrity of God's law and God's promises.[10]

This does not mean that the elect can lose their salvation. Those who are truly elect are held by God's grip on them, not merely by their own puny grip on God. However, while the elect are safe in God, it is quite possible to be self-deluded about one's own election. Thus, Peter calls Christians to make their calling and election sure (2 Peter 1:10).

---

10 Of course God insists that unrepentant people suffer Hell and damnation because the punishment of sin serves the glory of God (Matthew 13:14, Luke 19:27, Revelation 11:18). Christ wants to punish the wicked because such punishment serves the glory of God by providing the righteous motivation for God's justice. Rightly understood the destruction of the wicked serves as a goad to restrain wickedness and drive the savable wicked to Christ through the fear of the Lord. How does the damnation of the wicked serve God's glory? By demonstrating God's sovereignty over evil and wickedness. The punishment and destruction of evil is actually a good thing. By destroying evil God provides for the establishment of good. The only real issues here are the definitions of good and evil, and who has the right to make those determinations.

SEEK YE FIRST

So, how do we insure that we are serving Jesus Christ, which is nothing more nor anything less than glorifying God and enjoying Him forever?[11] By making our first priority to clearly understand the gospel of Jesus Christ faithfully, historically and sufficiently before we begin declaring and teaching the truth of the Bible to others. Jesus said that the gospel and Bible study are more important than food. We are to "seek first the kingdom of God and his righteousness, and all these things will be added to you." (Matthew 6:33). "Man shall not live by bread alone" (Luke 4:4). We must engage God's kingdom and His righteousness in our own lives, families and neighborhoods.

The church is not simply a social service agency, though it provides some social services. It is a gospel service agency. The church must always focus on its primary target market, to use contemporary marketing language. Our first and primary target market is Jesus Christ. Jesus Christ is the true "customer" of the church. He has bought us, purchased us with His blood (1 Corinthians 6:20, 7:23). We are the purchase of Christ's atonement. He bought us and is in the process of redeeming us in holiness for the glory of God. Jesus Christ is the only customer who is always right. Our worship and service must always please Christ first and foremost, not each other—nor the lost. Worship is not entertainment or amusement. It is the remembrance and celebration of a transaction, of Christ's purchase. And those who have not been purchased have nothing to remember or celebrate.

The church of Jesus Christ is not to appeal to the lost. Too often churches try to appeal to the styles and aesthetics of non-Christians as a means of establishing contact with potential converts. But such appeals simply bring greater acceptance of godlessness into the churches in the name of evangelism. The saved will eventually abandon the styles and aesthetics of godlessness, so there is no need to make such appeals. What people are won with is what they are won to. The church is to appeal to the world with the ultimate styles and aesthetics of the saved, of godliness, to indicate a clear difference between biblical life from godlessness.

The church is not to gather the lost, but to gather the saved. Unsaved people cannot worship the Lord because they neither know Him nor value Him. It's okay for unsaved people to be

---

11 *Westminster Shorter Catechism*, question 1.

involved in churches, but churches should not make themselves cozy with godlessness. The church is not to be or to appear to be like the world, it is to appear to be different—peculiar. It is to actually be different than the world. The values of the world and the values of the church are opposite, not similar (Romans 12:2, 1 Corinthians 2:12, 3:19, etc.).

The church must be customer-centered only in the sense of being Christ-centered. This is a critical insight because the church is not in the business of serving the people in the pews as if they were the customers of the church. Rather, the church is in the business of serving Jesus Christ, of making itself the object of Christ's desire—not the object of heathen desire. We are to serve Jesus Christ by making ourselves the object of His desire. We are to make ourselves what Jesus Christ wants us to be in the fullness of our sanctification (understanding that this only comes by the grace of God and the power and presence of the Holy Spirit). It is by doing these things that we will make the church attractive to those who want to please the Lord. And thus the church will grow in both numbers and in sanctification.

But if we appeal to the desires of those in the pews—and worse, appeal to the desires of the unsaved in the hope of getting them into the pews, the church will fail in her primary objective because she will fail to appeal to Christ. When the focus on evangelism supplants the focus on sanctification—growth and maturity—the church begins to aim at the lowest common denominator rather than the perfection we are called into (Matthew 5:48, Romans 12:2).

The Lord spits out churches that compromise their primary mission of preparing the Bride for the Lord (Revelation 3:16, 21:2). Such tactics attempt to bring in the godly by appealing to the ungodly, trying to do what pleases the Lord by appealing to the desires of lost sinners. This is critical because it runs counter to our current understanding—the lost are not the customers of Christ's church. Such tactics will not work. They cannot work. They will only perpetuate the confusion that dominates contemporary churches of every denomination.

Yes, of course we are to serve one another in the Lord. But that service is a by-product of our service to Christ, not a replacement for service to Christ. We must serve the right One, the One who is righteous. Then we must please the One we serve. Consequently, the pastor of a church is the servant of his church members only secondarily. He is first and foremost Christ's servant. Nor are church members to be servants of one another except secondarily. Our service must always be primarily directed toward the satisfaction of Jesus Christ. We are to be servants of Christ, not social servants of civil society at large.

This is a common misunderstanding. Churches are to be led, not simply by the will of the majority, nor by the desires of the lost, but by the Spirit of Jesus Christ. We are to be what Christ wants us to be, to do what Christ wants us to do, and to want what Christ wants for us. Unfortunately, too many churches have adopted a kind of constitutional democracy that promotes and encourages direction and leadership from the bottom rather than from the top, from the immaturity of the majority rather than from the maturity of the faithful.

BIBLE STUDY

How are we to accomplish this? Bible study. We always come back to this matter of Bible study. What I want you to see is that the concern for Bible study is not so much my concern, as it is God's. To claim Christ but neglect God's Word is to proclaim yourself to be a hypocrite, to say one thing but mean another.

Why should we study the Bible? So that we may "walk worthy of the Lord" (v. 10). The purpose is very practical. To walk worthy means to always keep obedience in mind, to follow Jesus Christ. However, Paul does not call Christians to blind obedience. He does not call God's people to mere obedience, not to obedience without understanding, but to the obedience that produces understanding. This is not the understanding of the world or of worldly ways, but the understanding of Scripture, of God's way.

We cannot neglect understanding—doctrine. Doctrine means understanding or teaching. We know that in order to understand spiritual things we must first be born-again. The foundation of the faith is regeneration in Christ. Upon that foundation, then, understanding and obedience support one another. Understanding grows through obedience, and obedience grows through understanding. They grow together or neither of them grow. They are in a kind of interdependent, reciprocal relationship.

Understanding and obedience work together in such a way that if you don't understand Scripture, working on obedience is the way to increase your understanding. And if you are failing to obey the

Lord in some area, working on doctrine—working to understand what the Bible teaches—will help facilitate increased obedience.

As if pleasing God were not a sufficient motivation, Paul suggests in verse 10 that by pleasing God we can be "fruitful in every good work," (obedience) and grow "in the knowledge of God" (understanding). Good works are the more obvious social benefits of faithfulness. Many people go wrong in that they want to cut directly to the benefits and forget about the discipline of faithfulness. By focusing on the benefits of faithfulness they neglect the disciplines of understanding and obedience. They want dessert before they have finished their green beans. Rather than doing Christianity God's way, people want to do it their own way. This has been a perpetual problem in both testaments.

People say, *Why waste so much time and effort struggling to understand and obey the Bible? It's too hard. Just do good things, and get by on what spiritual understanding you already have, or think you have. If the only concern is the bottom line (salvation unto good works), then just do good works. Who really cares about spiritual understanding anyway?*

Given today's standards, whose going to know the difference? This kind of thinking plagues so many Christians and churches today, and has for more than a century if not for the whole history of the church. But as much as good works are needed in today's world, and as much as this kind of thinking may make sense to you, it is not biblical Christianity.

I can imagine some people thinking, *So what? So it isn't biblical Christianity, according to some old, antiquated definition of Christianity. As long as the final product—good works—gets accomplished, what's the difference?*

The difference has to do with 1) actually doing good works, 2) the means by which good works are accomplished and 3) the end result. What is truly good can only be accomplished through the will of God. Anything done apart from obedience to Jesus Christ cannot be good. "All have turned aside; together they have become worthless; no one does good, not even one" (Romans 3:12, Isaiah 64:6). So, when people fail to live in obedience to Jesus Christ good cannot result—no matter how hard people work at it. Remember, Paul insisted that people "be filled with the knowledge of his will in all spiritual wisdom and understanding" (v. 9). When we ignore the fact that understanding and obedience are essential products of faithfulness, given as a fruit of regeneration, we fail to obey God's

Word. The difficulty is that we cannot claim to do God's will and fail to understand and obey Him at the same time. An error at this point grows into a tragedy of errors that culminates in damnation instead of salvation. That's the problem.

When we fail to understand and obey, we are not "strengthened with all might, according to His glorious power" (v. 11). When we do Christianity our way rather than His way our strength fails. Those who try to do it their own way find that their shortcut only leads them astray. But when we do it God's way our strength gives way to His strength and does not fail. Not only are good works accomplished, but salvation is assured.

When we are filled with the presence and power of the Holy Spirit we are filled with His patience and His long-suffering as well. Much of what God wants to accomplish are long-range things, multigenerational things, things that require patience and perseverance. God is not into quick fixes. Oh, He wants the world fixed, but He wants it fixed right, and that takes time. It also takes the knowledge and understanding that are produced by regeneration.

QUALIFICATIONS

Are you qualified for such service? Look at verse 12, "giving thanks to the Father who has qualified us to be partakers of the inheritance of the saints in the light." Paul suggests that qualification is necessary. To qualify for the Olympics, you have to perform well, do your best. But simply doing your best doesn't qualify you for the Olympics. Many fine athletes do very well, but never qualify. Why? Olympic athletes must be both gifted and chosen.

Unlike the Olympics, Christians are not chosen on the basis of their own performance, but on the basis of Christ's performance. God chooses according to His own will, not by our standards of good performance. Because God chooses on the basis of Christ's performance, our performance in Christ is guaranteed.

In addition, the Lord assures us that "whoever believes in Him should not perish but have everlasting life" (John 3:16). Our human responsibility is to believe, to believe with our best effort, to believe to the best of our ability, and to trust God for the result. Christians are not chosen on the strength of their belief, as if the act of believing makes people Christian. It doesn't! It can't!

Believing doesn't make you a Christian (Matthew 7:21-ff). Believism is a subtle form of works-righteousness. Rather, being a

Christian, having been reborn into the Holy Spirit makes people believe. We don't believe in order to be reborn. We are reborn in order to believe. Christians are reborn into belief, into the unity of truth that inheres in Jesus Christ, who alone holds all things together.

03 80

In Christ the many apparently divergent truths of the world are held together in the singularity of God. People do not chose to believe this, as if they first see Truth from some objective perspective and then mentally assent to it. No! Rather, people are swept into the love of Christ, who is the One who holds all things together (John 1:3). From that position, from inside the love of Christ, Christians look out to the world and its many truths and see only Christ. *Christos Singularis!*

3

THROUGH HIM

*For He has delivered us from the power of darkness and
has translated us into the kingdom of His dear Son; in
whom we have redemption through His blood, the
remission of sins. who is the image of the invisible God, the
First-born of all creation. For all things were created in
Him, the things in the heavens, and the things on the earth,
the visible and the invisible, whether thrones or dominions
or principalities or powers, all things were created through
Him and for Him. And He is before all things, and by Him
all things consist. And He is the Head of the body, the
church, who is the Beginning, the First-born from the dead,
that He may be pre-eminent in all things.*
—Colossians 1:13-18 (ESV)

J esus Christ has rescued His people from darkness. That means
that prior to rescue all people are in darkness. The resurrected
Lord appeared to Paul and said,

*I will rescue you from the people and from the Gentiles, But
rise and stand upon your feet, for I have appeared to you
for this purpose, to appoint you as a servant and witness to
the things in which you have seen me and to those in which
I will appear to you, delivering you from your people and
from the Gentiles—to whom I am sending you to open their
eyes, so that they may turn from darkness to light and from
the power of Satan to God, that they may receive forgiveness of sins and a place among those who are sanctified by
faith in me" (Acts 26:16-18).*

God rescues His people *from* darkness, which means that before the rescue they are in darkness and afterward they are no longer in darkness. They are taken out of darkness. They no longer walk or live in or do the things of darkness. They turn their backs on the darkness of the world. Yet, they continue to live in the world and among people who love darkness.

But those whom Christ rescues are transferred into the kingdom of Christ, God's Only Son, who is Lord and King of those He rescues. This means that everyone who gets rescued (saved) can testify about the difference between darkness and light. In addition, darkness is a universal experience.

What is this domain of darkness from which Christ's people are rescued? The Authorized Version translates the phrase as "power of darkness." *Power* (*exousia*) also means authority, jurisdiction, liberty, right, and strength. We might also think of this power or domain as a kind of influence. Christ rescues His people from the influence of *darkness* (*skotos*), from obscurity or shadiness. People cannot see things in the dark. It's like fog only darker. What is seen in the dark is seen poorly, if at all. Things are obscured in the dark. When it is dark we don't know what we are seeing because we can't see anything very well. Our imaginations run wild. And that's the point—we can't see anything in the dark and begin to rely upon speculation.

It's not just that we can't see Christ or we can't see Scripture or the things of the Spirit. We can't see *anything* clearly. Everything that we see is unclear, unfocused, indeterminate. Not just church things, not just godly things, not just biblical things, but everything. Does Paul really mean everything? Yes, everything.

When are God's people transferred out of the domain of darkness and into the kingdom of Christ? Does it happen right away when people are saved, at the very moment they realize that they have been overpowered by Holy Spirit to be rescued from Hell and damnation? Are they rescued from the realm and influence of darkness, into the kingdom of Christ, all at once, in an instant? Or does it take a while to get completely rescued?

This is a very important question because if it happens instantaneously, then God's people are done with the influence of darkness in an instant, never to be caught in the grip of darkness again. But if it takes a while to get rescued, to complete the rescue, then God's people are susceptible to the lingering influence of darkness during the time that their rescue begins and the time it is completed.

WESTMINSTER CONFESSION

The Westminster Confession[12] teaches that the rescue of God's people occurs in four steps: justification, adoption, sanctification, and glorification. The first step is God's. God does the justification, which is a kind of heavenly bookkeeping wherein Jesus Christ paid the entire debt that we owe for all of the sins we have accrued or will accrue in our lifetime. That payment was made upon the death of Christ over two thousand years ago. And it was accomplished in an instant like an electronic bank transfer. That debt is paid in full.

The second step involves the adoption of the sinner into the family of Jesus Christ. Webster speaks of adoption as an act of test-ament in which the adopted person is appointed or covenanted to be an heir, by the will, or on the condition of taking the family name. Adoption is both spiritual and worldly because the family of Jesus Christ is both spiritual and worldly. This adoption happens in the world, but is not of the world. "I do not ask that you take them out of the world, but that you keep them from the evil one. They are not of the world, just as I am not of the world. Sanctify them in the truth; your word is truth. As you sent me into the world, so I have sent them into the world" (John 17:15-18).

People are taken into the family of Jesus Christ spiritually by the Holy Spirit (Romans 8:14-17) and physically through member-ship in the visible church of Jesus Christ. Water baptism is part of adoption, as is baptism in or by the Holy Spirit. One is worldly, one is spiritual. One is done by the church, one is done by the Holy Spirit. Water baptism is a ceremony performed by the church.

Baptism in or by the Holy Spirit happens in an instant. The person is changed in an instant, but the change continues to hap-pen over a lifetime and beyond. So, it begins in an instant but isn't completed in an instant. The beginning point is the personal realiz-ation of God's justification by grace alone. And the continuing action is the activity of the Spirit through sanctification (growth and maturity). Baptism, like birth, marks the beginning of new life in Christ.

Adoption is a kind of bridge between the worldly and spiritual realities. The purpose of adoption is to provide access to the

---

12 The Westminster Confession, written in 1646, was among the first and most influential church agreements that came out of the Protestant Reformation. In the matters discussed here, it agrees with the Savoy Declaration (1658) and the Baptist Confession of 1689, and provided the mainline theology in the U.S. until the Civil War in 1865.

resources of God. As an adopted son or daughter, we have a legal right to share in the treasures or resources of the family of God as Father, Son and Holy Spirit. Adoption provides God's people with God's resources through inheritance (Romans 8:14-17).

Sanctification involves the application or use of God's resources to complete the transfer into the kingdom of Christ. The Holy Spirit leads, guides, provides and applies the treasures or resources of God to grow and mature the new adoptee as s/he prepares for the final stage of transfer into Christ's kingdom in glory, post-mortem. But all of this leading, guiding, providing and applying happens in this world, on earth, pre-mortem. The focus of the effort is the building of the church of Jesus Christ on earth.

Why does the church need to be built on earth? Because God's mission is to bring His kingdom to the earth (Matthew 6:10). In order to provide the growth and maturity of God's people for the final transfer into the kingdom of Christ (Ephesians 5:5). The church is a kind of launching station. It is one of the means that God uses in the process of salvation because God is not just saving individuals, He is also saving humanity itself. So, it is essential that the church be fully functioning, that it actually grow and mature Christians in this life in this world because the process of sanctification takes more than a lifetime on earth to complete.

This doesn't mean that people bring sin to heaven with them, but simply that this side of Christ's return no one on earth is completely sinless. No Christian is ever ready for the complete transfer into the kingdom of God during this life, no matter how young he was saved or how rapidly he matures. Salvation is of grace from beginning to end.

Perhaps, people are brought into perfection when they meet Christ in the air (1 Thessalonians 4:17), changed in a moment or a twinkle (1 Corinthians 15:52). If so—and it is so, the kingdom of Christ always has one foot in this world and one foot in Heaven (so to speak). It has to, in order to make the transfer from this world into the heavenly kingdom. The final stage of Christ's rescue from the domain of darkness is referred to as glorification. Glorification involves the final transfer into the kingdom of Christ, and occurs after physical death.

REDEMPTION

Verse 14 reminds us that in Christ, then, we have redemption and forgiveness of sins in this world in preparation for the next. So, when are God's people transferred out of the domain of darkness and into the kingdom of Christ? The process begins immediately, instantaneously upon the confession of Jesus Christ as Lord and Savior. The initial change is the most dramatic. And its completion or fulfillment is guaranteed from the beginning because God is sovereign and all-powerful, though it takes more than a lifetime to completely unfold. This guarantee of fulfillment is our hope and confident expectation.

Thus, salvation in Jesus Christ is not a possibility, as if it might or might not happen. It is a fact! Christ's death on the cross secured it. Therefore, salvation is not offered, it is proclaimed. The gospel is not *offered* to sinners, it is *proclaimed* to sinners. It's not that you might have salvation if only you give your heart to Jesus. But rather, "This Jesus, whom I proclaim to you, is the Christ" (Acts 17:3). It's a done deal, not an offer. The only issue is, Are *you* coming with Jesus out of darkness into His kingdom?

1 John 1:6 speaks to this issue, "If we say we have fellowship with him while we walk in darkness, we lie and do not practice the truth." If the gospel is merely offered, it may or may not be believed and accepted. But God's truth is true whether we accept it or not. We don't make God's truth true by accepting it.

The problem with the language of "accepting Jesus into your heart" is that it suggests that we are in control of Him, that we make a place for Him in our lives, rather than Him making a place for us (John 14:2-3) in His kingdom. Too many people mistakenly understand salvation to be a matter of making room for Jesus in their lives. On one level it sounds okay because we are so used to hearing it like that. You're at the crusade. The preacher offers the gospel of salvation. So, you go down the aisle to get a piece of the Lord to take home, promising you will make room for Him in your life.

The most insidious thing about this kind of Christianity is that it is almost true. A lot of people try to make room for Jesus in the darkness of their lives. They keep one foot in their life of darkness by partitioning off a little space for Jesus. While it may sound silly as I'm talking about it, one of the major problems in Christianity today is the compartmentalization of the faith. Our lives are segmented and fragmented already. That fragmentation, also called brokenness, is a function of sin. So, when someone "accepts" Jesus, Christianity or the church what is accepted is just another segment, another fragment to integrate into their lives. They create a "place" for it, for Jesus, for the church, which implies that such segmented faithfulness is not understood or practiced holistically. A compartmentalized faith doesn't inform or guide all of life. It's just a part of life, like an appendage.

I'm in control of my life, and I'll put Jesus here, or there. I don't take Jesus to work, don't take Him shopping, or to the movies. Church is the place for Jesus. We segment Him into the church and out of the culture, into our prayers and out of our hobbies.

CLOSE, BUT ...

This understanding of Christianity gets very close to the truth of the gospel, and it takes attention and discernment to see that it falls short. The problem is that this insidious idea is almost true and, being almost true, it seems pretty true while not being actually true. If an engineer designs a light switch so that the toggle mechanism almost connects the two wires that channel the electricity to the bulb, he has failed to design a working switch. Almost is not close enough.

Who are you to make room for Jesus? It's like making room for judge who issues a summons for you to testify before a grand jury. It's not a request subject to your convenience. We don't make room for Jesus so He can be a part of our lives. Rather, Jesus has made room for us so that we can be part of His life, so that our lives can be completely inhabited by Him. We have life in Him. You don't make room for a Boeing 747 in your apartment. Rather, you get aboard the 747.

To offer the gospel to sinners fails to make the proper connection with Christ because the sinner must then rely upon himself to complete the deal. Offers are always provisional, and the gospel of Jesus Christ is not provisional. The King does not offer, He commands. Of course, people may, and do, refuse to obey the command of the King. "Jesus came into Galilee, proclaiming the gospel of God, and saying, 'The time is fulfilled, and the kingdom of God is at hand; repent and believe in the gospel'" (Mark 1:14-15). Do you hear an offer? No. You hear a command. Yet, people may, and do, refuse to obey the command of the King. But their refusal does not remove them from the King's jurisdiction or from their own responsibility to respond.

The King is like a judge who issues a summons for you to

appear in court. It is not a request, but a command. And if you refuse to go, the judge will send his representatives and force you to appear. The judge can, and will, issue sanctions for your refusal to comply with his order, his request. In other words, just saying *no* to the judge does not make you free to disregard his "invitation." Ignoring the judge doesn't reduce his power and authority. Rather, saying *no* brings certain consequences.

And so it is with the gospel of Jesus Christ, the gospel of grace. It is freely given, not merely offered, but freely proclaimed. And it is to be freely received, received willingly, even gladly. But where it is not received sanctions—consequences—will follow. Maybe not tomorrow or next week, but they will follow as surely as winter follows spring.

> *Afterward he appeared to the eleven (the disciples) themselves as they were reclining at table, and he rebuked them for their unbelief and hardness of heart, because they had not believed those who saw him after he had risen. And he said to them, "Go into all the world and proclaim the gospel to the whole creation. Whoever believes and is baptized will be saved, but whoever does not believe will be condemned" (Mark 16:14-16).*

How can Jesus Christ provide redemption? Because He is God. "He (Jesus) is the image of the invisible God, the firstborn of all creation" (v. 15). To say that Jesus is the image of the invisible God is to ascribe to Jesus the attributes of God. The Westminster Confession teaches that God is "a most pure spirit, invisible, without body, parts, or passions, immutable, immense, eternal, incomprehensible, almighty, most wise, most holy, most free, most absolute, working all things according to the counsel of His own immutable and most righteous will, for His own glory; most loving, gracious, merciful, long-suffering, abundant in goodness and truth..."[13] This section of of the Confession makes the deity of Jesus Christ clear. Jesus is God incarnate.

It follows that since Jesus Christ is God, He is also responsible for the creation of the earth and all that is in it (Psalm 89:11). "For by him all things were created, in heaven and on earth, visible and invisible, whether thrones or dominions or rulers or authorities—all things were created through him and for him" (v. 16). Paul then repeats it for emphasis—all things were created through Him and

---

13 Westminster Confession of Faith, 2.1.

for Him. God's chief purpose is the exultation of His own glory. Humanity was created as the primary means of that purpose, to give God glory. Our chief and highest end is to glorify God and to fully enjoy Him forever.[14] We could sum up these two points by saying that God created all things for the purpose of His glory.

The "all things" of verse 16 can only be understood in relationship to the purpose of God's glory. Whatever exists has meaning only in relationship to God—proper meaning, real meaning, the highest meaning, the most fundamental meaning. This is much more important than I am able to make it. Nothing can be rightly or correctly understood apart from its relationship to God. This is what this verse means. *All* things were created through Him, or by Him, by His power. And *all* things were created for Him. It means that there are no things or facts apart from God-related things and facts in any area of human endeavor.

When someone tells you that you don't understand the facts or that you had better get the facts straight it means that the person telling you this believes that he has some additional information that sheds light on the situation that you don't know about. The new facts will cause you to reconsider what you think you know about the situation. They will give you a different perspective on the matter.

People see and assess the facts in the light of their beliefs. Beliefs always inform facts. We tend to see what we believe to be true. For instance, Creationists see the Grand Canyon and all of its factual data as proving the Flood. Evolutionists see the same canyon and the same facts, but see it as proof of evolution. How can this be? Their differing worldviews cause them to filter and interpret what they see differently.

Sometimes certain facts change what we believe, and sometimes what we believe changes the way that we see certain facts. The point is that belief and facts are always closely related. Our beliefs shape the way we see the world, the way we see the facts. And the facts that we see also shape our beliefs. We accept some things as facts and reject others based upon various beliefs we hold. It must also be granted that the facts that we don't see or accept also shape our beliefs because if we saw or accepted them we would believe differently. Our brains refuse to see facts that don't fit into our belief systems.

---

14 Westminster Confession, Shorter Catechism, Question 1.

The point I am trying to make is both subtle and difficult because it requires that we see the extent of our own human subjectivity. No one has an objective or neutral perspective from which to view facts. *Everything* is colored by our values and beliefs.

For instance, evolutionists look at the Grand Canyon and say, "Wow, look what a little water (the Colorado River) did over a long period of time (millions of years)." But Creationists look at the same Canyon, the same facts, and say, "Wow, look what a lot of water did is a very short time (Noah's Flood)." They are looking at the same "facts"—the Grand Canyon—but they see very different things because they believe very different things about the world and about God. Every "fact" is exactly like that. Facts are accepted or rejected on the basis of our beliefs. When you reject what I see as fact, you say, "That's just your opinion." People accept as facts only what supports their beliefs. Thus, new facts require new beliefs.

But the Bible tells us that *all* things, *all* facts, were created through Jesus Christ and for Jesus Christ, for His purposes. That means that *every* fact must be understood in relationship to Jesus Christ or it is not fully or correctly understood. Every fact exists for a purpose and the purpose for which a thing or fact was created determines its most important meaning.

Scripture tells us that everything was created for Jesus Christ, for His purposes (John 1:3). Everything, every fact, stands in relationship to Jesus Christ and seeing or understanding things in relationship to Jesus Christ opens up their primary meaning, their primary purpose, their objective factuality. Conversely, failing to see or understand how a fact is related to the glory of Jesus Christ will obscure its primary meaning and purpose. Again, *every* fact, *every* thing on earth and in Heaven can be properly and fully understood *only* in relationship to Jesus Christ because Jesus Christ is the Second Person of the Trinity and God, the First Person of the Trinity, is the Creator of everything. In the same way that a child is always related, and in important ways defined, by his parents, everything in the world is related and defined by God. Believers apply this insight to school, work, television, movies, government, war, *everything,* because that's what it means to believe.

"For by him all things were created, in heaven and on earth, visible and invisible, whether thrones or dominions or rulers or authorities—all things were created through him and for him. And he is before all things, and in him all things hold together" (vs. 16-17). Not only do all things hold together in Christ, but only in Christ do all things hold together. How many things? *All things.*

C3 80

How does this holding together or cohering happen? What are the physics of it? Scripture doesn't tell us that. But when people find themselves swept into Christ, when people see this coherence in Christ from the inside, from a position of belief, all sorts of other things fall into harmony with God's Word. The glory of God is the gravity of God, and that gravity holds everything together. *Christos Singularis!*

4

PEACE

For in him all the fullness of God was pleased to dwell, and through him to reconcile to himself all things, whether on earth or in heaven, making peace by the blood of his cross.
—Colossians 1:19-20 (ESV)

Here we discover the importance of the atonement of Christ and a brief description of how it works. This idea of reconciliation to God by the blood of the cross is a difficult concept. It is difficult, not because of what we don't understand about it, but because of what we do understand.

Because of Adam's sin all people are born into sin (Romans 5:12, 1 John 1:8-10). How can seemingly innocent newborn babies be sinners? People deny that this can be true. Nonetheless, the Bible teaches that all people are sinners from birth. Consider that Adam was the King of humanity, and that Adam's sin was a declaration of war against God. Because King Adam is at war all of Adam's children and future children are at war, though they themselves did nothing to cause the state of war. This was the human reality prior to Christ.

We are not sinners because we commit sinful acts, although we do. Rather, we commit sinful acts because we are sinners. The difference between these two perspectives is that if our sins cause us to be sinners, we could potentially stop sinning and thereby stop being sinners. But if we commit sin because we are sinners from birth, then the cessation of sinful actions, were it even possible, could not of itself eliminate either our guilt or our sinful character.

In the latter case, were we to stop sinning, which we can't but if we could, we would still be sinners because of the sins that we have done in the past. Our status as sinners would remain unchanged. Because we cannot eliminate our past, we remain sinners until we are legally declared forgiven and set free. We are forgiven our transgressions by the mercy of the judge. Having been forgiven, we are still guilty, but we avoid the punishment for sin. If we were not guilty, we would not need forgiveness. Our personal and corporate guilt as members of humanity is our reality, our actual situation. People must deal with this problem of sin if they are to avoid damnation. That's the human predicament given in the Bible, and it is staring us in the face in the midst of the multitude of crises we face as we enter the Twenty-First Century.

The difficulty is that we cannot eliminate sin by avoiding sinful actions. No matter how hard we try, history testifies against this possibility. But even if we could, we would still be guilty of past sins and we would still be sinners because sin is a character flaw, and is not simply determined by our actions. Because human character is sinfully flawed, we cannot stop ourselves from sinning, nor can we change the past.

This is part of the double-bind that God has put us in. We need to do something about our sin that we cannot do of or by ourselves. Left to ourselves, this problem is not solvable. Left to ourselves we are without the power to sustain or win a war against God. Left to ourselves we are destined for Hell because of Adam's sin, Adam's declaration of war against God. We have followed Adam in his sin, and without God's intervention we will simply continue on the highway to Hell.

A further difficulty is that we must satisfy God's sense of justice and fairness, not our own. Complaining that God is not fair because He has trapped us in a double-bind is useless because it does not address the problem. It is only a complaint that God is Judge and we are not. Nor can we change God's sense of justice. Rather, the solution to our problem must satisfy Him, satisfy God's sense of justice, whether we like it or not. He's in control, we aren't. And even if perchance we think we have a solution, it doesn't mean that God will accept our solution or that our solution will actually eliminate the problem. The real solution must satisfy God's sense of justice, God's understanding and requirements, not ours.

RECIPE

For example, a baker bakes a loaf of bread, and it turns out lousy. We go to the baker and ask him, *Did you follow the recipe?* He assures us that he did, so we continue our investigation. The recipe calls for whole wheat flour, but he has been out of whole wheat flour for a week. So, we ask the baker about it. *Well,* says the baker, *we're out of whole wheat flour so I substituted white flour, but I threw in a cup of bran.*

The point is that even though the baker thought he followed the recipe, and even made a correct compensation, he didn't actually follow it. He substituted ingredients for those specified by the recipe. He didn't actually do what the recipe said to do, though he thought he did. Add to this that apart from Christ the baker cannot know the difference between bran and sawdust and finds plenty of sawdust at hand and we come closer to our reality. The baker has mistaken sawdust for bran and included it in the bread.

Many people respond to God that way. For instance, God gave the Ten Commandments as a recipe for a godly life. In Christ we know that no one can obey the Ten Commandments perfectly and not even a little bit apart from the grace of God in the light of Christ by the power of the Holy Spirit. Jesus didn't rescind the Ten Commandments but provided the grace of forgiveness, instruction in righteousness and protection from damnation as we grow in the likeness of Jesus Christ, who did perfectly fulfill them.[15] Nonetheless, people, even saved people, substitute all sorts of half-baked measures for God's Law, and thereby fail to actually follow Jesus Christ. Yet, many think that they do.

For instance, not committing adultery was commanded in the "old days," which meant no sex outside of marriage. *But,* people say, *things are different today. People didn't live together back then.*

People try to split hairs about the differences between adultery and fornication, or claim that the world has moved beyond the mythology of the Bible. Everyone who has been involved in public education or contemporary culture knows the arguments. The excuses and justifications for sin are amazing.

People often make unauthorized substitutions in God's recipe for life in Christ, and then wonder why it doesn't work like God promised. Well, God's recipe for life only works like God promised if we actually follow the recipe, which we cannot do apart from

---

15 In the light of Christ Christians not only see the Ten Commandments differently, but fulfill them differently (i.e. the Sabbath). It's not that the the Ten Commandments changed, but that the regenerate have changed. Jesus dealt with this in the Sermon on the Mount. See *Rock Mountain Creed—Sermon on the Mount*, by Phillip A. Ross, Pilgrim Platform, Marietta, Ohio, 2010.

God's grace in the light of Christ through the Holy Spirit. And if we are going to follow God's recipe, our first responsibility is to understand the requirements of God's justice. That necessitates an understanding of the Old Testament. We must first learn God's Law, and then follow it, only honoring those amendments and corrections made by Jesus Christ. Again, such following of God's law apart from the grace of God and faith in Jesus Christ by the power and presence of the Holy Spirit through regeneration is impossible. Nonetheless, knowledge of God's law is commendable because it will bring people into God's double-bind and in contact with the gospel.

GOSPEL POWER

I'm not arguing against God's grace, not at all. I'm just pointing out that the gospel doesn't make any sense apart from being caught in God's double-bind. So, first comes the double-bind, the demand for perfect obedience, and the inability to comply. Like it or not, God has imposed this double-bind on all of humanity. Once a person realizes that he is in this double-bind, he understands that he needs help. The gospel is the power of God unto salvation for believers who acknowledge that they need God's help. But it is also the power of condemnation for unbelievers who don't.

This is just another way to say that God's law is for unbelievers (Exodus 12:49, Matthew 5:18), as well as for believers. God's promise is to reward obedience and curse disobedience (Deuteronomy 28). Like a watershed, God's eternal covenant has two sides, and between those two sides all humanity is bound to God's promises regarding either obedience or disobedience. Everyone is already involved, from Deuteronomy forward, first Jews and now the whole world. It is important that the law serves as a threat against lawlessness for everyone (Romans 13:4). The Ten Commandments will benefit everyone because they benefit society at large—humanity.

A common error today is that many people think that Jesus put an end to the Law, that God's Law is no longer in effect. "For Christ is the end of the law for righteousness to everyone who believes," said Paul in Romans 10:4. The Greek word for *end* is *telos*, which means the conclusion or purpose for which a thing is given. When I say that the end of marriage is procreation, I don't mean that the marriage is over when children are born, but rather that children are the purpose of marriage. In a very real sense the marriage is for the children.

Similarly, the word *end* does not mean that the Law is over and done with because Christ has come, but that Christ is the purpose or the perfection to which the Law points. Christ is the help we need in order to benefit from the law. With the advent of Christ the purpose or end of the Law is brought into view and achieved in Christ, by Christ. In Christ the law is no longer an impossible double-bind. Rather, it becomes useful in Christ. Christ satisfied God's demand for justice. He received the just punishment for human sin so that we can receive the just reward for His faithfulness. That means that in Christ we can do our best to live by God's law without the fear of failing, without the fear of receiving the ultimate punishment (damnation) for our failure to live it perfectly. In Christ there is grace and mercy, but only in Christ.

Christ said, "Do not think that I came to destroy the Law or the Prophets. I did not come to destroy but to fulfill" (Matthew 5:17) or complete the Law. How was this fulfillment or completion accomplished? By Christ's atonement for the sins of His people, by His death on the cross, "that He might reconcile them both to God in one body through the cross, thereby putting to death the enmity" (Ephesians 2:16) between God and man. Christ's atonement was then ratified by God through the resurrection of Jesus Christ as a sign and symbol of His acceptance of Christ's atonement.

BLOOD SACRIFICE

That is the biblical explanation of atonement. Yet, in the midst of our sinfulness people ask, *What kind of a God would require the death of His only Son, as a payment for the sins of a rotten people? What kind of beast is God, who demands blood sacrifice for atonement?*

Indeed, from our selfish and sinful perspectives we are not able to understand God's holy motives or divine wisdom whereby He developed the plan of salvation for humanity. God's intention from the very beginning has been the revelation of Himself as the Trinity (1 Peter 1:5). But to do this the first thing that had to be determined was the monotheism of God because apart from God's oneness the idea of His threeness cannot be differentiated from Paganism. God established monotheism through the Old Testament. In the New Testament God provided the advent of Jesus Christ, the Second Person of the Trinity and unleashed the Holy Spirit upon all flesh

(Acts 2:17). We are still involved with the fulfillment of that unleashing. It has begun but it is not complete.[16]

We cannot understand it because we are flawed sinners. Yet God calls us to understand it by faith through submission and obedience to Jesus Christ. "For by grace you have been saved through faith" (Ephesians 2:8). The refusal to submit to Christ is evidence of unwillingness to let go of sin, which is what being faith-less means. In such a case, God will not reveal the greater purpose of salvation because He knows that people will, in their sinfulness, only further misconstrue whatever truth He would give them.

But if we demonstrate to God our willingness to submit and obey, even though we don't fully understand (and no one does), God will begin to reveal His greater purpose to us as we grow spir-itually and become more able to understand God's truth. Because of our regeneration God trusts that the Spirit who has manifested in our own lives will help us understand God's will as we grow in faithfulness. Because we can only obey by the grace and presence of God's Holy Spirit through regeneration, our obedience is an indica-tion of the Spirit's presence in our lives.

But the truth of the matter is that reconciliation by blood sacri-fice is not a human idea and is repulsive to human understanding. It doesn't really make any sense to us, except that it is consistent with the Old Testament teaching of atonement. But from our sinful perspective the Old Testament idea doesn't really make any sense either, except that God instituted it and uses it for His own pur-poses.

It seems that the idea of blood sacrifice is a perfect way for God to test our willingness to rely upon Him and His Word alone, and to teach sinners to abandon their reliance upon worldly beliefs and ways of thinking. It boils down to the fact that we must submit to the logic of blood sacrifice for only one reason, because God said so. It's an authority thing.

The logic of blood is the biblical argument that the punishment for sin needs to satisfy God's justice. Our offense against God (sin) is ignoring Him and/or disobeying Him. Both are an attack on the Person and reality of God. If left uncorrected they lead to the death of God in our thinking and governance, and to the ultimate self-de-struction of humanity—eternal damnation. The logic of blood sacri-fice is that justice requires a life for a life (Exodus 21:23-25).

---

16 See footnote 7, p. 11.

God started with blood sacrifice to cover Adam's shame (Genesis 3:21).[17] It continued with periodic blood sacrifice of sheep, doves, bulls, etc. Then Jesus, the perfect man, received in His physical body the ultimate punishment for human sin in order to ultimately restore God's justice by providing the means of obedience and human longevity—God's Holy Spirit.

The logic of blood actually does make sense, but only in hindsight, only after one has engaged the way (Acts 18:25) of the Lord in earnest and the fruit of faithfulness has manifested in one's own life. It only makes sense because it is consistent with the Bible in the light of Christ. Apart from God's grace and mercy in Christ, God's justice seems exceedingly harsh. And that is how unbelievers see it. Apart from the light of Christ and the presence of the Holy Spirit through regeneration, it is a universal judgment against humanity by God.

At this point we begin to see the importance of believing in the infallibility of Scripture. If we cannot trust God's Word, then we cannot trust anything that God says about salvation because we ourselves cannot determine which parts of God's Word are trustworthy and which are not. Faithfulness begins with reliance upon God's Word or it doesn't begin at all.

Faith is not a leap in the dark as Kierkegaard suggested and Paul Tillich and the Existentialists capitalized on.[18] Rather, it is a step forward into the fog of reality. In the fog the next step can be seen, and maybe even a step or two down the road. But the distance is veiled in fog. Until one is out of the valley of the shadow (or fog) of death (Psalm 23:4) and into the light of Christ, things remain foggy. Christ is the light that dissipates the fog and the more we trust Christ, the more His light shines. The point is that in Christ more light is given over time as we grow in maturity.

So, we see from Paul's letter to the Colossians that blood atonement pleased God. God likes it because it is His idea, and it forces us to rely upon Him, which is the main point. God also likes it because it actually reconciles people and brings them into a relationship where they can receive and return God's love, which is also the main point. And further, it is not an idea that came to God after He saw that the Jews were unable to obey the Law. It is not God's backup plan. No, it was God's idea from the very beginning (Isaiah 41:26). He knew that no one would be able to obey the Law to His

---

17 The "coats of skin" required a blood (animal) sacrifice.
18 *A History of Christian Thought*, by Paul Tillich, Touchstone, 1972.

satisfaction, and that He would send His Son, Jesus Christ, after He had established some basic acceptance and practice of blood sacrifice through the Old Testament laws and Temple practices. The Old Testament teachings set up the New Testament understanding. Without the Old Testament the New Testament makes no sense, and apart from the New Testament the Old Testament cannot work. It is not a blessing, but a curse (Galatians 3:10).

It is important to see that Jesus' death on the cross was not God's Plan B, but that atonement by the blood of Christ was God's primary purpose in revealing the Law and establishing the Temple practice in the first place. The Law set up the gospel, and the gospel fulfilled the Law. God "prepared (it all) beforehand for (His) glory" (Romans 9:23).

CHRIST ALONE

For the same reason that reconciliation through the blood of Christ on the cross appeased God, our reconciliation depends upon Christ alone, for it was His blood alone on the cross, not ours. People sometimes wonder why Christianity is so exclusive. We say that salvation is by Christ *alone* and by no other. So, what about Buddha? And Confucius? And Mohammad? And all the rest? What about those people who have never heard about Jesus Christ?

The Christian answer is really quite simple. Buddha cannot save. Confucius cannot save. Muhammad cannot save. They are false teachers of false religions that will only confuse and lead people away from the only real salvation, which is by grace through faith in Jesus Christ.[19] But that does not mean that everything they teach is bad. No, some of what they teach is okay. Buddhism teaches people to clear their minds, and clear minds are good. Confucianism teaches people to honor their elders and families, and the Fifth Commandment (Exodus 20:12) is good. Islam teaches submission, but its god is not the God of the Bible, so Islamic submission is disobedience to the trinitarian God of the Bible.

Everything that each of these false religions teach (the whole of their teaching) is simply inadequate to avert the consequences of human sin. They all completely miss the mark. They cannot save. It is not that such teachings lead to Hell, but that they cannot avert the

---

19 It is essential for people to understand that apart from being genuinely born again *everyone* misunderstands who Jesus Christ is, how He works and what He is doing. See: *Marking God's Word—Understanding Jesus*, by Phillip A. Ross, Pilgrim Platform, 2007.

course of history that has already been set for Hell apart from Christ. People don't go to Hell because they are practicing Buddhism, Confucianism, Islam, etc. They are simply going to Hell because they are apart from Christ and His forgiveness. All who are apart from Christ will continue on the historic journey of this planet into Hell, without regard for their beliefs or traditions. Hell is home to the diversity of both godless and Pagan multiculturalism.

And what about those who have not heard about Christ? The Christian answer again is simple. They continue on the road or the train to Hell. And again unbelievers ask, *What kind of God would condemn people for something they have never heard of and can do nothing about on their own?*

We need to see that the reaction of the unbeliever is itself an expression of unbelief. It issues from a flawed understanding because what sinners believe about God, about reality, about themselves and about Christ is not true. But they don't know that it isn't true because their disbelief has blinded them to what is true (Romans 1). Everyone naturally thinks that they sufficiently understand reality, but they don't. If I believed what unbelievers believe about God, I wouldn't believe either. But I don't! I believe what I read in the Bible because I know how God has changed my own life and I find affinity with Scripture. The reaction of unbelievers is built upon false information or assumptions about God and the Bible.

SIN IS NATURAL

The person who thinks that God condemns people for something they have never heard of refuses to believe the evidence of sin in his own life, and which is common to all people. He refuses to acknowledge the reality of sin by pretending that people are born in a neutral state and are neither saints nor sinners at birth, that they are born unbiased. This is the modern doctrine of *tabula rasa.*[20] But the biblical truth is that all people are born sinners (Romans 3:23). The Bible teaches that people come into the world with a natural bias toward sin, that it is hard wired into the human psyche. The unbeliever neither believes nor understands this, yet Scripture

---

20 *Tabula rasa* (Latin: blank slate) refers to the epistemological thesis that people are born without any built-in mental content and that knowledge comes from experience and perception. Proponents of this idea favor the nurture: side of the nature versus nurture debate regarding human character. The idea appears as early as the writings of Aristotle and was popularized by John Locke. However, it contradicts the Bible (Ephesians 1:3-5).

teaches it. Believers know that it is true because, believing the Bible, they see their own natural bias toward sin. And what is more, they know that Christ can and has made a significant difference in their own lives.

Scripture goes on to tell us that everyone knows the reality of sin because (in a sense) God placed it in our chromosomes—definitely, figuratively and perhaps even literally. Everyone is born into sin. No one needs instruction to know how to sin. It's natural. Paul told the Romans that everyone has an adequate acquaintance with their own human sinfulness, so all are "without excuse" (Romans 1:20). Nonetheless people deny it. Several factors contribute to the reasons that so many people deny the reality of sin, but they all boil down to the simple fact that they don't want to believe it.

They don't like the implications of it, so they choose not to believe it. Sinners go to great lengths to dream up rational explanations for everything, rationalizations that do not make reference to God, in order to write God out of their minds (i.e, the Big Bang Theory of creation, the Theory of Evolution and the many systems of unbiblical philosophy and religion). Rejecting God makes people feel better about themselves because they think that it gets them out from under obligation to God, out from under the demand for obedience and consequences of disobedience to God. The rejection of sin is an affirmation of pride and belief in one's own superiority to God or the Bible because they think that they have succeeded in these efforts.

But just because people don't believe something does not mean that it isn't true. Once we believe, God proves the truth of His promise by His actions in our lives. He changes us in the likeness of Christ. We know it's true because God said it is true, and Christians experience its truth in their own lives. Nonetheless, God said it, and that's enough to reveal that it is true. God is the author of truth, and all truth is of God. God doesn't lie. God changes people in such a way that they can see His truth in their own lives.

WHAT ABOUT THEM?

So, what about all those people who don't believe, or who have never heard of Jesus? Well, they are *our responsibility*! God calls those who do believe to spread the news to those who don't, to teach them, to convince them, to persuade them, to encourage them to believe. It doesn't matter why people don't believe, they are the responsibility of believers. We need to be doing all we can to reach them with the good news of Jesus Christ.

People ask, *What about those who have not heard about Christ?* But anyone who asks that question and is not at the same time actively engaged in reaching such people with the gospel is not a faithful believer, and needs to hear the gospel himself. Such a person is using the question as a means to dodge God's call to faithfulness and evangelism in his own life. The argument he espouses (that God is unjust to condemn people who haven't read the New Testament) works to make a case against the gospel. The question is an attack on the truth of the gospel. Any believer who asks the question is called to answer it, and not just intellectually. He must answer it with willing and obedient service inasmuch as he actually understands the issues. The asking of the question is itself the call to service to go and reach those who haven't heard, who don't believe. But the truth is that people don't have to go very far to find people who haven't heard the truth about Jesus or who don't believe it.

Obviously, more is implied by hearing the gospel than simply hearing the name of Jesus Christ or the facts of His story. By hearing the gospel we mean responding in faith to Christ. The five letter word *Jesus* is not a magic talisman. It is not a matter of barking the word *Jesus* at people. It's a matter of presenting the gospel to people in a way that makes sense. But it must make sense to *you* before you can explain it to anyone else. Indeed the effort to make sense of Scripture and the various conundrums in it fuels our own prayer and spiritual growth in the process.

Theology is not a finished process of those who know teaching those who don't, but is more a conversation about God by interested people. Everyone learns and everyone teaches. Yes, some people are better at it than others, and so some explanations become more common. But understanding God is not like learning math, where one person instructs another in the mechanics of God. Rather, understanding the God of Scripture is a matter of loving God enough to take the time to delve into Scripture and discuss God with others.

It is more a process of abiding with God and with other believers, of bearing God's uncomfortable truths, of being changed by them, and appreciating the change. Others can be helpful, but it is mostly a personal journey. So, the responsibility of the faithful is to understand the gospel and then to share their understanding with others. In the process of that sharing, people are then changed, both speaker and hearer.

Too many people who call themselves Christians can't make sense of the gospel because too many preachers can't either. The sad truth is that the gospel isn't being preached or heard in most churches. The weakening of Christianity is not the fault of God or Jesus or the Bible. It is the fault of Christians. So, if you know someone who hasn't "heard" (Matthew 11:15) the truth of the gospel, it is your responsibility to tell him about it. You don't even have to become a missionary. Just talk to your neighbors. There is much work to do! The harvest is upon us (Matthew 9:37).

The promise that God makes to His people is that we will have peace through reconciliation by the blood of Christ (v. 20). We've talked about the blood of Christ, but what about this peace? We need to understand that God's peace does not mean the absence of trouble and difficulty. God's peace is not the simple absence of hostility, but is the hard work of reconciliation. There can be no peace apart from reconciliation with God and with one another.

The Greek word translated *peace* (*eirēnopoieō*) is a Greek version of the Hebrew word *shalom*. Shalom is not mere peace, but includes a sense of wholeness and harmony. Biblical peace or shalom always requires a satisfying understanding of God's purposes and reconciliation among all (the whole) of the various positions and perspectives found in Scripture. This integration is found only in Christ, only in the Trinity of God in Christ.

Jesus said, "These things I have spoken to you, that in Me you may have peace. In the world you will have tribulation; but be of good cheer, I have overcome the world" (John 16:33). Difficulties and troubles will continue for Christians as long as this world continues. God uses them for our growth and good. The peace of Christ is peace with God, a confidence that, in spite of the troubles and tribulations of this world, our eternal security is assured.

Eternal security doesn't mean that we can do whatever we want because we have God's stamp of approval. But rather, because God will accomplish what He wants to accomplish, and having become a witness to Christ's resurrection through regeneration, we find that we actually want to do what God wants us to do. That is our assurance. We are sure that God will do what He wants to do and that He has actually gotten a hold of us. That assurance, then, fuels our understanding of the gospel, which in turn provides additional confidence to trust in Christ's faithfulness and in His power to bring salvation to all of His people. By trusting Christ and acting on that trust, our understanding grows, which gives us more reason to trust Christ even more, which provides more understanding, *etcetera ad infinitum.*

Trust leads to understanding, understanding leads to service, to the work of reconciliation, because to be a Christian is to be in service to the Lord. Genuine Christian service issues out of peace because it is based upon the peace of Jesus Christ, which is the fruit of reconciliation.

ন্নৈ৺

To reconcile means to bring into consonance or accord, to recover unity and harmony among formerly or apparently divergent things. Complete reconciliation in Christ comes as people are caught up (1 Thessalonians 4:13) into the singularity of Christ and forever changed by the power of *Christos Singularis.*

5

GROUNDED & STEADFAST

And you, who once were alienated and enemies in your mind by wicked works, yet now He has reconciled in the body of His flesh through death, to present you holy, and blameless, and above reproach in His sight—if indeed you continue in the faith, grounded and steadfast, and are not moved away from the hope of the gospel which you heard, which was preached to every creature under heaven, of which I, Paul, became a minister.
—Colossians 1:21-23 (ESV)

Those who are in need of reconciliation are those who are unreconciled enemies of God. And who might those unreconciled enemies of God be? Everyone begins this life as unreconciled sinners. Everyone stands in need of reconciliation to God until they, in fact, receive reconciliation through the blood of Christ. No one is exempt. No one stands outside the need for Christ's reconciliation.

In essence Paul said that there are two categories of human beings: the reconciled and the unreconciled. This means that the reconciled were also unreconciled before they became reconciled. The language here sounds awkward because I am trying make a point that is completely obvious, yet often overlooked. Paul said in verse 21 that all people were enemies of God in their thoughts and practices before they received the grace (gift) of reconciliation by the blood of Christ.

Another way to say it is that if Christ has not changed your sinful thinking and habits, you are either unsaved or unsanctified. If you still prefer worldly values and vices, your salvation may be in question. Sure the difference between being saved and not being saved is like night and day. But sunrise does not happen in an instant. Sanctification takes time. The sunrise is not the end of the day. Those who are saved are actually changed. They grow. They are aware of both their new values and their old values, and consciously strive to let the old go. Reconciliation happens in an instant, but sanctification unfolds over a lifetime. Paul spoke of his own struggles in Romans 7. The point is that those who are saved struggle against their sins, they don't celebrate them as gifts of God.[21]

Since Paul was arguing against false teaching in Colossae, his point was that this personal change that is brought about through reconciliation by the blood of Christ is obvious only to those who have experienced it, only to those who have been born-again, only to those who are led by the Holy Spirit. And this was the very thing that was disputed or twisted by the false teachers.

The false teachers at Colossae were syncretists who were working to combine ideas from various religions and philosophies with Christian truth. This heresy was also called Gnosticism which taught that salvation came by way of secret knowledge, a knowledge that was added to the gospel by the Gnostics. While it is true that salvation—reconciliation, belief and the understanding of Christ that follows it—does not come to everyone, it is not true that it is the result of knowledge (secret or public) or of any mixing of biblical Christianity with anything. Christianity stands alone and apart from all other religions and philosophies. Unfortunately, syncretism, Gnosticism and Universalism have enjoyed a great revival in America to the point that they provide the dominant religious perspectives in America today. And we are awash in their foul backwaters.

The difficulty that Paul deals with is the challenge of trying to convince people that they were wrong when they didn't think they were wrong. Have you ever thought you were right about something and later discovered you were wrong? Before you discovered that you were wrong, you didn't see why you were wrong, and couldn't admit it. But once you accepted the fact that you were wrong, once

---

21 There is a movement in the church to accept unrepentant homosexuals as church members and officers. However, the unrepentant are banned from such participation, but not because of their sin. Sin is not the problem. The problem is the lack of repentance. All Christians are sinners and all must repent of their sins. Repentant homosexuals renounce the sin of homosexual behavior, just as repentant liars renounce lying and repentant thieves renounce stealing, etc. Homosexuality is not okay with God in the same way that lying, stealing, extortion, etc. are not okay. Like it or not, that is what the Bible teaches.

you understood how you were wrong, you changed your thinking. At some point your error became clear to you, and you changed your thinking in light of it.

What Paul was arguing here was that all human thinking is wrong from the outset. The only way that human thinking can be right is to receive Christ's reconciliation personally and experientially, and then to ground all further thinking in God's Word. Only in as much as human thinking is grounded in God's Word, can it be right. Only in as much as the presuppositions of our logic are biblical, can we be right in our conclusions.

The traditional way of saying this is that Christ is our only righteousness, only in Christ can people be right. Paul said that Christians are "found in Him (Christ), not having (their) own righteousness... but that which is through faith in Christ, the righteousness which is from God by faith" (Philippians 3:9). Paul argued against those who were "ignorant of God's righteousness, and (sought) to establish their own righteousness." Paul elsewhere accused them of not submiting to the righteousness of God (Romans 10:3). That submission is the key to understanding the gospel.

By submitting to Christ, Christians abandon their own authority and logic, and submit to God's authority and logic, to the authority and logic of the Bible. It is very easy to impose our own thoughts and ideas on the Bible and think they are biblical. But we must not do that. We must, rather, conform our thoughts and ideas to the Bible by believing the Bible to be completely true and trustworthy. This is the faith we must bring to our reading of Scripture. We must bring "every thought into captivity to the obedience of Christ" (2 Corinthians 10:5). Every thought! Not just at church, not just on Sunday, not just thoughts about so-called spiritual things. But every thought must be brought under the authority of Christ through Scripture.

TALK VS. WALK

There is a great deal of difference between understanding what I just said and putting it into practice. But the truth is that what I have said cannot be understood until it is put into practice. And far too few Christians actually practice bringing every thought into captivity to the obedience of Christ! Those who don't practice it, at best, misunderstand it. That misunderstanding then produces what

Paul calls false teaching. It produces a gospel that is no gospel. He also said that "the gospel which was preached by (Paul) is not according to man" (Galatians 1:11), but according to God.

Paul said that all Christians begin life alienated from God. "All have sinned and fall short of the glory of God" (Romans 3:23). In sin and alienation all Christians were once God's enemies—enemies because of their wrong thinking and their refusal to submit every thought to the obedience of Christ. Paul said that God's enemies are those who do not want to submit to Christ.

Paul called all baptized Christians to continue in the faith. Does this mean that some Christians might not so continue? We all know people who have left Christianity, who once considered themselves to be Christians, but no longer do so. That's the reality. Whether this means that Christians can lose their faith is a complex question. The short answer is *no*, but people can fool themselves.

Nonetheless, Paul addressed all who had been "reconciled in the body of (Christ's) death" and said that they would be presented "holy, and blameless, and above reproach in His sight *if...*" (vs. 22-23). If what? If they "continue in the faith, grounded and steadfast, and are not moved away from the hope of the gospel which (they) heard." Paul encouraged, even required, the faithful to remain faithful and not change their minds because of any additions, deletions or variations of the gospel, no matter how right such additions, deletions or variations may seem.

Paul told them not to be confused by new (or contemporary) ideas, but to hold fast to the original truth of the gospel. There's nothing wrong with new ideas, as long as they are grounded and steadfast in God's Word. Paul was not trying to throw out every new idea. Rather, he distinguished between new ideas that were biblical and those that were not.

INNOVATION

Paul himself was the chief innovator of new ideas in his day. His understanding of reconciliation by the blood of the cross itself appeared to be a new idea to the Pharisees, though it was grounded in and faithful to the Word of God. The Jews attacked Paul because they thought that he was being too innovative with his talk about Jesus being the Old Testament Messiah. Paul's caution to remain faithful to the original gospel was not an attempt to retard progress. He was cautioning people against a very real and very common error, an error that is still common today, even among Christians.

Paul cautioned the faithful to "not (be) moved away from the hope of the gospel" (v. 23) because he observed that people were in fact being drawn away from the gospel. Nowhere does Paul teach or suggest that once people are saved, they can believe whatever they want. Rather, everywhere Paul taught and suggested that people who believe what they want (according to their own thinking) are not led by the Holy Spirit. To be led by the Holy Spirit requires surrendering our own opinions, and conforming to God's opinions, not perfectly but increasingly over time.

How can we apply this today? Paul suggests that faithful Christians should not live by their own opinions, but on the basis of Scripture. Christ calls Christians to rise above their own opinions. Christ does not call His people to a diversity of opinions about religious matters. Rather, Christ calls His people to unity of mind and spirit (1 Peter 3:8). Christians are to have the "mind of Christ" (1 Corinthians 2:16).

The dictionary says that an opinion is a belief based upon what seems to be true, valid, or probable to one's own mind. It is a belief that is based on one's own thoughts, feelings, and experiences. However, the Bible teaches that human opinion is hopelessly flawed because of sin. Human thoughts, feelings, and experiences are always grounded in sin, not in righteousness. Consequently, Christians must not be governed by their own opinions and beliefs, but by Christ's opinions and beliefs revealed in Scripture. In Christ there is diversity of people types, but unity of mind and spirit.

Being governed by Christ is a fruit of reconciliation (Matthew 5:24). It only happens when people submit to Christ, when they submit to Christ's reconciliation by the blood of the cross. It only happens when people are born-again, when people are washed in the blood of Christ. Not when they are awash in the backwaters of syncretism and Gnosticism, but when they are saved—justified and sanctified by the blood of Christ.

The practical application of the gospel is to quit thinking that you are always right, to doubt yourself and your own beliefs, and to study the Bible until all your beliefs are in line with Scripture. We live in a very strange time, a time in which practically everyone thinks that he understands the truth about God, about religion and about the Bible. Yet, most people don't really think about God or study the Bible. Christians think they are doing well when they read one or two popular Christian books a year. Not that that's bad, it's not, not necessarily, depending on what people read. The major Christian bookstores are no longer owned by Christians, which means that they are profit-driven rather than prophet-driven. The bottom line is sales, not truth, popularity, not integrity.

Getting a foundational understanding of the Bible and a faithful, historical biblical understanding of the issues in our day is a huge task! It takes time. Like eating an elephant, it must be done in small bites. The trick to completing a big job in small bites are the disciplines of perseverance and consistency. Even so, it can't really be done at all unless and until you surrender yourself, your heart, mind, soul, and strength to God's Holy Spirit.

I'm not suggesting salvation through Bible study. Rather, I'm suggesting that biblical understanding is a fruit of sanctification, that those who are saved have a thirst for God's Word. How can people learn to thirst for God? How can people learn to want God? Can people change their wants and desires? I honestly don't know if it is possible. Of course desires change. But do we change them? Or does God change them? If we don't like a particular food, we can force ourselves to eat it so we will get used to it. But do we ever really come to the point of liking it? We can better tolerate it—sure. But like it? Can a leopard change its spots (Jeremiah 13:23)?

And yet desires change, people change. However, apart from regeneration people only become more of what they already are. It is the power of regeneration, of being born again, that changes people into something else and for the better, for Christ. But how do people get born again? If the second birth is anything like the first one, we do not do it to ourselves. It is something that happens to us, not something we cause to happen.

The message of the gospel is that Christ has come, died for our sins, for the sins of the world. Christ satisfied God's desire for justice and released the Holy Spirit upon the world for regeneration. In other words, being born again is not something that people can look forward to. It is something that people have by faith, or don't. People don't realize something and then get born. They get born and years later they look back and make their realizations, or not.

So how can people get it? I don't know, but you gotta wanna.

The application is to let go of those beliefs that do not line up with Scripture and to hold fast to those that do. The practical application is to know Scripture because God wants to change what you believe, so that it matches what He believes. God loves His people so much that He will not leave them as they are.

ᙅᙓ

God conforms people to His thinking by drawing them into Christ, the Word of God where Father, Son and Holy Spirit cohere in union with Christ and His people. God's gravity draws people in. Yet, all personal identity remains intact, and is augmented by the others in the singularity. *Christos Singularis!*

6

THE HOPE OF GLORY

I now rejoice in my sufferings for you, and fill up in my
flesh what is lacking in the afflictions of Christ, for the sake
of His body, which is the church, of which I became a
minister according to the stewardship from God which was
given to me for you, to fulfill the word of God, the mystery
which has been hidden from ages and from generations, but
now has been revealed to His saints. To them God willed to
make known what are the riches of the glory of this
mystery among the Gentiles: which is Christ in you, the
hope of glory.   —*Colossians 1:24-27 (ESV)*

Earlier Paul told the Colossians that through faith in Christ
there is reconciliation to God by the blood of the cross, and
that this basic message of the gospel is unchanging. Therefore, people should hold fast to it and not be moved from it, even in
the light of what might seem to be acceptable arguments to the contrary. The church is to be leery of human knowledge that is not
grounded in and faithful to the gospel of Christ revealed in Scripture.

Paul previously claimed the authority of Christ as the basis of his
preaching. His authority came to him by divine appointment. Christ
had called him and commissioned him to preach. Here Paul
summoned his own experience to testify to his authority. In essence
he said that he was able to rejoice in the sufferings he had experienced because of his fidelity to the gospel of Christ and because of the
fruit his ministry produced. He had not preached in vain. His preaching led many to Christ, whose reconciling blood brought forth the
fruit of the Spirit. That fruit, then, was evidence of his authority and
of God's blessing.

Paul did not say that his own suffering was redemptive. People are saved and will then suffer for Christ. Jesus said that Christians should expect persecution because the world persecuted Him (John 15:20). Paul did not say that he had been saved because he had suffered for Christ, but only that God had blessed his faithfulness in spite of the suffering it had caused him. Only Christ's death on the cross redeems, not Paul's suffering, nor our own.

We might wonder today why faithfulness would produce suffering? We know that Paul had been slandered, maligned, beaten, run out of town, and imprisoned. But why? Why all the fuss? Why bother persecuting Paul or any other Christians?

There is no doubt that all this happened to Paul because of his steadfast faithfulness. In fact, his faithfulness was revealed by his suffering. Few American Christians experience real hostility to the message of Christ today, though hostility is growing. Satan has perfected modern resistance to the gospel by teaching people to ignore it. Satan has succeeded in convincing many people that they need not be concerned with Christ.

How has Satan done this? By promoting the understanding that truth is relative, that there is no objective truth. Secularists have inoculated people against Scripture's claim of absolute truth. If truth is relative, then the desire to discover it and live by it is unimportant. People believe that whatever they think is their truth and whatever I think is my truth. So what's the big deal about truth? Everyone has their own truth. Don't they?

RELATIVE

The problem is that if truth is relative, it is insignificant and does not match its own definition. A relative truth is no truth at all. It is a truth that changes meanings depending on ... whatever. And so the bulk of Americans do not outwardly oppose Christianity, they simply ignore it. They consider it to be insignificant. Even when people profess to be Christian, they often ignore its truth claims. Too many people today do not know how to blush (Jeremiah 6:5). People, even self-professed Christians, fail to consider the seriousness of the gospel or the extent of sin. People take their faith lightly, insignificantly, as if it were a minor thing. By confessing Christ but not the absolute truth of Scripture, people actually deny the Christ they profess to affirm (Matthew 7:21-ff).

When people begin to *seriously* oppose Christ again a great revival will break out! When Christianity is officially deemed to oppose current civil law, as is beginning to happen around the issue of homosexuality, a great hue and cry will come in response. Serious opposition to Christianity will get people thinking about the issues, and will spur faithful Christians to mount a countervailing and equally serious defense in the public square that will shake people to their very foundations.

Christianity has already won every argument that history and science have been able to throw at it, though atheists deny this. But atheists don't actually understand God. So they don't understand absolute truth. Atheists seldom argue against the actual God of the Bible because they don't know Him! So, they argue against straw gods of their own imaginations or the straw gods that litter history.

Where people seriously oppose Christ enough to seriously engage the Bible, He is able to make His case and win hearts by defeating falsehood. When people care enough to seriously oppose Christ will they seriously study the Bible and the issues. Opposition apart from serious study is mere bigotry. God is not afraid of serious disbelief and uses it to expose disbelievers to the serious arguments of the gospel. He is not afraid because He knows that faith comes by hearing (Galatians 3:2-ff), by seriously wrestling with the issues.

But when people choose to ignore God or Scripture and His truth claims they close their ears and their hearts to the hope of the gospel by not caring. They don't ever hear the real gospel and reject what they think the gospel is before they actually know what it is. They simply don't bother to listen to it in the first place. They think they know what Christianity is all about, but what they know is almost always a truncated version of a shallow and false gospel.

The gospel of Jesus Christ provides an effective treatment for human sin and depravity. It is the only solution to the difficulties of the human predicament, that predicament being the fact that humanity is stuck in a very long historical cycle of boom and bust, cultural development that is based upon sin and leads to the loss (thievery) of capital.[22] The predicament is that our approach to human development to date has incorporated depravity, decay, and decline because it is approached apart from Christ, because it

---

22 The original idea of boom and bust belongs to Carl Marx, one of the chief architects of Communism. Markets are driven by greed and fear. Greed is bullish, and fear is bearish. Neither are endemic to Capitalism, but are functions of sin. The effectiveness of Capitalism makes it a target of the greedy. As Christ rids the world of sin, the markets will stabilize and become engines for social stability.

incorporates truth and error, God and Belial, Christ and Satan.

PROGRESS

What do I mean? For instance, the passion for development that produced the industrial revolution resulted in great damage to the environment and may threaten the quality of human life. What was once great and noble, the passion for freedom that led to the development of technology and progress, when pursued without Christ, without the discipline of Christian faithfulness (righteousness and the impact of righteousness on science and technology), has undermined society by damaging the ecosystem upon which life itself relies. If the recent past is an indicator, it is unlikely that the damage is permanent. But time will tell.[23]

The fact that some industrialists claim to be Christian, or even if they actually are Christians, doesn't necessarily mean that they operate their businesses on Christian principles. Christians are often more conflicted than non-Christians because of the issues Paul discussed in Romans 7. The non-Christian does not have the New Man to contend with, and can simply be united behind the Old Man in opposition to God. Regardless, sin has been imposed upon the environment by human greed and selfishness through the efficiencies of modern technology.

The analogy points to industrial pollution, for instance, as an end-result of unrestrained freedom, or freedom apart from Christ. Faithful Christians would engage industrial production differently than faithless Pagans. Why? Because their worldviews are different, and different at every point. Thankfully, over the past few decades great progress has been made in diminishing much ecological damage. But the cost of this effort has encroached upon human freedom and independence. We have come to learn that we cannot be absolutely free and independent, that is, free apart from Christ because we are interdependent.

We are interdependent with one another, with other nations, with the environment, and with what is beyond the environment. The environment of the earth is dependent on lots of things, and God holds them all together (John 1:1-17). And God sent Christ, so we are also dependent upon God in Christ. It is not just that Chris-

---

23 The debate about global warming or climate change is currently raging. Pollution is a problem. Nonetheless, our ability to reduce man-made pollution over the past 50 years has been remarkable. Much reduction of pollution has been accomplished, and will no doubt continue.

tians are dependent upon God in Christ, but the whole human race is dependent upon God in Christ, believers and unbelievers alike. The difference is that unbelievers don't believe it. But their lack of belief does not change the fact.

Today, then, there is a rash of noble sentimentality about inter-dependence. As people once had a passion for independence, people now have a passion for interdependence. And it is the ideo-logy of interdependence that now champions the relativity of truth. But it need not.

Earth Day provides an example of what I mean. Here is how this kind of relativity works: In order to get along with one another, we think that we have to allow every possible perspective to believe itself true. In our passion to establish cross cultural relationships, which are necessary for our interdependence, we mistakenly think that interdependence requires social or cultural diversity. So we accept various falsehoods—false beliefs, false gods, silly cultural traditions, etc.—in the name of diversity. But in doing so we have thrown out objective truth because objective truth will testify that some people and some cultures are right and some are wrong in what they believe. And that realization then causes offense and brings stress to the relationships that foster our current belief in diversity and interdependence. We as a culture have failed to see that in Christ there is more than sufficient diversity of humanity, that Christianity is not a cookie-cutter religion.

The relativist complains, *Who are you to say that I'm not right!*

If all truth is relative, there is no standard by which to evaluate anything. So people don't evaluate. They just accept whatever any-one believes as being true "for them." But such a position makes a mockery of reason and logic. Something cannot be true for me and not true for someone else. Of course, people have different tastes and preferences. But truth is not a function of taste or preference. People are in the habit of speaking as if truth is relative, so they couch their ideas and sentences in ways that support the relativity of truth and undermine its absolute character. Depending on com-mon language or common usage for the definition or description of ultimate Truth is simply inadequate. And thinking that it can be adequate is an act of disguising truth with relativity. Such thinking belittles God and inflates man.

If truth is relative we can only bounce from one set of human values to another. But from the objective perspective of God's truth,

Christ calls us to abandon our human values and take up God's values, biblical values. That's just another way of saying that God calls us to believe in Jesus Christ, to believe the gospel, to believe the Bible. Not to simply say that we do, but to actually do those things. And doing so requires the abandonment of our own values, the abandonment of our personal assumptions about life and truth, and particularly to abandon the godless, secular values that are ingrained into us through the media and government education. Biblical values and truths are as close to perfect objectivity as human beings can come because they transcend various cultures and historical epochs. The Bible holds its value over time.

Paul's understanding of reality is that man (humanity) is not the head. Christ is the head, and the church is the body of Christ. The body does not have its own values, but lives in submission to the head, to Christ. This simple model of reality is redemptive. But few people actually believe it. This is also true for the church, for Christians. Those who are not Christian have usurped the headship and authority of Jesus Christ in that God has given all authority to Christ (Matthew 28:18).

The application of this is to believe the gospel. But if we (society) were to actually believe the gospel, we would not live as we presently live. If we were, by the grace of God and the power of the Holy Spirit, to actually believe and live by biblical values, we would freely and willingly submit to God's Law in the light of Christ. We would honor the Sabbath, honor our parents, abandon our romantic indulgences, and cease to covet Madison Avenue. Things would be very different, would they not?[24]

I'm not trying to chastise anyone, or to take away what people value or the things that they enjoy. I'm simply trying to point us to Christ's values. But in pointing this out, I am often vilified as the bad guy, Mr. Negative!—as if the guy who points out the elephant in the room is the guy who put it there. Nor am I suggesting that I have *the* answer. I'm simply raising issues that need careful consideration.

So often we think that if only we can have a little positive encouragement that we are doing something right, then we will have the strength to continue. We look for self-affirmation, for

---

24 Christians can neither revert to Old Testament law, nor abandon it. Rather, God's law must be understood and honored *in the light of Christ*. Christ fulfilled God's law, and that fulfillment means that Christians are no longer bound by the law, but that doesn't mean that the law is no longer useful. The purpose of the New Testament is to better understand and honor the Old Testament *in the light of Christ*. Much work still needs to be done in this area.

indications that we are on the right path so that we will have the strength to make it through another week. That seems to be what most Christians want, and that's the way that most pastors preach.

But Christ says that there is no hope in self-affirmation, no hope in the ways of the world. Christ calls us to give up the ways of the world, to give up our desire for self-satisfaction and worldly success, to give up our passion for self-fulfillment and worldly achievement. We must come to see that the only hope that will really satisfy is the hope of God's glory, not our own. We must seek the hope that is given by Christ, and abandon the false hope that builds our self-esteem at the expense of truth. The hope that satisfies is the hope that comes from obedience through the grace of God and the blood of Christ. That hope comes, not from human lips, but from the mouth of God, from Scripture.

In Christ there is great hope. Apart from Christ there is no hope. In false belief there is only false hope. And so the hopelessness of the world without Christ is a great goad to faithfulness. The hopelessness of the world should create a hunger and thirst for righteousness. The hopelessness of the world should frustrate us and drive us into the arms of Jesus. Christ is then the answer to that hunger and the satisfaction of that thirst.

But where such hunger and thirst do not exist or are denied, Christ is neither valued nor sought. Where the world has its own hope, it lacks Christ. To seek hope from anything other than Christ is to turn away from the hope of Christ, the hope of salvation, and the reality of regeneration. These are the problems that unbelievers must face.

Believers have a different problem. Believers must be aware that Satan loves to dress the hopes of the world in the robes of Christ, to confuse believers about the true nature of Christian hope in order to poison the well of the church. Satan's best gambit has always been to confuse the hope of Christ with the hope of the world, knowing that immature believers will easily default to their well-worn worldly desires and turn away from Christ—*in the name of Christ!* This is why Paul spends so much time correcting theological errors. Most of Paul's letters were written to correct an errant church. Satan loves to muddy the water.

THE MAIN PROBLEM

In regard to salvation, there are no gray areas. It is Christ or

Hell! The primary problem in our day is that people do not believe themselves to be sinners, and the suggestion that they are greatly offends them. People neither think themselves to be sinners, nor admit the consequences of sin. Therefore, they have no interest in salvation, in Christ or in faithfulness to Him. They think they don't need salvation. And as long as they think that they don't need what Christ provides, they will not listen to or hear the gospel. It is a conspiracy of ignorance where people ignore truth and Jesus Christ.

That's fine for you, they say, *You can believe in Jesus if you want to. But I'm okay just as I am.*

Of course, some of them want their children to learn about religion. They reassure themselves that they don't need it themselves, but they send their kids to Sunday School or Vacation Bible School or church camp, etc. And the kids get just enough religion to inoculate them from it. We live in a difficult time and in a difficult place to speak of God's truth in Jesus Christ. But speak it we must!

The primary purpose of preaching the gospel in every age is to help people understand that they are not okay, that they stand in need of a Savior. And that the only hope for the world is the glory of Jesus Christ. And in spite of the difficulties, that is exactly what we must do. In spite of the difficulties, the age we live in is no different than other ages because people's hearts are always the same.

The gospel is the only remedy for the unbelieving heart. The gospel is the same yesterday, today and tomorrow. So, the message we share must also be the same yesterday, today and tomorrow.

CB&O

The Hebrew word for *glory* (*kâbôd*) literally means weight, which is a function of gravity—the universal force of attraction. The glory of God is His gravitas, literally His gravity, from which nothing can escape, and by which He brings people into His orbit. Thus, we participate in God's function of holding reality together by giving God glory in worship. *Christos Singularis!*

7

WARNING & TEACHING

Him we preach, warning every man and teaching every man in all wisdom, that we may present every man perfect in Christ Jesus. To this end I also labor, striving according to His working which works in me mightily.
—Colossians 1:28-29 (ESV)

Paul preached "Christ crucified, to the Jews a stumbling block and to the Greeks foolishness, but to those who are called, both Jews and Greeks, Christ the power of God and the wisdom of God. Because the foolishness of God is wiser than men, and the weakness of God is stronger than men" (1 Corinthians 1:23-25).

There was something very unsettling about Paul's preaching. Not only were the Scribes and Pharisees uncomfortable with Paul, but they were able to stir up the common people against him as well. The response to Paul's preaching was mixed at best. Some heard him and were convicted unto salvation. Others became offended and angry.[25]

As a church we must come to an understanding of this response to Paul's preaching of the doctrines of grace, or we will succumb to the liberal tendency to alter our message to insure that no one is offended. This is how people change the gospel to suit themselves. This is no imaginary concern. It has plagued the church in every age, and ours is no exception. It is not only a concern in our time, but a real concern in every city. Few are the churches that have not fallen to some perversion of the gospel. Indeed, the progressive revelation of Jesus Christ (1 Peter 1:7) suggests that the gospel will be better understood and the church more faithful over time.

One of the things we must come to terms with is that the wisdom

---

25 For more on this theme see: *Acts of Faith—Kingdom Advancement*, Phillip A. Ross, Pilgrim Platform, 2007.

of God is not like the wisdom of the world. I have been concerned about this theme for some time now because it is a major concern in our day and in our churches.[26] There is a false belief afoot today that suggests that all Christians need to do is to profess belief in Christ as Savior and they are saved. Just say the words and it's a done deal.

The problem with this false belief is that is suggests that people are saved by their profession of faith. If that is the case, salvation is a matter of works, of speaking the right words. The problem with this false belief is that it arrests the process of sanctification (growth in grace) by suggesting that salvation is the main thing and spiritual growth is an option. It fails to understand that sanctification often comes from struggles and difficulties that we try to avoid. It separates spiritual growth from salvation in an unhealthy and unrealistic way.

While profession of faith is necessary, it is not the means of salvation. Rather, profession of faith is only a response to salvation. It is the evidence of salvation, it does not cause it. Furthermore, once God's grace has been received, spiritual growth begins and does not stop. In response to God's grace, Christians *want* to worship. They *want* to pray. They *want* to study their Bibles. They *want* to fellowship with other growing Christians. The key here is that Christians *want* to do these things. And people always have time for the things they want to do.

Salvation involves the conversion of the will. That means that when people are saved, they actually want to do what God wants them to do. It is not a matter of duty. Born-again Christians do not worship, or study the Bible, or fellowship together because they know they should, but because they want to. They value these things. They hunger and thirst for them.

DESIRE

So, if you don't have a personal desire to worship and pray and study your Bible, you may be in great spiritual danger. If you find yourself making excuses like *I'm too busy, I'm too tired, its too cold, its too late*, then you must face the possibility that you don't really want to do these things because you don't really value them. By definition, to value something is to treasure it enough to make

---

26 See: *Arsy Varsy—Reclaiming the Gospel in First Corinthians*, Phillip A. Ross, Pilgrim Platform, 2008, and *Varsy Arsy—Proclaiming the Gospel in Second Corinthians*, Phillip A. Ross, Pilgrim Platform, 2009.

time for it. By definition, what people don't value, they don't make time for.

I've presented this situation in a particular way because it will be helpful to trust your salvation, but doubt your theology, to trust Scripture but doubt our own understanding. We must trust Christ for salvation. It is His doing, and He has completed it on the cross and before the tribunals of God Almighty. We must trust that the salvation of God's people is certain.

But many Christians struggle with spiritual growth. Don't trust my observation about this, test yourselves. Can you name the Ten Commandments? If you can't name them, how can you possibly claim to honor them? Where are they in Scripture? Can you recite John 3:16? What about Romans 3:23? Or Romans 6:23? What did Jesus teach about election? What about predestination? Grace? Reprobation? Atonement? Providence? Perseverance? Assurance of salvation? It is not that people need to know these things in order to be saved, not at all. Rather, it is that pleasing Jesus means loving the things that He loves, and He loves Scripture and theology. Understanding these things is for all Christians because God wants all Christians to grow and mature (Ephesians 4:11-16).

These are fine tests for mature Christians, but what about immature Christians? Well, immature Christians don't have the depth of understanding that mature Christians have. But they will have the desire to learn. In fact, the immature (new Christians) often have more passion for study and learning than the mature, who have satisfied many of their desires to understand. So, these tests are good for the immature as well because they will inspire them to learn and grow.

Too many people think that they don't need to know these things unless they plan to be a minister. That's Satan talking. That's a cop-out! That's an excuse! And it's not true. These things are not for ministers alone. They are the basics. Without them there can be no real understanding of God or Christ or Scripture, and no significant spiritual growth. Christian growth comes in two forms: obedience and understanding, and they are related. That relationship is mutually interdependent. Like love and marriage, you shouldn't have one without the other. They belong together.

Liberals think that theology is just for ministers, and that it's not really important. Liberals believe nothing because they know nothing. They don't care about doctrine, about what the Bible actually teaches because they don't think it's important. But theology is the foundation of the faith. Born-again Christians will desire to know what Scripture teaches.

"Be ready to give a defense to everyone who asks you a reason for the hope that is in you" (1 Peter 3:15). Christians must be able to explain what they believe. As we think about the possibilities that face us, we must be able to tell people what we believe, and why. They're going to ask, and if we don't know they will pass us by. God's people know what they believe.

Paul warned everyone. He warned people of God's impending wrath, so that he could teach them about God's amazing grace. He warned them of the dangers of a lazy faith, so that he could inspire them with God's call to commitment. He warned them about believing falsely so that he could teach them to believe truly.

Paul tells us here that warning and teaching go together in the church, that a faithful church will both warn and teach, and that a faithful people will both heed his warning and learn his doctrine. There is nothing bad or wrong with warning people or telling them that they are wrong. Teaching involves both encouragement and correction. Both are required to teach faithfully.

Paul called the church to "teach every man in all wisdom" (v. 28). We must know that the wisdom of God is not the wisdom of the world. "Because the foolishness of God is wiser than men, and the weakness of God is stronger than men" (1 Corinthians 1:23-25). God's wisdom is opposed to, different than and in conflict with the wisdom of the world. Failure to understand this leads people away from God. Such failure makes people think that they are pursuing God when they are actually pursuing the world.

SCIENCE

Theology is not science. Science can be either faithful or unfaithful to God's Word. When science is built upon the foundation of Scripture, employing God's values and respecting God's limits, it is faithful. When it ignores God's Word, it isn't.

In our day worldly science has employed capitalism to produce modern technology. There is nothing wrong with technology. There is nothing wrong with capitalism. There is nothing wrong with science. But when these worldly enterprises are not used in the service of God, then something is very wrong. Something is wrong because modern technology is the most powerful force ever unleashed in the world, apart from God. When such a power is employed in the service of greed, or lust, or human ambition it opposes God and can do great damage. It's like a scalpel in the hands of a child.

The point is that God's wisdom and the world's wisdom locked horns long ago in a great struggle for dominance.[27] The bad news is that, not only are you on the battlefield, but your heart is the prize for which they struggle. The good news is that Christ has already won the war, but the bad news is: not for everyone. The good news is that your concern about these things suggests that *you* have been claimed by Christ. But you need to be sure because the struggle is intensifying.

Paul's purpose evidenced in verse 28 was to "present every man perfect in Christ Jesus." Perfect! Not just okay. Not just saved, but perfect in Christ. The Greek word translated *perfect* here is *telios*. It means lacking nothing necessary for completeness, human integrity and virtue, full grown and mature. It was Paul's job, and every preacher's responsibility, to help Christians grow in sanctification, to grow spiritually. Spiritual improvement must be the constant companion of every Christian.

Spiritual growth means much more than the practical application of God's Word to everyday living. Certainly, application must be practical, and we must practice our faith every day. But the application of God's Word does not simply mean that people are to blindly apply what they hear from the pulpit.

APPLICATION

What I'm trying to get at may be seen by asking the question, *Apply what?* What are you to apply? Are you to apply what I tell you to apply, in the manner that I tell you to apply it? Or are you to apply what you understand to be true from your own study of Scripture? Are you not primarily to apply your understanding of God's Word to your own life as you grow in faithfulness? Of course you are!

Each person must apply the wisdom that God gives him to his own life. How can you apply the wisdom that God gives me? I am called to share what I've learned with you, of course, and I pray that it might be helpful. But you can't coast along on my understanding. How can my understanding or some application I suggest be appropriate to all your varying life circumstances? God knows what you

---

27 See: *The Long War Against God: The History and Impact of the Creation/Evolution Conflict*, Henry M. Morris, Master Books, 2000.

need to apply in your life, and He will make it clear to you. Personal application is the function of the Holy Spirit.

The application of your spiritual understanding to your life produces spiritual growth. A person who tries to apply a preacher's understanding to his own life is a fundamentalist. Fundamentalists are forever trying to live by someone else's rules, someone else's insight and understanding, and it doesn't work. It leads to legalism of the worst kind. If I were a fundamentalist I would tell you exactly what to do with your lives by giving you all kinds of practical applications of Scripture for you to follow. But I'm not. So, I won't.

Paul said that the preacher's job is to guide the understanding of his people, and allow them the freedom to apply their own understanding to their own lives in obedience to Christ. Do you see the difference? The preacher's job is to teach biblical principles and stories (and to provide adequate examples, for sure). The preacher's job is to teach the Bible and its doctrine, to help people understand what the Bible teaches.

To do this effectively the preacher must be free to follow where God leads him. Paul said that the preacher must be free to pursue and teach and preach biblical truth, to go where it leads, and not be overly concerned that this or that person will dislike this or that biblical doctrine. The preacher, as Paul modeled, must have the commitment to follow God's truth wherever it leads, to trust that he is under the direction of the Holy Spirit. And his congregation must have the commitment to allow him that freedom. But not blindly!

Pastor and people are to be in covenant and discussion about the Bible and its teachings. The church is not a one-man show, but a community effort led by God's Holy Spirit. Pastor and people are in this thing together. To accomplish this end, the pastor must take the lead by submitting to God's truth, come what may. And the people must engage that truth with their pastor. Paul said, "To this end I also labor, striving according to His working which works in me mightily" (Colossians 1:29).

Will you allow your pastor to follow God's leading? Will you take the responsibility to not follow blindly, but to search the Scriptures to insure that his leading is of God?

C3&)

The Truth of God's Word is a singularity in that it is the only Truth in this world that is completely and absolutely true. And yet, its Truth is complex, multifaceted. All truth belongs to God or refers to God because God is the creator of all things. He ordered all things by the unity of His decree, the authority of His Son and through the power of His Holy Spirit into the amazing diversity of His creation. He is one, yet three. *Christos Singularis!*

8

HIDDEN TREASURES

For I want you to know how great a struggle I have for you and for those at Laodicea and for all who have not seen me face to face, that their hearts may be encouraged, being knit together in love, to reach all the riches of full assurance of understanding and the knowledge of God's mystery, which is Christ, in whom are hidden all the treasures of wisdom and knowledge. —*Colossians 2:1-3 (ESV)*

P aul wrote to the church at Colossae because he wanted them to know what a great struggle (*agōn* or *conflict* in the Authorized Version) he had for them. He had been struggling on their behalf to maintain the purity of the gospel message of salvation by grace alone, which had come under attack at Colossae. He wanted them to know that the difficulties he had while struggling against false teachers and false doctrines was for their benefit.

And for that very reason he was clarifying the doctrines of grace so that they could take up their own defense and better engage the controversy themselves. He wanted them to know that commitment to Jesus Christ was not without struggle and conflict in the world, that commitment to Christ would always be a source of conflict because the world hates Christ and His truth (John 7:7, Matthew 10:25). Paul wanted them to know that he was in the midst of conflict because he was teaching Christ's truth.

Paul was preparing them because as they grew in grace they would find themselves also enmeshed in the conflict between the world and Christ. The struggle against false teaching was not unique to Paul, nor to the Christians at Colossae, nor at Laodicea (Revelation 3:14-ff), but was and is a reality for all Christians everywhere at all times, past, present and future. The more faithful you are, the more

Satan and the world will attack and/or belittle you.

Paul was aware that he was working on behalf of the Colossians. His efforts were also for all who had not met him face to face (v. 1), for those in Colossae whom he didn't know personally, but also for those down the corridors of history whom he would not have the opportunity to know—us. Paul was struggling for the integrity of the gospel on behalf of all Christians.

But why must there be struggle and conflict? Isn't Jesus the Prince of peace? Isn't He loving and gracious and merciful? Why are Christians always stirring up trouble? Why can't Christians just get along with everyone? Of course Jesus is all of these things, loving, gracious, merciful, peaceful and more—righteous, just, and perfect. It is the "and more" that troubles the ungodly. It is not that Christ or in this case Paul stirred up trouble. All Paul did was to teach the "whole counsel of God" (Acts 20:27). Paul proclaimed Christ's righteousness, justice and perfection, which causes the light of Christ to shine in the dark recesses of our sin. In Christ our sins are revealed. They cannot be hidden, denied or ignored.

OFFENSE

The problem was, and still is, that biblical truth offends and upsets the ungodly because of the biblical teaching regarding sin and Hell. People don't like the idea that they are sinners or that sinners are headed for eternal Hell. And it is the reaction of the ungodly to such biblical truth that stirs people up. People don't like being held responsible for their own sin, much less Adam's. They then create conflict and difficulty for the saints, as they struggle against God's judgment and demands for justice and recompense. God's love, grace, and mercy pose no problems. The world and its hoards of godless people love these things. But God's identification of and judgment against sin and His demand for justice are the sticklers. They are part of God's "stone of stumbling and a rock of offense" (1 Peter 2:8).

Jesus said, "Do not think that I have come to bring peace to the earth. I have not come to bring peace, but a sword." (Matthew 10:34). It is very important that we understand that Jesus did not say that He was bringing violence and bloodshed. The sword that Jesus wields is the sword of the Word, not a sword of steel, but "the sword of the Spirit, which is the word of God" (Ephesians 6:17). The sword of Christ is sharper, more discerning, than any sword that the world knows. "For the word of God is living and powerful, and sharper than any two-edged sword, piercing even to the division of soul and spirit, and of joints and marrow, and is a discerner of the thoughts and intents of the heart" (Hebrews 4:12).

Jesus came to bring peace, but He knew that God's way would initially upset and offend people and that they would react strongly to His teaching, even violently at times. He knew the history of the prophets. But it was, and is, critical to hold fast to God's truth even when people have such adverse reactions to it because it will ultimately bring the only lasting peace possible. The only sustainable peace this world will ever know is peace under the influence and authority, the grace and mercy of God through Jesus Christ.

The sword that Jesus wields is the sword of discernment, it is the sword of purification that cuts away from our hearts that which is wicked and evil in God's sight. It cuts away the sin and enmity that keeps people from reconciliation with God and from one another. God's peace requires reconciliation with God on His terms. And God's sword, God's Word, provides real reconciliation. The battleground of this conflict is the human soul, our hearts and minds, our values and beliefs. Christ is out to change our hearts and minds, to change our values and beliefs, not abstractly, but concretely, in order to change the way we think and live, the way we relate to God and to one another.

Jesus did not mean that He or His people would initiate worldly war, and any suggestion of that is categorically mistaken. Rather, as Paul said, "we do not wrestle against flesh and blood, but against principalities, against powers, against the rulers of the darkness of this age, against spiritual hosts of wickedness in the heavenly places" (Ephesians 6:12). The battle that Jesus brings is a moral battle, a spiritual battle, a battle of wits and wills, of values and beliefs, a war of thoughts and ideas, of presuppositions and premises that will serve the purposes of God's love and unity in Christ. It is a personal matter, but not merely so because it spills out into our social relationships. So, it is also a social matter, a political matter. Nonetheless, it is a battle, a struggle filled with conflict. The struggle is real and the conflict is real because Satan is real.

RECONCILIATION

But inasmuch as this battle for God's truth asserts the priority of discernment and moral purity, its greater purpose is not scriptural separation and alienation among men, but the drawing together of people in faithfulness. God's truth offends the unfaithful, but it also encourages and unites people through faithfulness. Those who are not in unity with Jesus Christ turn away because they are unfaithful. Christ is the door into Christian unity (John 10:9). Christ's priorities necessitate the reconciliation of men to God first, and then, only on the basis of that reconciliation, can the faithful be fully reconciled to one another. Complete reconciliation is not possible apart from Jesus Christ. Reconciliation to God cannot be avoided, and when it is sufficiently engaged reconciliation between other faithful people falls into place.

Complete reconciliation only occurs in Christ. So, those not in Christ cannot be fully reconciled, not with God and not with one another. The problems with the ecumenical efforts toward Christian unity to date have come because the people seeking such reconciliation with other Christians and denominations have not been sufficiently reconciled with God. They (we) have put denominational reconciliation ahead of their (our) own personal reconciliation with Jesus Christ. They (we) have put organizational and administrative unity before personal and spiritual unity. They (we) have been motivated by empire rather than kingdom.

To be reconciled with Jesus Christ is to be reconciled with all who are in Him, all who are under His authority. So, wherever reconciliation fails it fails first and foremost with Christ. If we are to see reconciliation with others, it must first be established with Christ, which means that we must be reconciled with and through Christian trinitarianism because that is the reality of God.

When people receive God's grace and give themselves to reconciliation with God, they are then blessed with the presence, power, and encouragement of the Holy Spirit. Spiritual encouragement comes from only one source, the Holy Spirit, who enlightens Scripture. We must derive our spiritual direction and encouragement from Scripture in the light of Christ by the Holy Spirit, and not succumb to the temptation of fundamentalism or legalism. The temptation of fundamentalism and/or legalism is the temptation to receive direction and encouragement from other people, to feed on the scraps of moralistic platitudes applied to Scripture that make us feel good about ourselves, that make us feel spiritually superior, but fail to fully convict us of our own deeper sin and drive us into the ever-loving and unifying arms of Jesus Christ. Fundamentalists and legalists are often plagued with the residual sin of spiritual pride, thinking that their faithfulness makes them better than others. But it doesn't.

Again, the main characteristic of religious fundamentalism or legalism is the attempt to achieve personal spiritual progress by riding on the coattails of someone else's wisdom, someone else's understanding and application of God's Word, trying to live by the understanding and practices of others, rather than turning directly to the Lord through Scripture for personal understanding, guidance and application.

Don't get me wrong. Faithfulness does in fact make us better than we used to be when we were less faithful. But we must not slip into the pride of life that suggests that we are better than others, or that our faithfulness will merit us anything in the eyes of God. Jesus taught us that when we have done all that we have been commanded, to say, "We are unworthy servants; we have only done what was our duty" (Luke 17:10). Faithfulness is not the grand culmination of Christian living. It is the starting point, the floor not the ceiling.

DUTY

We live in such a faithless generation that we find that people in the world are honored and rewarded for simply doing their duty. We are so used to people not doing their duty, not performing according to their job specifications that we honor people who do because they are so rare. But this is not the way God does business and not the way things should be. God expects everyone to do their respective duties. Doing your job is not heroic. Heroism is going above and beyond duty.

Christians are not free to do whatever they want, or to believe whatever they like, not at all. The ordinary duty of all Christians is to conform their beliefs and practices to Scripture. Where biblical words and terms are not understood, we are not free to define them as we like. Rather, we must allow Scripture itself to define its own words and set its own terms. The temptation for many people is to take the easy way by letting someone else figure it out, and then try to duplicate their beliefs and practices in their own lives.

If you correctly understand me, you will see that this criticism cuts broadly across the face of current Christian and Evangelical belief and practice. Too many people try to follow someone else's teaching, some famous Christian or other. But Paul told us not to do that. Where there are differences of opinion, we must turn to the historical testimony of the church (other faithful Christians) and take care not to side with one or another famous figure without understanding the issues and the biblical truth ourselves. We must study the issues until they are clear to us.

Paul reminded the Corinthians that there had been quarreling among them, among various believers. "What I mean is that each one of you says, 'I follow Paul,' or 'I follow Apollos,' or 'I follow Cephas,' or 'I follow Christ.' Is Christ divided? Was Paul crucified for you? Or were you baptized in the name of Paul" (1 Corinthians 1:11-13)? His point was that we are to follow Christ alone. Sure, others can provide helpful advice and guidance. Nonetheless, our allegiance, our unity is in Christ alone. That is where our hearts and our heads need to be—with Christ alone.

READING SCRIPTURE

Of course, reading Scripture correctly is difficult. It takes time and practice if we are going to mine Scripture for all its precious gems, cut them properly and set them into our lives. Let me say two things about understanding Scripture correctly, biblically, that might sound contradictory but are not.

First, concentrate on Scripture itself. Read the Bible. Don't waste time with the milk of daily devotionals that present fragmented and romantic—if marginally biblical—moralizations. So many of these productions are fluff, and whose main purpose is to make people feel good about themselves so that they will buy more of them. They are habitual in the same way that certain drugs are habitual. They make you feel good for a while, but over time they retard growth and maturity. Too many good Christians have gotten bogged down in this murky, sticky sea of milk and syrup, and not grown in Christian maturity. Christian publication in our day is more an industry than a ministry, more business than service. So, read Scripture regularly and methodically, and choose your supportive materials carefully.

Second, don't think that you have to reinvent the wheel of biblical understanding. Because the Bible is hard to read correctly and profitably, we need to take advantage of the help that is available. But what kind of help you choose makes all the difference in the world. My recommendation here is to let history do the heavy lifting of testing and discernment. Of course, no reading apart from the Holy Spirit will be fruitful.

So, read the Christian classics, the old stuff. Follow where the Holy Spirit has gone before. (I'd say begin with the classics, but nearly everyone has already begun somewhere else!) It is not as difficult as you might imagine. Standing on the shoulders of our Christian predecessors will bless you beyond your greatest expectations because their faithfulness and usefulness has been proven to be of value. But don't get stuck in them. Always return to Scripture.

New Christians should not begin with contemporary literature. Contemporary literature always assumes more than new believers know. Trust that the new thing that God is doing in this time is always the same old thing that He always does in every time. Often, Sunday School curriculum is the worst. New Christians need to be grounded in historic faithfulness in order to develop biblical discernment. But don't believe me! Turn to Scripture, turn to the Christian classics and learn for yourself the faithful testimony of God's people. Experience for yourself the satisfaction of a deeper walk with the Lord. Here, in the annuls of history, Christians will be knit together with the faithful of every age. Here your life will be sewn into God's quilt of faithfulness and you will be encouraged like never before.

Yet, another caution must be mentioned because antiquity alone is not a sufficient reason to trust a book or author. Heresy has plagued Christianity from the outset. And before that it plagued ancient Israel as can be seen throughout the Old Testament.

HIGH CALLING

Paul calls us to "to reach all the riches of full assurance of understanding and the knowledge of God's mystery" (v. 2). That's a high calling. Paul wanted all Christians to reach the full assurance of personal understanding. Understanding of what? Understanding of God's Word, understanding of the gospel of Jesus Christ, understanding of the Trinity, of "Christ in you" (Colossians 1:27). We must understand what the Bible teaches—Christian doctrine. We must be assured that we understand it correctly, biblically, historically. And the only way to do that is to drink from the deep waters of historic Christian testimony, and not be content to play on the shallow shores of contemporary Evangelicalism.

It is not that we must go into the deep water, but that when we awaken in Christ we find that we are already in the deep water. The Bible is deep water. We are to be in union with Christ, who is in the deep water. So, we must trust Christ and help each other. No Christian should swim alone. Christians are on the buddy system, "two by two" (Mark 6:7) cautioned Jesus. So, find a buddy and engage the process. Hold fast to Christ alone, who will not let go of you.

What awaits us is the "knowledge of God's mystery" (v. 2). Paul said that God is an ultimate mystery, yet we can be assured of knowing the hidden treasures of God's mystery, not completely of course, but adequately. This is the great secret of the ages, Scripture itself is the Rosetta Stone that has unlocked the mysteries of the world, and the Holy Spirit unlocks the mysteries of Scripture. Those mysteries unfold through the correct understanding of the Trinity, the most mysterious of all Christian doctrines. The Trinity stands at the center of Christianity and differentiates it from all other religions. Get the Trinity right, and you will get it all right, again, not perfectly right, but adequately right.

Paul proclaimed to all the great secret of the Scriptures—salvation by grace alone through faith alone in Christ alone according to Scripture alone. Christ alone, yet three in one. One, yet Three. Christ Himself is the seed of faith. Planted by God's decree, Christ Himself took root in the Old Testament, and fulfilled God's plan of redemption as Jesus died on the cross. Christ Himself then sent the Holy Spirit to invade the hearts and minds of people everywhere to give them new birth, to awaken people to the reality of God in our midst—Emmanuel! This seed, this mystery is planted in minds and hearts by the Holy Spirit through regeneration and is watered through gospel obedience.

The first act of obedience for all Christians is to claim baptism. Paul wrote to Titus, "he saved us, not because of works done by us in righteousness, but according to his own mercy, by the washing of regeneration and renewal of the Holy Spirit" (Titus 3:5). However we understand baptism, it is a washing that both cleanses and waters our souls, our hearts and minds. Baptism not only cleanses the soul, it waters the Seed (Luke 8:11; Romans 4:16, 9:8; Galatians 3:16, 1 Peter 1:23; 1 John 3:9).

This is the seed, planted and washed (watered), that grows in faithfulness in the light of Christ. Paul said that understanding these things is the fruit of salvation (Romans 6:20-22). Jesus told us that by their fruits we will know them (Matthew 7:20). Those who bring good fruit will carry on, and those who do not produce good fruit will be carried out "and thrown into the fire" (Matthew 7:19). We must understand that fruit here does not refer to numbers. It does not suggest a quantity. Rather, the emphasis is on goodness, on quality. And goodness refers to biblical morality, right action, right activity, but also right understanding and teaching because action follows thought (Matthew 5:22). We think about a thing before we do it. And whatever we think about we usually end up doing. So, the key to right morality is right thinking.

Jesus said that people cannot understand the Scriptures before they are saved, that understanding comes by God's grace, not apart from it. "Whoever is of God hears the words of God" (John 8:47). Those without ears to hear cannot hear because they do not listen with the ears of the Holy Spirit. "He who has ears to hear, let him hear" (Luke 14:35). And at the same time, simply being saved is not a guarantee that a person understands Scripture correctly. "For everyone who lives on milk is unskilled in the word of righteousness, since he is a child" (Hebrews 5:13), cautioned Paul. The Jews, who had been saved out of Egypt, had been feeding on milk for too long, said Paul. Their spiritual growth had been arrested by shallow beliefs.

Through Christ God has granted the gift of salvation, and Paul testified that personal understanding of Scripture follows on the heels of that gift. This is only to say that in the light of Christ Scripture makes sense. Paul testified to the Ephesians that God "chose us in him before the foundation of the world, that we should be holy and blameless before him. In love he predestined us for adoption as sons through Jesus Christ, according to the purpose of his will, to the praise of his glorious grace, with which he has blessed us in the Beloved" (Ephesians 1:4-6).

That's the secret! And God unlocked it Himself by sending His Son, and His Son sent the Spirit, and the Spirit animates the faithful. Paul went on to say that, not only is grace alone through Christ alone the key to salvation (remembering that God alone is Three in One, One in Three), but that we need all the knowledge that is provided in God's Word. This is not an advocation for primitive culture, it is a call for mature biblical culture.

God's Word, the Bible, is alone sufficient for salvation and for faithfulness. But that sufficiency does not preclude the development of things not mentioned in Scripture. Rather, it forbids various ways of living, various character expressions, various ways of being human, being God's people. For instance, Paul said "do you not know that the unrighteous will not inherit the kingdom of God? Do not be deceived: neither the sexually immoral, nor idolaters, nor adulterers, nor men who practice homosexuality, nor thieves, nor the greedy, nor drunkards, nor revilers, nor swindlers will inherit the kingdom of God" (1 Corinthians 6:9-10). This sort of primitive, unrighteous morality is excluded from biblical culture.

This means that God's faithful people must rest assured that Scripture alone is sufficient, not only for salvation but for abundant life (John 10:10). It means that, while God provided the key to understanding the secrets of Scripture, there are still things that are beyond the understanding of faithful Christians. We can understand God's Word adequately, but not completely. And we must be content with what God gives us. Over time, as we grow in maturity and sanctification (personally and culturally) we will be given more as we understand more completely. As we practice what God gives us, as we do what we understand to be right, God will give us more. But if we fail to act on what God has already given, we cannot expect any more knowledge or wisdom.

We need to learn to live the truth that God has already given. The Lord has not given us a heavy burden. Yet in our pride and our greed, in our self-centered short-sightedness we too often reach for what we cannot grasp and grasp for what we cannot hold. We too often live beyond our means, beyond our bounds, beyond our abilities. And doing so makes us stressed and unhappy. It damages our environment and our relationships with others. It is a reflection of our damaged relationship with God through Christ. Tired and weakened by our unmanageable lifestyles, the stress of life without Christ clouds our thinking and we make increasingly poor judgments, which in turn drives our stress levels higher, which further clouds our thinking, and round and round she goes.

We need another way. Our current way of life, our contemporary world culture, is unsustainable. That is the message that God is telling us through our current world financial crisis. The godless system or way of life we have created, driven by the banking industry, is bankrupt and unsustainable. Our culture is riddled with greed, graft and corruption, selfishness, sexual immorality and sin. We have crossed the tipping point. If we as individuals and as a people would abide by God's Word, we would not be caught in the current web of dilemmas and crises.

The way out and the way of prevention are the same. Christ is the Way and there is no other. The burden is upon those who are in

Christ to show the Way. It's not magic, nor mystical. No special equipment is needed. It is not a matter of going somewhere else. It's a matter of blooming where we are. We are already where we need to be. We are already where we can do the most good. There are no obstacles to faithfulness, other than those we put in our own way. Satan himself is not an obstacle, not really. Christ has already defeated him. He only tricks us into fooling ourselves by thinking that he is a formidable obstacle. We can't defeat him, but Christ has. So, his defeat is assured as we abide in Christ.

In order to grow in our knowledge and understanding of God's Word we must also abide by what we learn. It is not that Christianity has been tried and has somehow failed. But rather, Christianity has only ever been seriously considered by a few, and has been rejected out of hand by most. But it has never actually been fully engaged by any social order. No historical social order has ever been fully committed to Jesus Christ. Since Christ's own day—and before—the saints have struggled against falsehood and the forces of evil. The wheat and the tares have always grown together, side by side. This is the source of Christ's conflict with the world. God is growing a crop of righteousness through Christ alone, and Satan has sown unrighteousness in God's field.

But one day, perhaps sooner than we expect, perhaps not, the great harvest will come. It seems clear to me that we are currently living in the midst of God's judgment. This has always been the case. It is time to learn what God is teaching. Rather than deny that it is God's judgment because it isn't as bad as it could be, we should accept it as God's chastisement and thank Him that it is not as bad as it could be. Some day it might be that bad, and on that day it may be too late to repent.

For now we must work the works of him who sent Christ while it is day; night is coming, when no one can work (John 9:4) Again Jesus spoke to them, saying, "I am the light of the world. Whoever follows me will not walk in darkness, but will have the light of life" (John 8:12).

CɜƐꝋ

The Trinity is not a singularity in the sense of being a black hole. God is light (1 John 1:5), not darkness. However, unbelievers do not recognize God or His kingdom or His light (John 3:3). So, for unbelievers God appears to be darkness, not light—perhaps even a black hole. They think that believers are trapped by their belief, in the same way that light is trapped in the event horizon of a black hole. They don't realize that they are projecting the imagination of their own unbelief. As light dawns, darkness and the things of darkness disappear from reality into the event horizon of God's waxing light. *Christos Singularis!*

ROOTED AND ESTABLISHED

I say this in order that no one may delude you with plausible arguments. For though I am absent in body, yet I am with you in spirit, rejoicing to see your good order and the firmness of your faith in Christ. Therefore, as you received Christ Jesus the Lord, so walk in him, rooted and built up in him and established in the faith, just as you were taught, abounding in thanksgiving.
—Colossians 2:4-7 (ESV)

P aul had been in conflict because he was defending God's truth against falsehood. He acknowledged in v. 4 that the conflict arose because there were people who were trying to deceive the Colossian church about the nature of faith and grace. Paul said that there was a danger that they could be deluded with "plausible arguments" (or "enticing words," v. 1, Authorized Version). It was an effort to disrupt the peace and unity of the church with good sounding but wrong interpretations and explanations of the gospel.

Differences of opinion were expressed even in Paul's day. Yet, while Paul called attention to some differences of opinion, he also pointed to the fact that genuine unity is possible, but only in truth. Unity is a product of God's truth. To be in unity is to be in submission to and in harmony with God's truth. And yet, God's truth stands against the opinions of men.

Truth is not built piecemeal, a little here, a little there. Truth is not constructed from the bottom up. Truth is not something that we need to construct. Rather, God has given it. It is a given, not a construct. It is holistic, not piecemeal. God's truth is revealed by the Lord through Scripture, illuminated in the light of Christ by the power and presence of the Holy Spirit. God's truth is whole and perfect from its inception by God. Truth is always perfect, or it is less than truth. Obviously, I am speaking of *the* Truth, not *a* truth.

The summing up of the opinions of men is not at all like God's truth because God's truth is whole and unified from the start. Human opinions and ideas are not. The human effort to build the whole truth from partial truths that we understand is destined to fail because the whole truth is more than the sum of its parts. Our job is not to build or construct truth on the basis of our opinions or findings. Rather, our job is to reflect God's revealed truth (Scripture in the light of Christ) in our own thinking. We are to be faithful to God's revealed truth. Christian unity is the sharing of covenantal commitment to God's revealed truth. It is love of God and love of the brethren, understanding that love is not a warm feeling but a commitment, not passion but loyalty, not abstract but concrete, not intellectual but actual.

ECUMENISM

There are many people today who believe that each denomination, even each religion, contains part of the whole truth, that each religion is true in its own way. And further, that the whole truth requires taking what is true in each denomination (and too often different religions, as well) and developing a composite based upon them all. Ultimate Truth is thus understood to be like a patchwork quilt. This allows each faith perspective, each denomination or religion, a limited place in the sun. Understanding Truth as a whole is then considered to be a matter of believing them all together with a kind of all-enveloping faith perspective that embraces the truth of all by assenting to the truth of each. This is the methodology of Unitarianism, Universalism and multiculturalism, and is opposed to Christianity at every point.

This theological perspective is the falsely tolerant religious perspective that proclaims that all denominations, all religions and perspectives lead to God, that all roads lead to Rome (so to speak), that all religious beliefs lead to salvation. This idea is that there are many paths that lead to the top of the proverbial mountain, and that it doesn't matter what path is taken, only that one reaches the mountaintop.

This is the dominant theological perspective in America today. It is the unspoken theology of the American Civil Religion[28] and the

---

28 Bellah, Robert Neelly (Winter 1967). "Civil Religion in America." ... *Journal of*

Supreme Court as it works to impose this particular religious perspective upon modern American society, in that its various
decisions consistently reflect this worldview. It is the unspoken but
assumed truth perspective of the Court and of contemporary American civil society and all of its various institutions.

Curiously, while this perspective accepts all religious beliefs, it
also categorizes and marginalizes religious belief in general in such
a way that, while religious belief is tolerated, it is rendered power-
less and ineffectual because of its relativity. This process of intellectual religious castration eliminates all ultimate truth claims of all
religions and makes this kind of generic religious belief functionally
equivalent to secularism.

It amounts to the a priori rejection of religion and religious
considerations across the board. It actually trumps all other religious perspectives or beliefs with its own commitment to relativity
by rejecting all claims of ultimate truth other than its own, which
are assumed and not stated. It amounts to the denial of God and
ultimate truth. Yet, it is itself a religious belief about God that is as
ultimate and absolute as any other. Because of its ultimate beliefs,
its axioms and assumptions, Universalism claims to honor all religions and beliefs. Nonetheless, it is not Christian by any biblical
measure. It is, at best, syncretism and a denial of the First Commandment. It passionately, consistently and comprehensively pro-
secutes its own beliefs, its denial of God and hatred of Christianity
in the public realm.

Of course there are some similarities between the various
denominations and religions, which is to be expected because
people have a common Creator. The various religions represent different perversions of God and His Word. Nonetheless, God has
been in the business of opposing and deposing false religions and
false gods, including universalism, perhaps even *usually* universalism, from the most ancient of days.

For instance, the First Commandment reads, "You shall have
no other gods before me" (Exodus 20:3), thus demanding that
God's people have a common loyalty to the God of the Bible alone.
Christian unity is the covenantal commitment to God and to His
culture, to the knowledge and values given through Scripture, freely
shared and publicly proclaimed as ultimate truth. Until quite
recently Christians have had the individual, corporate and political

---

the American Academy of Arts and Sciences 96 (1): 1–21.

freedom to publicly proclaim this simple and essential truth. Of late, however, many people have found it to be so offense as to work to ban its mere public mention.

READJUSTMENT

The conflict that Paul had been involved in had to do with protecting God's truth from human modification. It is a conflict that has never actually been settled, and probably never will be completely settled until the Lord comes again. We sinful human beings are forever trying to reinvent or readjust God's truth to suit our own thoughts and desires, rather than adjusting our thoughts and desires to conform to God's truth. Sin causes us to misperceive and misunderstand reality. Human perception is biased toward its own concerns. And when we deny sin, we deny our own misperception and misunderstanding, our own self-centeredness, and think that God's Word must be adjusted to fit into our own thinking rather than adjusting our thinking to fit God's Word.

The whole purpose of Scripture is to reveal God's truth and nail it down so that we in our limited perspective and creative sinfulness don't succeed in changing God's truth to suit ourselves. The point is that biblical truth is culturally transcendent. It applies to all human cultures, all human societies through all time. God's truth is not limited to any one period of history or subculture, but is for all people at all times, regardless of any regional, historical or social distinctives. "Jesus Christ is the same yesterday, today, and forever" (Hebrews 13:8). God's truth is absolute and eternal (Psalm 15:4). It doesn't change to suit the times. Its ultimacy is the foundation of human unity. People change, God doesn't. People grow, God doesn't.

CIRCULAR REASONING

The primary mode of attack by those who have opposed God's truth always involves the use of "persuasive words" (v. 4), arguments that are apparently reasonable and valid. Arguments that seem to be true. However, the only way to know whether such arguments are actually true or not is to compare them to Scripture, the only source of ultimate truth. Where they oppose Scripture, they are not true. But how do we know that Scripture is true? By faith, study and personal experience. And how do we know that our faith is true and our study is correct? By the testimony of Scripture and history and the Holy Spirit through regeneration.

But isn't this circular reasoning? Yes. But isn't something wrong with circular reasoning? No, not necessarily. Sometimes our reasoning can be wrong, but all reasoning is circular in the sense that its purpose is to prove an initial premise. The conclusion of a logical argument can only be as valid as its initial premise. There are some very smart people who have thought up some very reasonable arguments for challenging the ultimate truth of God's Word. They usually argue that God's Word is not objective, eternal and culturally transcendent, that it is not universally applicable but is bound to the culture and time of its original writing. But, in fact, all they are doing is assuming as their initial premise that God and His Word are not true and then proving the same by appealing to reason and logic. Isn't that circular reasoning? Yes.

Of course, believers do a similar thing because circular reasoning is unavoidable. The process of reasoning simply justifies an initial presupposition. Believers assume as our initial premiss that God and His Word are true, and we prove God's veracity by appealing to Scripture, supported by reason/logic.

The difference between these two rational processes is both subtle and critical. Apart from regeneration by the power and presence of the Holy Spirit, the difference between these perspectives remains illusive. The critical difference comes when the eyes of faith see the reality of God's Word come true in the believer's own life. When God changes a person's own heart and mind, God's reality and veracity are no longer doubted. The changed heart and mind become the proof for the existence and reliability of God.

FREEDOM

Some people say that The Ten Commandments were fine for people in the old days, but they just aren't practical today, thinking that Jesus' ministry and teaching somehow put an end to or changed God's law. While it is true that Jesus has set the faithful free from the condemnation of the Law, He did not suggest that people are free to ignore it. The faithful are free from it because their faithfulness, their love of Jesus Christ, intends to keep the Ten Commandments. And though that intention is not perfectly fulfilled by us sinful human beings this side of glory, the faithful are covered by Christ's love, His righteousness and God's forgiveness, in the interim.

In Christ the faithful are free from the burden of the Law in the sense that we are now free to practice the Law, knowing that salvation does not require perfect conformity to the law, but knowing that we can practice only in the genuine love of Jesus Christ. In Christ, then, we are free to practice God's law out of our love of the Lord in the assurance of becoming who God has called us to be, rather than out of the fear of failure to measure up to God's expectations and consequent damnation.

What has changed in Christ is our actual situation of being condemned and without assurance, to being redeemed and given the assurance of Heaven, of eternal life. This involves a huge change regarding our relationship with and attitude toward God. We change, but God doesn't. Nor does it eliminate or reduce God's expectations. What changes in Christ is our approach to God and the way we live in obedience to His Word, His law (His expectations).

We are not free to ignore God's law. Rather, we are free to strive toward complete obedience to it, knowing that our obedience will not be perfect. But neither will we be condemned by our failure because we have been claimed by the blood of Christ. We can plead for God's mercy by the blood of Christ, not because of anything we have done, but because of what Christ has done on the cross. The advent of Christ and His fulfillment of God's law does not represent a change on God's part. God always planned for Christ's redemption. So when it came, it was not a change of God's plan, but a fulfillment.

Paul further said that the truth of Christ did not depend upon his (Paul's) personal presence (v. 5) with the Colossians. Paul did not need to be there in person for them to know God's truth. Nor did they need to wait for him to come. The truth was not his to reveal, but God's. The Holy Spirit alone reveals God's truth. And because Paul knew that they had already received the Spirit, he could rejoice from a distance regarding God's success in their midst, knowing that while they might lose track of God's truth, God would not lose track of them. God would complete what He began.

But neither did they have to wait for Paul to come to Colossae before they could mount a defense against what they knew to be false. He told them that their best defense was to walk in the truth, to actually live by God's law in freedom and joy, knowing that while they could not do it perfectly, they could do it adequately in Christ, and joyfully grow in faithfulness day by day. That was not only their best defense against falsehood, but was their best means of evangelism as well. Their faithfulness and genuine love of Christ would fill them to overflowing and spill out into other relationships.

ORDER

Even though Paul wasn't there, he rejoiced in their "good order and the firmness of (their) faith in Christ" (v. 5). Paul charged them to maintain order (discipline) and faithfulness in the church. Church order is not merely the expression of orderly worship and effective procedures, but is also the moral order of personal faithfulness. The order of worship and church procedures is to be built upon the foundation of the personal moral order of church members, much like a house is built upon a foundation. Paul's desire to see their good order was the desire to see them live personally and corporately by the moral order of God's Law.

Paul was arguing, not merely for personal discipline, but also for discipleship, for the teaching and learning of God's order. Discipleship is not an individual sport, but requires team effort. Discipleship requires both teachers and students. One cannot be a disciple without being a student in a teacher/student relationship. Nor can one be a discipler without being a teacher who is actively in a teacher/student relationship. In fact, being a disciple of Christ means being a student of one and a teacher to another. Christianity lives in the midst of these teaching and learning relationships.

As we look around our world today and see the growing moral crisis, evidenced not only by the collapse of the financial markets and rampant dishonesty across virtually all sectors of society and the general lack of common courtesy, we Christians must take responsibility for this situation. It is the result of the failure of God's church to be what God has called her to be. Thus, the remedy is for God's church to be what He has called her to be. God's people are charged to be His moral agents in the world, and we have failed in this regard. We have failed to be people who disciple others in the benefits and obligations of life in God's world. Christianity is the universal antidote for immorality and social collapse.

To disciple people requires a long term personal relationship focused on the task of teaching them how to read and profit from God's Word. Such a relationship requires significant amounts of time spent together in worship, prayer, study, fellowship, and service. Discipleship requires friendship, but more than friendship.

Discipleship requires fellowship. While friendship requires mutual affection and trust, fellowship requires common values and virtues. Friends can agree to disagree, fellows cannot. Fellowship is more demanding than friendship, more binding and more covenantal.

Fellows are covenantally committed to common beliefs, common assumptions and a common faith. Christians can disagree with one another, but we must not fool ourselves into thinking that an agreement can in some way be founded on a disagreement. An agreement to disagree is neither an agreement nor a disagreement, but a temporary truce that results in something that is neither hot nor cold (Revelation 3:16).

If you are involved in such a relationship, either as a student or a teacher, then hats off to you. But the sad truth is that most Christians today are not. The sad truth is that most Christian parents do not even disciple their own children! Most church families today think they are too busy for such time consuming relationships. Even if they have the time, they don't have the personal commitment to Christ to see it through. And what is more, parents no longer believe Christian discipleship to be their responsibility. Too many Christian families have relinquished the responsibility to disciple their children to the Sunday School or youth group, thinking that people they don't really know will be able to undo in an hour a week what governmental indoctrination, media (TV, Internet, radio, etc.) and the counsel of godless immaturity has done in forty, fifty, eighty or more hours a week. Such thinking is madness!

RESPONSIBILITY

The responsibility for the failure of the churches in our own day and in our own families must rest squarely upon ourselves and upon our churches. The churches themselves are guilty of pandering to the world, to the values and activities that draw people away from Christ! Most Christians are guilty of neglecting their own personal discipleship. Most adult Christians are not actively involved as a student under a teacher, nor are they teaching Christianity to anyone else, not even their own children.

This gaping hole in the fabric of Christianity provides the greatest opportunity for Christian renewal, revival and reformation of our time. We must abandon the desperation that seeks the return of some imagined Great Awakening or some other grand spiritual drama that fans the flames of passion and excess. Rather, we must stake our claim to the slow, deliberate, consistent and comprehensive commitment to the ordinary study of God's Word. We must learn it right and teach it right to our own children, regardless of their age (or ours).

The burden is upon parents and grandparents because people learn by teaching. The burden of leadership was given to elders, not simply those who hold a particular church office, but to those who have been wizened by time. And conversely, we haven't learned a thing until we can teach it. Christians are to practice this teaching on their own children (1 Timothy 3:4-5).

So, when does the responsibility of parenting begin? It begins long before the birth of a child. And when does the responsibility of parenting end? It does not end because your children are always your children. Sure, as adults our own children often don't like or appreciate our advice about their beliefs and behavior in the light of Scripture. They didn't like it any better when they were young! Age is not a factor because people are never too old to learn. They may be too stubborn, but not too old.

No one ever outgrows their need for parental love, nor do parents ever escape the responsibilities of parenthood. The parent/ child relationship is eternal. Parents remain parents and children remain children regardless of age or time. Of course people grow and mature, and growth changes the relationship, but it does not end it. Parents have the responsibility to teach and disciple their children. Yes, it gets harder as they get older. That's why the Bible recommends that discipline be firmly established when children are young. But whether or not that happens, parents are not relieved of their spiritual responsibility for their children, young or old.

The Fourth Commandment is valid all our lives, "Honor your mother and your father" (Exodus 10:12, Matthew 19:19). The relationship between parents and children is an eternal relationship. It has eternal joys, eternal consequences and eternal responsibilities. Both parents and children are involved in the relationship, and both have duties and responsibilities. When should we stop teaching our children or honoring our parents? Never. When should our responsibilities as parents or children end? Never. The relationship changes over time, of course. It is different when our children are small than when they are tall, different again when they are adults with families of their own. But it always exists, even in death. A dead father is still a father.

I know that nobody wants to be a meddling mother-in-law or

an interfering grandfather. But where in the Bible does God relieve parents of their responsibility to teach their children? Nowhere. Sure, it's difficult, it's awkward, it's usually uncomfortable. It is no easier or less awkward when the children are young. If you avoided it while they were young, that is exactly why you avoided it, because it's hard. The point is that Christian relationships and responsibilities do not end at 18, or 21, or 35, or any age.[29] We are in it forever because God is in it forever.

GRATITUDE

> *"Therefore, as you received Christ Jesus the Lord, so walk in him, rooted and built up in him and established in the faith, just as you were taught, abounding in thanksgiving"* (vs. 6-7).

If you are rooted in Christ, then the nourishment that you draw from Him will show up in your fruits, in your actions and behaviors. If your actions and behaviors do not reflect the love and discipline of Christ, you need to check your roots, check your fundamental beliefs and values. When people are not rooted in faithfulness, when they have not been built up in Christ or established in the faith, when people have not been taught the Bible, they cannot abound in thanksgiving. You can't get blood from a turnip! Nor can people abound in thanksgiving apart from being rooted, built up (*epoikodomeō*—reared or taught) and established (stabilized) in Christ.

This is the long-neglected job of Christians. This is where the church has failed and where it must pick up the proverbial ball and begin again. We have failed to root, to build up, to establish and teach our own children. The churches have dropped the ball, as have Christian families. That ball needs to be picked up.

Of this verse Calvin said that "ingratitude is very frequently the reason why we are deprived of the light of the gospel, as well as of other divine favors."[30] To be ungrateful is to be unsatisfied with what God has given. It is the refusal to be thankful to God, the

---

29 This is not an invitation for grandparents to teach their grandchildren things that contradict the children's own parents. Christ is aiming at a united front between grandparents and parents in order to sustain the idea of parental authority. Rather, this is an invitation to for grandparents to teach their own children, even when those children are adults.

30 *Calvin's Commentaries*, XXI, Baker House, Grand Rapids, Michigan, 1993, p. 179.

refusal to live with a sense of gratitude or to be appreciative.

Appreciation requires discrimination. It requires the ability to discriminate, to recognize and draw fine distinctions. The differences between a thing of high quality and a thing of low quality are often small matters of detail that reflect large differences of substance.

The difference between living faithfully and not living faithfully is a matter of quality, of character, of caliber and timbre. A high quality life, or excellence of character, is characterized by elegance, refinement and accomplishment. While these things are often thought to come from wealth, they don't. Not really. They are learned skills, but not everyone who studies them learns them. Why not? Because their mastery involves more grace than effort, more gift than purchase. They are character qualities, not things that can be bought and sold.

DISCRIMINATION

Elegance reveals a sense of beauty that is ingeniously simple, both efficient and direct. Elegance is not derivative. Elegance must always be authentic or it is not elegant. Whatever it is, it cannot be bought. It's a grace, a gift. And yet, to a degree, it can be taught—learned and improved. It can be rooted, built up and established.

Refinement involves a process of removing impurities in order to make a thing pure. Think of gold. In terms of Christian character, we are talking about the abandonment of impure thoughts and habits. Christians are called to personal refinement, not snootiness or uppity presumption, nor pomposity, but the real thing, the authentic thing. Refinement is an art, and art can be learned and improved. It's a matter of practice. It can be rooted, built up and established.

Accomplishment, applied to character, reveals a commitment to discipline. For instance, an accomplished musician has mastered his instrument by way of personal commitment, discipline and practice. The accomplished person has gained skills and abilities through hard work and training.

And yet, the truly accomplished have exceeded their training by discovering their gift. The truly accomplished are often described as being gifted. All Christians are gifted by God with various graces for the world, for use in the world. And yet discovering our gifts of grace always involves the hard work of discipline, training and commitment. The gift is given, but making something of it is hard work. It too can be rooted, built up and established.

Interestingly, those who are genuinely elegant, refined and accomplished are thankful and grace-full. Over the centuries people have turned these things into the crass privileges of the rich, as if they can be bought and sold. People have made them more a function of vanity than humility. And so we tend to associate them with wealth and privilege.

But this is backwards. It is not the way it actually works—arsy varsy. It is not that the wealthy have access to elegance, refinement and accomplishment, but that elegance, refinement and accomplishment usually produce wealth. While wealth cannot buy superior character qualities, superior character qualities usually produce wealth. These qualities are the same qualities that make for a good worker, i.e., honesty, integrity, consistency, etc. And good work habits increase income. People may not get rich personally, but as a general rule, people with good work habits do better than people without good work habits.

There are two primary reasons for ingratitude. Some people are ungrateful to God because they think they deserve more than what they have been given. They feel cheated because they covet what others have, and justify their coveting by insisting that justice means equal results rather than equal opportunity. Others are ungrateful because they deny God and refuse His grace. The ungrateful are unaware of the fruits of God's grace. In either case ungratefulness is an expression of disregard and disobedience to God.

In contrast, obedience to God, which is faithfulness to Jesus Christ, is both fulfilling and joyful. To trust the Lord for salvation is satisfying beyond description. Jesus Christ died on the cross in order that we can live our lives in Him. His death paid the price for our redemption. In Christ we are free of the burden of the law—not free from the law itself, but from its burden and punishment.

In Christ we enjoy the gift of grace, the satisfaction of obedience and the assurance of salvation. This joy is not an empty promise nor a thoughtless, emotional effervescence, but is a Rock-solid commitment to God's truth that is nothing more than the assumption that God's Word is true—because it is!

CB80

At the center of a singularity is infinite gravity. Even with all of our advanced science and math, we don't really know what gravity is. We simply observe its result, which is attraction. And it works best when a large body like the earth attracts smaller bodies like people, or when the sun attracts the earth and planets. And the larger the body, the greater the gravity. So, people would weigh more on Jupiter because it is larger. Imagine the attraction that God, who is infinite, has upon people. Who can resist? Who can escape God's gravity? *Christos Singularis!*

10

HABITS & TRADITIONS

See to it that no one takes you captive by philosophy and empty deceit, according to human tradition, according to the elemental spirits of the world, and not according to Christ. For in him the whole fullness of deity dwells bodily, and you have been filled in him, who is the head of all rule and authority. —*Colossians 2:8-10 (ESV)*

George had passed the Civil Service exam and it was his first day on the job. The Post Office assigned him to a walking route in a residential neighborhood. As he approached 698 4th Street he noticed that the yard was fenced. The gate was closed, and on it hung a sign, *Beware of Dog*. George detached his mace spray from his belt and held it loosely in his free hand as he opened the gate.

"Beware" (v. 8, Authorized Version), said Paul. Be on your guard, be alert. Paul was aware that danger was near, that caution was required. Paul was in the process of sharing the gospel with his friends at Colossae when he told them to beware, to see to it that they were not fooled by falsehood.

But be aware of what? Of being taken captive by philosophy (*philosophia*), said Paul. Strong's tells us that Paul's concern was sophistry, a deliberately invalid argument displaying ingenuity in reasoning in the hope of deceiving someone—and specifically Jewish sophistry. When you share the gospel with people do you caution them to beware, to be careful that they are not deceived by the persuasive arguments of powerful, popular and influential people who will try to lead them astray? The chapter introduction of *The Reformation Study Bible* (Ligonier Ministries, 2005) says that Paul was "struggling with a Greek-influenced form of Jewish philosophy that viewed Christians as still vulnerable to spiritual forces."

When Paul said *philosophy*, he meant Greek philosophy, and Greek philosophy is Platonic, and Platonic philosophy is the foundation of Western Civilization.[31] But Paul wasn't merely struggling against Greek philosophy, but a Greek-influenced form of Jewish philosophy. Paul was struggling against Old Testament misunderstandings because that is the Jewish source book. And if Paul was struggling against both Greek and Jewish forms of philosophy, he was struggling against the syncretism of Greek philosophy and the Old Testament. It provided an alternative explanation of the Old Testament in terms of Greek rationalism. Or another way to say it, perhaps, is that it was a godless or Pagan (non-trinitarian) interpretation of the Old Testament, rather than a Christian (trinitarian) interpretation of the Old Testament, which is what Paul was teaching and advocating.

Paul alerted his hearers to two potential spiritual dangers: 1) vain philosophy, and 2) empty deceit. The word *philosophy* means love of knowledge or love of wisdom, the love of intelligence and wit. From the root *phileo* it also suggests brotherly love or humanism, in the sense that it is human centered love. We know that Scripture encourages the faithful to love, adore and obey God's Word (Psalm 1, Psalm 119, etc.). Scripture also teaches the difference between godly wisdom and worldly wisdom.[32] Godly wisdom uses assumptions, presuppositions and definitions from Scripture, and worldly wisdom uses assumptions, presuppositions and definitions from the world, from personal experience and other sources that exclude, ignore or denigrate Scripture.

WISDOM & FOLLY

The difference between godly wisdom and worldly wisdom involves two classic but opposing approaches or methodologies of investigation, two different ways of thinking, of seeing or understanding things. Worldly wisdom prefers to trust personal experi-

31 "The safest general characterization of the European philosophical tradition is that it consists of a series of footnotes to Plato." *Process And Reality*, Alfred North Whitehead, Free Press, 1979, p. 29.
32 See *The Wisdom of Christ in the Book of Proverbs*, by Phillip A. Ross, Pilgrim Platform, Marietta, Ohio, 2006; *Arsy Varsy—Reclaiming the Gospel in First Corinthians*, by Phillip A. Ross, Pilgrim Platform, Marietta, Ohio, 2008; *Varsy Arsy—Proclaiming the Gospel in Second Corinthians*, by Phillip A. Ross, Pilgrim Platform, Marietta, Ohio, 2009.

ence over Scripture. It evaluates Scripture on the basis of personal experience or personal knowledge. Godly wisdom, on the other hand, prefers to trust Scripture over personal experience and knowledge, and evaluates personal experience on the basis of Scripture. The one method adjusts Scripture to fit personal experience so that experience guides Scripture. The other adjusts personal experience to fit Scripture so that Scripture guides experience. The issue is which is leading and which is following: Scripture or personal experience.

It's not always easy to tell, but it is important. The difference between wisdom and folly is like getting bitten by a dog, in that getting it wrong will ultimately be painful, and can sometimes be deadly if the dog is rabid. Failure to discern the difference always means the failure to discern the root biblical message that God is sovereign. Failure to discern the difference is to usurp or assign the function of sovereignty elsewhere.

This was Eve's error in the Garden that led to the Fall, and it is the natural tendency of everyone ever since. The Serpent used sophistry to trick Eve. He offered Eve an intentionally invalid argument, and she bought it—and then sold it to Adam. That argument and its methodology has wormed its way into the hearts and minds of people ever since. Indeed, human history since the Fall has been about the struggle between two arguments, two ways of thinking, two different philosophies or worldviews, that of God and that of Satan, that of godliness and that of worldliness.

Secondly, Paul warned of "empty (*kenos*) deceit," blatant falsehood that is devoid of truth. It is empty or vain because it amounts to nothing. It does not lead to salvation, but that doesn't mean that it isn't harmful. Empty deceit is like building a bridge with substandard materials or inaccurate engineering. It may look good, but it will not hold up over time. The vanity of a worldly foundation is both costly and dangerous, though it looks good. Worldly ways are ways that seem right in our own eyes (Proverbs 12:15, 21:2). Whereas, godly ways are ways that are right in God's eyes (Exodus 15:26).

Paul suggested two ways to identify vain philosophy and empty deceit. It operates "according to human tradition" and "according to the elemental spirits of the world" (v. 8). "Elemental spirits" is a poor translation of *stoicheion*, which literally means a fundamental order or arrangement, and is also translated as *element, principle,* and/or *rudiment*. Paul was referring to philosophical principles or guiding methodologies that are not biblical. In particular Paul was arguing against rationalism in its Greek forms and any other form it might take. Paul didn't discredit all tradition, nor all philosophy—only the traditions and philosophies of men. Those traditions and philosophies that are not grounded and saturated in Scripture—in the light of Christ, and not in the light of Greek philosophy or some other form or humanistic rationalism.

TRADITION

The Pharisees asked Jesus about this matter, "Why do your disciples break the tradition of the elders? For they do not wash their hands when they eat" (Matthew 15:2). God requires spiritual purification (sanctification). But the Pharisees had concerned themselves with ritual rather than genuine purity and sanctification. Jesus answered them, "And why do you break the commandment of God for the sake of your tradition?" (Matthew 15:3). Note that their traditions, the way that they interpreted and understood Scripture. What became the *Mishnah* among the Jews took precedence over God's biblical commands. Jesus told the Pharisees that they had misunderstood the primary philosophical perspective of the Bible, that they had imposed their own misunderstandings upon Scripture. To some extent, they had been in the process of rationalizing their misunderstanding of the Old Testament with Greek philosophy or some other godless perspective.

Whatever else Gnosticism was, its origin was Platonic. The roots of Gnosticism began some 400 years before Christ. The point being that Gnosticism and its variants were not merely New Testament phenomena, but had older roots that may suggest a tradition of Old Testament Jewish Gnosticism or syncretism, as well.

Jesus wasn't arguing that people shouldn't wash their hands before they eat. Rather, He was arguing that hand washing is not a substitute for righteousness. God calls His people to genuine personal righteousness, not mere obedience to rules (laws). Rules and laws are fine, but they should not circumvent God's purposes. We should not confuse method with purpose, but we do.

WORK

Let me illustrate. Needing an automobile to get back and forth to work is one thing. However, we shouldn't get distracted (or lost) with the features of an automobile. Automotive styles and accessories often distract us from our transportation needs. Before long we find that our purpose in having an automobile is no longer to simply use it for transportation, but the purpose of our work is to pay for our feature-loaded automobile. The car, formerly a means to work, has become the purpose of work. The work has become the means of the car rather than the car being a means of the work. They have switched places as means and end.

There's more. Christians are called to consecrate our work to God, no matter what our job. We are to dedicate our work to God. Work is a blessed privilege given by God for His purposes. After all, He is the boss in this scenario because He gave us everything, including the work. So, our work is primarily for His purposes, His glory, and secondarily for the happiness and health of humanity. It is nice when our health and happiness are in harmony with God's purposes. But it only works this way when people are engaged in their work as a calling from God, only when we use our work to further the kingdom of God.[33] We are to be used by God to accomplish His purposes. We are not to use God to accomplish our purposes.

This doesn't mean that everyone has to be employed in church work or missionary evangelism. It means that every Christian should view work as a calling to promote God's kingdom on earth. It is not a function of our work, but of our attitude, our orientation. I'm talking about an attitude, not a particular kind of work. Almost any work can be done to the glory of God.

God's kingdom is exceedingly broad (Psalm 119:96), and involves a wide variety of jobs. However, too many people today are not working for the glory of God. Too many *Christians* today are not working for the glory of God, but only to maintain their lifestyles. The ends and means of our work have changed places, and we need to return to the original plan, God's plan.

When we change purpose (end) and means, when we lose sight of God's purpose and substitute our own for His, we are then guilty of transgressing the command of God for the sake tradition. At that point we have sold our birthright for a mess of pottage (Genesis 25:31-34). I'm not saying that people need to go out and quit their jobs. I'm saying that people need to change their attitudes toward God, toward work and toward worldliness.

What is at issue here is not about the world per se or the things

---

33 God gave Adam work in the garden before the Fall. Thus, work is not a curse resulting from the Fall. However, the Fall did result in God's curse that made work much more difficult (Genesis 3:18-19).

of the world, nor it's technological baubles and bangles. It is about our purposes regarding work. The issue is using our work, our employment, for the sake of the kingdom of God, rather than using God to justify a worldly lifestyle. Again, God is not against wealth, but neither is He for it. Rather, wealth is a means to an end, not an end in itself. Too many people work hard in order to live the kind of life they think they deserve, and then go to church and ask God to bless their self-centeredness. They go to church expecting God or the preacher to make them feel better about themselves so they can continue doing what they're doing. They want God to bless them, to bless their self-centered, godless lifestyle, their self-made traditions, rather than being a blessing to God through their work and their lifestyles. People don't have to change jobs to be of service to God. They have to change their attitudes, their hearts and minds, their priorities.

> "Now we command you, brothers, in the name of our Lord Jesus Christ, that you withdraw yourselves from every brother who walks disorderly, and not after the teaching which he received from us" (2 Thessalonians 3:6).

Here Paul commanded Christians to follow the traditions of the apostles rather than any other traditions. Paul was talking about their work habits, their life habits, their orderliness. He linked the concern about the traditions of men with work—employment. The tradition of God is not idleness, but industry. God gave Adam a job in the Garden. God's tradition is not working simply to earn money, but earning money to support the work of God's kingdom.

Again, God's kingdom is exceedingly broad and incorporates all kinds of work. So, we are not to throw out all traditions, only the traditions of men, only the worldly traditions, humanistic traditions, Pagan traditions, self-made traditions. We are to discard those activities that we do in our work and play that draw us away from God, away from Scripture, away from those things that do not serve God and are not authorized by God.

EXPERIENCE

Secondly, the basic principles of the world (v. 8) are all those principles that are derived from experience rather than from God's Word. Please understand that God is not opposed to experience or science (the exploitation of experience), but is opposed to ignoring and/or subverting principles that are given in His Word. Paul was pointing to the same issue here. Rather than stressing the application of traditions or principles, he was emphasizing the principles from which godless traditions come. Paul doesn't simply forbid greedy and selfish actions, He forbids the rationalizations or principles we make up to justify living greedy, self-centered and godless lives.

The basic principles of the world that Paul argued against here were in some sense the principles of works-righteousness—self-justification, the principles of humanism and godlessness. A modern modification of the idea of works-righteousness is the belief that we can live however we want as long as we can afford it, that our being able to afford it justifies it. Modern works-righteousness is the belief that our ability to do a thing provides the only justification we need. Today, works-righteousness manifests as an "I deserve it" attitude, a "just desserts" attitude. Today, people are not trying to do things that will justify them before God. Today people justify themselves and do whatever they want before God.

Rich and poor alike believe this principle. The rich live it, and the poor covet it. The rich rationalize, *I can do thus-and-so because I can afford it.* The poor dream about winning the lottery so that they can then afford to do whatever they want. God is lost in the hustle of modern living, and gladly so. People don't want what opposes their selfishness or their covetousness. Today, covetousness has become an art form.

No! Don't! Stop!

Thirdly, Paul warns us against all of the various ways of living and believing that are "not according to Christ" (v. 8). Here Paul provided a negative injunction. But people don't like negatives! They didn't then and they don't now.

Today, there is a great demand for positive Christianity. Everything church related has to have a positive spin or it isn't considered to be loving. So there has been a concerted effort over the past fifty years or so to repackage Christianity in a positive light. Sermons, Bible studies, music, etc., have to be upbeat. Everything has to be sweet and light and nonthreatening. Whatever in the Bible that is not perceived as positive, affirming, accepting, etc., is overlooked, denied or denigrated, as if God used to be nasty, mean and threatening in the Old Testament. But now in Christ God is nice, kind and loving, as if the New Testament God is different from the Old Testament God.

The difficulty is that the negative spin that people complain about is a major element of the Bible. The Ten Commandments are sometimes called the "shalt nots." People don't like them because they are negative. And they are! They forbid various beliefs and behaviors that people naturally do.

The human conscience is a restraining force. Conscience itself provides a negative function. Conscience performs a limiting or governing function, not an expansive function. People refrain from things because of their conscience. We don't do things because of our conscience. People are not conscientiously motivated to do drugs or lie, cheat and steal. That's not how it works. The conscience restrains. The Ten Commandments restrain belief and action. In this regard Christianity has a strong negative element, if restraint is understood as negative. But is restraining evil a negative thing?

People complain that the church is against everything. People want to be for things. Christians are tired of being against everything. Well, Christianity is for Jesus. It is for love and for justice as well. But without Jesus, love isn't love and justice isn't just. The church is for truth. But without Jesus, truth is not true.

The Bible is negative because, while God loves us just as we are, He is out to change hearts and human nature. He loves us so much that He won't leave us just as we are. And once He has changed us, He wants us to keep changing, keep growing "till we all come to...the measure of the stature of the fullness of Christ" (Ephesians 4:13).

Of course, God is not always negative, and neither is the church. But God does put many things in negative terms, in the language of forbiddance. The church then brings the fullness of God's Word to bear upon people, all of it, both the positive and the negative. A faithful preacher must preach all of the Bible. And when people are not accustomed to hearing negatives, they sometimes seem to hear nothing but the negatives. One *shalt not* seems to stand out in a paragraph of praise.

CHRISTIAN BARTERING

The thing that we must see is that the negative admonitions of the Lord lead to a positive life in Christ. For instance, in the flesh it's hard to find anything positive to say about Jesus' death on the cross. It was messy, painful, and unjust. Yet, it was a necessary part of salvation. Christ died for us so that we can live for Him. He died for your sin, so you can live by His righteousness. He wants to trade futures with you. You trade-in what you believe for what He believes. It's a simple swap, your judgment for His, your future for His. It's an act of faith.

People want to know how to make this trade. How does it work? How can I do it? Books have been written describing the best techniques of salvation. One says that you've got to walk the aisle. Another requires the sinner's prayer, or a show of hands with every head bowed and every eye closed. Some have refined (or summarized) the process and come up with various spiritual laws. Others use a variety of salvation steps, as if salvation is mechanical. Some require that you speak nonsense, others that you believe nonsense. Just walk the aisle, do the steps, raise your hand, speak in tongues, and bam! It's done. Once saved, always saved. It's done and I'm good to go do whatever I want. Been there, done that.

While some of these things might sometimes be helpful, they are all the traditions of men. The truth is that there is no specified way to come to Christ. "For by grace you have been saved through faith. And this is not your own doing; it is the gift of God" (Ephesians 2:8). By grace there are no special techniques or steps that can assure or improve salvation. But also, by grace there are no special problems or sins that can keep anyone from salvation, save one —the unforgivable sin (Matthew 12:31).

Jesus said, "Come to Me, all you who labor and are heavy laden, and I will give you rest" (Matthew 11:28). Coming to Jesus is a positive action. It is a moving forward. It is sweet and light. But that is not all it is. It is also a baptism into Christ's death. It is a dying to sin and self. It is a forsaking of the former things. It is discipleship and discipline. It is the love of God that produces willing, heart-felt obedience to God's law.

It is the not doing or the abandonment of unrighteousness. It is not getting involved in sexual immorality, not engaging idolatry, adultery, homosexuality, theft, greed, drunkenness, revelry, swindling, slavery, deceit, perjury, "and whatever else is contrary to sound doctrine" (1 Timothy 1:10, 1 Corinthians 6:9-10). It is not a lot of things, but it is not merely negative. It has a negative component. Yet these negative injunctions make a positive impact on people and on the world. Not engaging them is a source of joy, of happiness.

Apart from Christ people have the wrong idea of happiness. Apart from Christ people have the wrong idea about who they are. Apart from Christ these are the very things that people do with their freedom (idolatry, adultery, homosexuality, theft, greed, drunkenness, revelry, swindling, slavery, deceit, perjury).

The world thinks that these things are positive, that they are fun, that they are a necessary part of being human. The world says that these are the things that make us human, that make us interesting, and that we need to engage these things to embrace our humanity. But God says, "Thou shalt not!"

☙❧

While God is light, sin is darkness. So, whatever black holes are they have darkness in common with sin. It is an important commonality because sin also operates like a black hole. There is a dark center that attracts everything in its orbit. The closer to the center of the darkness, the greater the attractive forces. And at a certain point (going over the event horizon), there is no coming back. People are often attracted to attractiveness itself, as if there is a "high" involved with being caught up in something bigger than one's self. And there is! This is why it is essential to discern light from darkness, good from evil before the attraction becomes overwhelming. *Christos Singularis!*

11

CIRCUMCISION BY CHRIST

In him also you were circumcised with a circumcision made without hands, by putting off the body of the flesh, by the circumcision of Christ, having been buried with him in baptism, in which you were also raised with him through faith in the powerful working of God, who raised him from the dead. And you, who were dead in your trespasses and the uncircumcision of your flesh, God made alive together with him, having forgiven us all our trespasses, by canceling the record of debt that stood against us with its legal demands. This he set aside, nailing it to the cross. He disarmed the rulers and authorities and put them to open shame, by triumphing over them in him.
—Colossians 2:11-15 (ESV)

It is impossible to speak of the significance of circumcision by Christ without in some way referring to the reality of circumcision as the Jews understood and practiced it. Circumcision in the Old Testament was a procedure that surgically altered the physical character of individual men. It imposed a surgical alteration of the human reproductive system upon infant boys. From a purely physical perspective, it appears to have little to no purpose, and modern medicine considers it to be nothing more than a personal religious preference.

The religious symbolism, however involved, is quite complex and centers on the doctrine of the covenant, God's primary point of contact with humanity. Because circumcision involves the human reproductive organs, the use of which is strictly governed by God through Scripture through the covenant of marriage. Circumcision is a symbol of God's covenant and functions as a human reproductive governor or regulator, and has everything to do with human families and reproduction. What-ever else circumcision is, it involves a covenantal message from God about human reproduction and human cultural sustainability, in the sense that circumcision was the central symbol of God's covenant. In the long run, God's covenant, now in Christ, will prove to be the only foundation for sustainable families, churches and civil societies. Indeed, this is the central message of the Bible.

The practice of circumcision required a heightened perception of and commitment to God because God required circumcision of His Old Testament people. Yet, we must remember that Old Testament circumcision anticipated the coming of Christ and symbolized a greater revelation of God's love that the Messiah would bring. The circumcision of the heart (Deuteronomy 10:16) involves the removal of a kind of callousness toward sin and ultimately an end to corruption and sin. This is true not merely of circumcision, but of the whole of God's covenant with humanity because that is what circumcision represents.

THE FLAP

The "circumcision of Christ" (v. 11) is related to the circumcision of the flesh, in the same way spirit is related to flesh in biblical literature generally. It must also be noted that it is not simply an Old Testament/New Testament difference. There is an important analogy between the pruning of unneeded skin and the pruning of unholy attitudes regarding the circumcision of the flesh and the circumcision of the heart. One provides a mark of God on the body and one on the heart. Only one's wife (ideally) is an enduring witnesses to the mark on the body, and only the Holy Spirit, who is another kind of covenant partner, is the enduring witness to the circumcised heart.

Various references to the circumcision of the heart provide a key element of Old Testament doctrine: "Circumcise therefore the foreskin of your heart, and be no longer stubborn" (Deuteronomy 10:16); "And the Lord your God will circumcise your heart and the heart of your offspring, so that you will love the Lord your God with all your heart and with all your soul, that you may live" (Deuteronomy 30:6), etc. We often forget that circumcision of the heart is an Old Testament doctrine, and mistakenly think that it was introduced by New Testament baptism.

This is the circumcision that Paul referred to when he said that circumcision by Christ is "made without hands" (v.11), indicating that there is a corresponding process of pruning back the callousness of the human heart. Note that a callous heart can only be circumcised by God. What the Jews outwardly did to the flesh by way of a ceremony, Christ does inwardly to the heart in reality.

Traditionally, then, heart circumcision is celebrated in Christ's church through the ceremony of baptism. Yet it needs to be noted that Christian baptism remains an outward ceremony of the church regardless of the mode or the candidates. The same issue between the outward sign and the inward reality has continued into the New Testament ceremony of baptism.

Yes, baptism is a better symbol of the better covenant (Hebrews 7:22), but the same external/internal issues remain. In the same way that all Jews are circumcised,[34] but not all those who have been circumcised are faithful to their Jewish heritage, so also, all Christians are baptized,[35] but not all baptized Christians are faithful to their Christian calling. In fact, only people who have been engaged in a promise like circumcision or baptism can be guilty of unfaithfulness. People can only be unfaithful to a former promise. Being unfaithful requires the breaking of a former promise. So, if that initial promise has not been made either by you or on your behalf, you cannot be unfaithful to it.

It is shortsighted and inadequate to understand God's promise in an individualistic way, as if the promise exists only between God and particular individuals, and is valid only if and when particular individuals sign on the proverbial dotted line. When we do this we are assuming a legalistic and individualistic interpretation of God's promise—God's covenant, when God harbors no such strictly individualistic interpretation.

God always deals with people on the basis of the reality of the Trinity, and the Trinity provides for the reality of individual and corporate being simultaneously. Within the unity of the Godhead are the individual divine Persons of the Trinity—one, yet three.

---

34 Women participated in circumcision through the authority of covenantal headship, wives via their husbands, daughters via their fathers, through the reality and representational character of biblical authority.

35 The baptism of women and children, of households (Acts 16:15, 18:8, 1 Corinthians 1:16), symbolizes the expansion of God's mission from the Jews to the whole world. Baptism symbolizes the fact that through Jesus Christ everyone has direct access to the throne of grace (Hebrews 4:16) without undermining the representational character of authority.

Similarly, in union with Christ are the individual persons of Christ, the Holy Spirit and the individual. The persons and personalities retain their unique characters and are differentiable. The analogy is not perfect, but it is both adequate and substantive.

That reality is His own trinitarian character and our likeness and/or reflection of His essential character, His image. The point is that God's promise involves God the Father, God the Son and God the Holy Spirit on His side, and individuals, families and nations on our side. Thus, God's promise, God's covenant is both an individual promise and a social promise. John Donne was right, "no man is an island." God's promise and salvation are equally and mutually for individuals, families and nations because of God's trinitarian character and our likeness to it. Consequently, God's covenant covers everyone, law abiders and law breakers.

CEREMONY

Paul linked the ceremony of Christian baptism with the ceremony of Jewish circumcision in verse 12. The circumcision of Christ is symbolized in baptism as a dying to sin and a resurrection to the spiritual reality of Christ. Baptism symbolizes that Christians follow Christ into personal death and resurrection. The ritual of circumcision was an act of covenant obedience on the part of Jewish parents in honor of God's covenant promise to their children. Similarly, the Sacrament of infant baptism is an act of covenant obedience on the part of Christian parents in honor of God's covenant promise to their children. The ceremony does not guarantee the fulfillment of the promise. It simply brings the children into a growing awareness of the covenant so that they can only disregard it as a act of overt unfaithfulness.

God said to Abraham, "As for you, you shall keep my covenant, you and your offspring after you throughout their generations. This is my covenant, which you shall keep, between me and you and your offspring after you: Every male among you shall be circumcised. You shall be circumcised in the flesh of your foreskins, and it shall be a sign of the covenant between me and you" (Genesis 17:9-11).

Paul was concerned here with the connection between circumcision and baptism, not with the proper mode of baptism. He wasn't talking about immersion or sprinkling here and to read that discussion into these verses is an error. Paul's concern here was to indicate that the purpose of circumcision and the purpose of baptism are the same. Both ceremonies point to the inward reality of conversion and regeneration, of new life in Christ, and of faithfulness.

Paul's argument in this regard is often defended as the superiority of spirituality over legalism, or of spirituality over ceremonies, and correctly so. Those in Colossae who clung to the legalistic and ceremonial concerns of Jewish circumcision had closed their eyes to the greater reality of God's ability to convert hardened hearts. In the same way, we don't want to fall back on legalistic concerns ourselves by thinking that Paul's point here was about the proper mode of baptism. Paul was not here concerned with ceremonial exteriors, but with the interior reality of a circumcised heart. So, we need to understand his concern to be the necessity of all Christians to have circumcised hearts, the kind "made without hands" (v. 11).

Too many people read these verses and get sidetracked by various legalistic concerns about the baptism ceremony and lose sight of the fact that baptism as Paul speaks of it here is a spiritual act of God, a death and resurrection, a "putting off the body of the sins of the flesh by the circumcision of Christ" (v. 11). While the symbolism of the ceremony is important, the reality of what God does in the human heart is Paul's key concern here. How can you or I or some priest perform a circumcision without hands? We can't. And that was Paul's point.

The central element of circumcision was not the ceremony, not the procedure, but the reality of a circumcised heart, the result of which made people significantly less stubborn toward God.[36] We often forget that the ceremony of baptism is not the whole of baptism. In the same way that there is more to marriage than the wedding, there is more to Christian discipleship than baptism. The Old Testament referred to this by specifying the difference between circumcision of the flesh and circumcision of the heart. The New Testament points to the same difference when it differentiates baptism and baptism by the Spirit (Matthew 3:11, John 1:33, Acts 1:5).

The Hebrew word used by the Lord in Deuteronomy 9:6 to describe the Jews as stiff-necked is sometimes translated as *stubborn* (*qâsheh*), and literally means churlish, cruel, grievous, hardhearted, impudent, obstinate, and troublesome. The Jews were not chosen to be the host of God's covenant because of their particular

---

36 Sanctification is not complete or perfect in this life, but it does increase over time with practice.

suitability to God's salvation program, but because they as a people were particularly indisposed toward the Lord. God did not choose the Jews because they were especially prone to faithfulness, but precisely because they were prone to unfaithfulness. They provided a kind of worst case scenario. If the Lord could convert the Jews, anyone could be converted. And He did.

Paul was saying that, as important as the ceremonies of the church are, we shouldn't trust in the ceremonies of a local church to make salvation real—and they are very important to the success of God's plan of salvation. Local churches don't make salvation real for anyone. And yet, at the same time, salvation cannot be real apart from the Universal Church, the Body of Christ.[37]

Only Christ saves, and Christ saves people *into* the Universal Church, and ideally into a local church, as well. Salvation doesn't make sense—can't make sense—unless and until Christ has circumcised the heart. The unredeemed can talk about God's salvation with all of the eloquence and ostentation they can muster, but they are clouds without rain (Jude 12) because they speak in vain. Their words are empty apart from the reality of a circumcised heart or baptism by the Holy Spirit.[38]

ALIVE!

Verses 13-14 tell us that God "has made (us) alive together with Him, having forgiven (us) all trespasses, blotting out the handwriting of ordinances that was against us, which was contrary to us, and has taken it out of the way, nailing it to the cross." Paul said here that God's Old Testament law was a kind of I.O.U. held by God for the sin of Adam. Adam's sin incurred a debt and God holds the note, which means that God can either foreclose against the debt owed or forgive it.

Foreclosure is what people refer to as judgment, where God finds a person guilty, unrepentant, and without adequate representation. Such a person is damned to eternal punishment and removed or barred from habitation with God. Christians, on the other hand, are also judged and found guilty, but have repented and do have adequate representation by Jesus Christ. Christians

---

37 Church and Body are capitalized to refer to the universal, mysterious, triumphant, eschatalogical and spiritual Church, as opposed to a local church.

38 This is not to be confused with speaking in tongues. It simply refers to regeneration. For more on tongues, see: *Arsy Varsy—Reclaiming the Gospel in First Corinthians*, by Phillip A. Ross, Pilgrim Platform, Marietta, Ohio, 2008, p. 274-285.

are, then, forgiven and invited into habitation with God in Christ.

This concept is not at all mysterious or other worldly, but in fact is very similar to the national debt that the United States is currently generating, in that we are creating a debt for the generations who will follow us, a debt that will be inherited by our children and grandchildren who did nothing to incur it. Our children who will inherit our debt will have done nothing to deserve it, yet it will be theirs. In fact, the similarities should give us great pause.

According to the Old Testament, people owe obedience to God, the lawgiver. God's covenant specified in Deuteronomy 28 that when people obey God, they will receive God's blessings, and when they don't, they will receive God's curses. In order to receive God's blessings, then, people owe obedience to God's law. That is the central point of the covenant. God's covenant is an agreement that covers both human obedience and human disobedience to the law. God has promised blessings for law abiders and curses for law breakers. All people fall into one or the other of these categories, which means that God's covenant or promise pertains to all people at all times and in all places. It is a universal law, an eternal covenant. Though God first gave it to the Jews, it has been given to the whole world through Jesus Christ, though many people continue to reject it.

The Jews lived under God's law and were blessed or cursed according to their obedience. The history of the Jews in the Old Testament has clearly demonstrated that God can and will keep His promises by blessing Israel's obedience and cursing Israel's disobedience. The history of the Old Testament provided a record of their failure to obey God and the final destruction of the Temple and Jerusalem that resulted in A.D. 70. The destruction of Jerusalem confirmed that God would fulfill His promises even if it meant the destruction of His own people and their covenant and the establishment of a new covenant and a new people. In the process of that destruction, though, God passed His promise forward to Jesus Christ, who is the savior of the nations, of the world.

FORGIVEN

Paul argued that because Christ is the second federal head of humanity (Adam was the first), Christ's obedience to the law has eliminated the debt owed to God (v. 14) for those in Christ. Adam's disobedience in his role as federal head incurred the debt, Christ's obedience unto death on the cross in His role as federal head elim-inated it. Because of their respective human headship positions, both the debt incurred by Adam and its forgiveness secured by Christ function through inheritance. The debt has been inherited by the children of Adam (all humanity), and the forgiveness is inher-ited by the children of Christ, by Christians.

The situation is as if God had provided humanity a house—a home, a habitation for humanity. Adam's sin, then, destroyed the relationship between man and God. So, God threw him out of the free habitation and began charging him rent. God made him work for his keep (Genesis 3:19). The Old Testament sacrifices served as a kind of perpetual payment of this rent, but were unable to change the renters into owners.

As renters humanity owed God perfect obedience as the pay-ment for their habitation. But because human beings are so far from perfection, we could never be anything but renters who con-tinuously make payments according to the Old Covenant. Our efforts or works—if they were acceptable to God, which they aren't (Isaiah 64:6)—could never pay all our rent to God. The debt we owe is greater than our ability to ever repay it because our relationship to God is that of a tenant. We lack the ability or the down payment to become owners rather than renters. That's our situation under the law, the Old Covenant. This is the Old Testament dilemma.

But Jesus, who has the right to human headship, by grace, by birthright and by works, by having perfectly obeyed the law, has promised to pay our entire debt. He then gave His life as a down payment (2 Corinthians 1:22, Ephesians 1:14). Because of Christ's human Headship, His down payment on the cross and His promise to return to complete the transaction, Christians are relieved of their debt to God inasmuch as they are in Christ. We have been released from a debt we could never repay, and thus are free in Christ, but only in Christ. Our freedom in Christ does not, however, mean that we are free from all obligations. Those who owe their freedom to Christ are obliged to Christ for their freedom.

Still, an old question lingers: For whom did Jesus die? Jesus' life and death effects everyone on earth, but not in the same way. When Jesus became fully human, He changed the definition or character of humanity as a whole. The advent of Christ clarified the doctrine of the Trinity and demonstrated the trinitarian character of humanity because of His humanity. In a sense, the analogy of man as a renter was transformed into man as an owner by Christ's advent and the change of covenant administration. A new note was drawn up with Christ as the guarantor.

Christ made a down payment to God (His life) for controlling (and ultimately full) ownership of the human habitation (the whole earth) with God. Humanity as a whole, because of Christ's advent, because of the humanity of Christ and federal headship of Christ, has now become the corporate mortgage holder of this habitation. Ownership was transferred from God to Christ. Christ is now (since His ascension) in the process of buying our individual mortgages, or incorporating individuals into His company, the Church. He's buying them out.

He has the capital to purchase everyone's mortgage note or indebtedness, and will eventually take possession of it all. Some people willingly surrender their notes, and willingly come under the New Agreement (Covenant). They join the company and work for their new Boss (Jesus Christ). Others will fall into foreclosure because of their inherent inability to meet their mortgage demands, at which point Christ will acquire their habitations and evict the unwilling and uncooperative tenants.

So, did Jesus wipe out the debt for everyone, or only for some? Scripture's answer is that He wiped it out for everyone who believes. Unbelievers are still in debt to God because they will not receive the gift or acknowledge that Christ did what He did. Believers, on the other hand, are now in the habitation business with Christ. They have no debt because Christ bought their mortgage. They are now partners with Christ in a commonly owned habitat corporation, and continue to work for the welfare and improvement of the corporation by faith (Ephesians 2:8).

Unbelievers continue to be under the Old Testament law, only now (since Christ) as mortgage holders rather than renters. Their mortgage is greater than their ability to repay it. Failure to pay the mortgage makes them liable to foreclosure and recipients of God's curses, which are destruction, death and damnation.

But believers are under grace because believers acknowledge the fact that Christ has purchased their mortgage and burned it. The habitation is ours inasmuch as we keep it free from other liens. But while the habitat is a free gift of God's grace, it comes with certain obligations, just as home owners have more obligations to the home than do renters. We have obligations not merely to Christ Himself but stewardship obligations to the habitat as well. Home owners, unlike renters, are responsible for the maintenance of the dwelling.

Wouldn't you be thankful if someone paid off your mortgage and burned the note? Why would anyone reject such a gift? The analogy suggests that while Christ agreed to pay our debt, the time in which we presently live, the church age, is the time in which the deal is being concluded. It will be brought to completion when Christ returns. At that time all the notes will be recalled, the final papers signed, Christ will take His purchase home, and take possession of His earthly habitation, and God will foreclose on all unbelievers.

FORECLOSURE

Some people don't believe. They don't believe that God would make such a deal with Jesus. Or they don't believe that Jesus was able to make the necessary arrangements with God. Or they don't believe that Jesus' obedience unto the cross was sufficient to cover their debt. Or they don't believe that there was any debt to begin with. Or they don't believe that God holds their mortgage. Or whatever.

The bottom line is that they don't believe in the sufficiency of Christ. And, because they don't believe it, they don't have the faith that Jesus can or will take care of it. So, they haven't given Jesus their mortgage papers. They simply ignore or deny the whole deal between God and Jesus Christ. Not believing it, they don't see it, and not seeing it, their blindness becomes their confession that it has nothing to do with them. It is not that Christ has abandoned them, but that they refuse to accept the gift of grace in Christ. For whatever reason, they don't want it.

When Jesus returns to complete the deal, He won't have their mortgages because they didn't give them to Him. Adam still holds them. So, when God forecloses they will lose their homes and be cast into the street. But those who have submitted their mortgages to Christ will be saved from God's foreclosure. That's what Paul means when he said that the "certificate of debt" (or I.O.U.) that God holds for Christ's people was nailed to the cross. It has been taken care of, paid in full.

Paul argued elsewhere (Romans 6:1-2, etc.) that this does not mean that Christians are now free to "party hardy!" Christians are not free to do whatever they want. It only means that our debt has been transferred from judgment apart from Christ to mercy in

Christ. The faithful are now in moral debt to Christ. We are free from God's foreclosing judgment, and now morally obliged to Christ's gracious mercy. We are now free from God's old demands, from God's demand for perfect obedience in this lifetime, and are free in Christ, free to shower Christ with our gratitude, thankfulness and obedience. No longer driven by fear of the Lord, we are now driven by gratitude to be all that we can be in Christ.

Paul said that when Jesus purchased the note of our indebtedness, He removed the authority of the principalities and powers. He has removed the authority of the worldly forces that God sometimes uses to enforce His foreclosing judgment. These are the same principalities and powers that Paul wrote to the Ephesians about: "For we do not wrestle against flesh and blood, but against principalities, against powers, against the world's rulers, of the darkness of this age, against spiritual wickedness in high places" (Ephesians 6:12).

These principalities and powers mistakenly think that God still holds the note of indebtedness against us. They contend Christ's authority to do what He did, His purchase of the note of human indebtedness from God with His down payment on the cross. They deny the authority of Christ and work to make their agents deny it, too. They want people to continue thinking that they are in debt to God because debt is their power. One person's debt is another person's power. So, as long as people think that they are in debt to God, the principalities and powers have power over them.

But when Christ paid the debt, that power was objectively nullified, canceled. However, only as humanity learns who the real mortgage (covenant) holder is do they stop giving power to the old mortgage enforcers. Interestingly, those old mortgage holders actually served under God, but apart from Christ, apart from the Trinity.

While God has transferred ownership to Christ, the old enforcers (religious beliefs, customs, leaders, etc.) have not willingly given up their position and power. And even though that power is nothing more than people kowtowing to them, and is nothing in itself, it endures until that kowtowing stops. And it stops as people accept Christ and give Him glory. It stops through the act of worship. It stops by giving glory to Jesus Christ as Father, Son and Holy Spirit. It stops by not giving glory to the principalities and powers.

Because Jesus has stopped foreclosure on the faithful, the forces of foreclosure cannot actually foreclose against the faithful.

The faithful don't own their own notes, but have been bought out by Christ. But more than that, said Paul, Christ has made a public spectacle of His triumph over the principalities and powers in order to attract a greater number of people to His gracious salvation (1 Corinthians 4:9) The public spectacle was like an advertising campaign to get the Word out that planet earth is under new management. We are today still part of that public spectacle, part of God's evangelism program.

By canceling the record of debt that stood against us with its legal demands Christ set it aside. By nailing it to the cross He disarmed the rulers and authorities and put them to open shame. Christ's triumph is their shame because in the light of Christ's righteousness their sin and trickery are clearly seen for what they are.

God has already begun foreclosure proceedings. So, our own houses best be in order, which means that Christ needs to be holding your mortgage. Lord, make it so!

CঙৎO

Money is often mistaken for God. The Bible calls it idolatry, and this problem has been around forever. People often think that money can solve their problems. But it can't. It's only a tool, and tools can be used or abused. People even think that money is the solution to poverty, that poverty is a condition caused by the lack of money. But it's not. Giving money to poor people doesn't solve their problems. Poor people don't understand money and can't manage it. Giving money to the poor is like pouring it into a black hole. Jesus knew this (John 12:8). The poor need a correct understanding of reality, and that means abandoning superstitions and embracing the trinitarian God of reality. *Christos Singularis!*

12

SHADOW & LIGHT

*Therefore let no one pass judgment on you in questions of
food and drink, or with regard to a festival or a new moon
or a Sabbath. These are a shadow of the things to come, but
the substance belongs to Christ. Let no one disqualify you,
insisting on asceticism and worship of angels, going on in
detail about visions, puffed up without reason by his
sensuous mind, and not holding fast to the Head, from
whom the whole body, nourished and knit together through
its joints and ligaments, grows with a growth that is from
God.   —Colossians 2:16-19 (ESV)*

Therefore" (v. 16), Paul concluded an argument made in the
preceding verses. What argument? Paul had been arguing that
Christians are free and forgiven in Christ. In Christ we are free
from "philosophy and vain deceit, according to the tradition of men,
according to the elements of the world" (Colossians 2:8). In Christ we
are free from superstition and ignorance, free from the ideology that
masks itself as wisdom and intelligence, particularly the intellectual
wisdom of the college/university/academy. The Lord has nothing
against intelligence, of course. In fact, He prefers it. But what passes
for intelligence in this world is little more than pride and self-sancti-
fication tethered to this or that unbiblical assumption.

SABBATH

"Therefore" said Paul, "let no one judge you in food or in drink,
or in respect of a feast, or of the new moon, or of the sabbaths" (v.
16). He was simply acknowledging that in Christ neither the Old
Testament festivals nor Pagan celebrations had any significance. The
Sabbath commandment (Exodus 20:8) requires special treatment

here because it is included in the Ten Commandments. Christ's ful-fillment of the law brought, not the *end* of the Sabbath, but the ful-fillment of the *purpose* of the Sabbath, which is rest in God, and is only possible in Christ. So, the Sabbath observance shifted from Saturdays to eternal or perpetual rest in Christ. The emphasis is no longer a particular day, but on Christ Himself, who is the fulfill-ment of the Sabbath.

These celebrations (feasts, new moons and a particular Sabbath day) were mere shadows that vanished in the light of Christ. They don't matter. They are immaterial. They are non sequitur. It doesn't matter if you do and it doesn't matter if you don't. He was saying that Jews were free from the Old Testament demands of festival participation, just as former Pagans were free in Christ from think-ing that they could manipulate God with their festivals and cere-monies. Christ overshadowed it all.

Whatever evaluation of faithfulness people associated with par-ticipating in festivals, ceremonies or diets were useless in the light of Christ. From Christ forward faithfulness would be a measure of conformity to the gospel, not conformity to the old social mores of diet, festival or celebration attendance.

The teaching of the Sabbath played an important part of Old Testament culture. Sabbath observation was still important for Christians, but not as narrowly defined as previously understood by the Jews. It was summed up in the general command to worship and rest, to find refreshment in worship and fellowship. Its purpose was the expression of freedom in God and was never intended to put people in a legalistic bind. It was never intended to strangle the Spirit out of faithfulness, as had happened prior to Christ.

Undoubtedly, Paul was also responding to the fact that Christi-ans had been gathering on Sundays for Christian worship since Christ's resurrection. Paul's general argument was that one day was no better or worse than another (Romans 14:5). The original Old Testament Sabbath ideal was not what was being done in Israel. It has been perverted by the Pharisees. Nonetheless, in the light of Christ, it simply dissolved, not that the idea of Sabbath rest is unimportant. It is! But it's importance is no longer tied to a specific day. There was nothing wrong with honoring the Sabbath on Sat-urdays, but neither was it required on Saturdays.

Nor was anything particularly necessary about worshiping on Sundays. The particular day of the week didn't matter any more because in the light of Christ Christians were called to live out their worship of the Lord day by day, hour by hour, minute by minute. In Christ worship was no longer compartmentalized into this or that day, but is now understood to be the foundation of faithfulness and godliness. But neither was there any reason not to follow the Christian community practice of gathering on the Lord's Day, on Sunday. And because it was common practice among the churches even in Paul's day, it should simply be honored. There was no reason to change it and good reasons to keep it.

The weekly pattern of work and rest is still beneficial. People are creatures of habit, of patterns and cycles—night/day, inhale/ exhale, fall/winter/spring/summer, etc. It is the nature of the earth and the creatures of the earth to conform to various patterns. We who live in the environment of the earth are tied to its cycles and patterns. The idea of a day of rest, of taking a break from work, is still a good idea. It is not an arbitrary rule. Rather, it serves our human nature. It is helpful, beneficial, good for body and soul. And it should be a source of joy and pleasure. If our experience of the Sabbath isn't a joy and a pleasure, something is wrong. Christ is the fulfillment of the Sabbath.

BODY

In verse 17 the English Standard Version does a disservice by translating the Greek word *sōma* as *substance*. "These are a shadow of the things to come, but the substance belongs to Christ" (v. 17). It is not that *substance* is inaccurate as an idea, but that it fails to point to the body of Christ. The discernment of the body of Christ is critical to being faithful. According to Paul in 1 Corinthians 11:29, "anyone who eats and drinks without discerning the body (*sōma*) eats and drinks judgment on himself."

The Authorized Version translated verse 17, "which are a shadow of things to come, but the body is of Christ." The contrast between shadow and substance is useful and important. Old Testament shadows gave way to the substance of the gospel, to the reality of Christ. But Paul was talking about the *sōma* of Christ, and given Paul's lengthy and explicit contrasts between *sarx* and *sōma* in 1 Corinthians,[39] Paul undoubtedly had something particular in mind He was not talking about Christ's substance or reality in a general or philosophical way. In contrast to the various shadows of the Old

---

39 See: *Arsy Varsy—Reclaiming The Gospel in First Corinthians*, Phillip A. Ross, Pilgrim Platform, 2009, p 211.

Testament, Paul placed the body of Christ, not simply the idea of Christ's substance. The word *is* in the Authorized Version has been added by the translators. The Greek simply reads *sōma Christos* or body Christ, with an implied *of*.

And what is the body of Christ? The church! In opposition to the shadows and ceremonies of the Old Testament now stands the body of Christ, the church. It's not some philosophical idea of substance as opposed to essence or shadow. It is not an abstract idea, but is the very life blood of the Christian community, set apart and gathered together. It is hearts "knit together in love" (Colossians 2:2). It is "living stones" that are "built up as a spiritual house, to be a holy priesthood" (1 Peter 2:5). It is walking "in the light, as he is in the light" and having "fellowship with one another" (1 John 1:7). It is not some spiritual ideal suited only for heaven, nor a mere idea intended for philosophical reflection. It is here and now, in Christ. It is the reality of the church, not the idea of the church.

Why is this important? Paul wrote, "Let no one disqualify you, insisting on asceticism and worship of angels, going on in detail about visions, puffed up without reason by his sensuous mind, and not holding fast to the Head, from whom the whole body, nourished and knit together through its joints and ligaments, grows with a growth that is from God" (vs. 18-19). Paul's allusion to qualifications suggests that there are qualifications regarding membership in the body of Christ. Some sort of compliance is involved. While salvation is by grace, body membership is through faith. The gift and the response cannot be separated. They are two sides of a single coin. It is not that one side causes the other, but that grace and faith are fused together.

Paul was here arguing against the idea that being a Christian has anything to do with asceticism, angel worship, visions or pride in sense perception (some sort of hypersensitivity or superior discernment). The Colossians were being drawn away from the gospel by Gnostics who had been teaching that the path to superior spirituality was through some or all of these various things. To which Paul responded, Hogwash! Apart from the central tenets of the gospel they are all idolatrous.

ASCETICISM

Asceticism is the idea that through renunciation of worldly pleasures, of bodily functions, it is possible to achieve a superior spiritual or intellectual state. The obvious problem here is that such an idea is a matter of works-righteousness. Asceticism is a kind of works-righteousness, which is completely contrary to the gospel of grace. Yet at the same time, there is a kind of self-denial that accompanies faithfulness. Jesus told his disciples, "If anyone would come after me, let him deny himself and take up his cross and follow me" (Matthew 16:24).

There are several ways that this self-denial differs from asceticism. First, it doesn't lead to a higher spiritual or intellectual state or status. The values of the kingdom are the opposite of the values of the world. So, Christ defined higher status with what is considered to be lowly service; "whoever would be great among you must be your servant" (Matthew 20:26). Christian service leads to submission and self-denial, not superiority.

Second, Christian self-denial is not a matter of deprivation, but of joy. Christian self-denial is not a matter of sensory deprivation, not a matter of submission to pain or difficulty for the sake of physical mastery, nor of the denial of bodily functions like food or sex. It is none of that. Rather, Christian self-denial is not self-focused at all. It is other-focused. It is a matter of being a servant, not for self-improvement purposes, but for the sake of others. It is the sacrifice of self-concern altogether. It is not denial and sacrifice in order to please God or to qualify for salvation, though it does please God and is a fruit of salvation. But that is not the right motivation. It is not about "me," not about the person doing the sacrifice. It's about others. It is the joy of serving others that leaves self-concern behind.

ANGEL WORSHIP

Paul also argued against the idea of angel worship or the worship of superior beings. In Christ, all worship is directed to God alone, to the Trinity—Father, Son and Holy Spirit. Worship directed to anything or anyone other than God is false worship and must be abandoned. Of course, God is trinitarian. So, worship of God follows along trinitarian lines. It is worship of the Father, of the Son and of the Holy Spirit, all in one and one in all.

Angel or spirit worship, on the other hand, has always been a ploy of Satan to obscure and interfere with the authentic relationship between God and man, and has always been denounced by the God of Scripture. God dealt with this matter by forbidding worship of anything but Himself in the First Commandment.

Christians are commanded to worship God alone, as the Trinity. So, there is an element of truth to the idea of worship, but the object of worship is critical. There are two elements involved in worship. We must worship the right God and we must worship the right way. Both the object of worship and the methods of worship are prescribed. The reason for this is that the whole purpose of humanity, the reason why we are here at all, is to worship God. Not just the hour or so on Sunday mornings, but our entire lives are to be directed and circumscribed by worship, the glorification of God in Christ on earth. Such worship is the practice of eternal Sabbath rest in Christ.

VISIONS

Paul also argued against visions, actually against "going on in detail about visions" (v. 18), against "intruding into things which he hath not seen" (Authorized Version). Each of these translations provides a slightly different understanding of this concern. Paul was indeed opposed to what passed for mystical visions and experiences of the Gnostic variety, which included Old Testament or Jewish Gnosticism, Greek Gnosticism (also known as Greek philosophy), and Pagan Gnosticism. Salvation was not a function of knowledge or experience, but of grace alone. People were/are not saved on the basis of what they know. Nor does salvation produce a special kind of knowledge or perception. Christians are not smarter than other people, though we do have a different perspective.

Genuine salvation actually produces genuine faith in God. And faith in God is something that the unfaithful don't have. It is experiential and does have a profound effect upon one's knowledge and experience. God gives the faithful ears with which to hear and eyes with which to see. Paul knew about faith and its effect because his own salvation had given him faith.

Paul even had visions of being caught up in the third heaven (2 Corinthians 12:2). But he spoke sparingly and only under duress about it because he knew that such things are liable to inflammation and exaggeration. The Authorized Version translation, "intruding into things which he hath not seen," suggests that Paul was arguing against ungrounded and unnecessary speculation, a particular penchant of the Greeks and those who have followed their patterns of thought.

SUPERIORITY

The last thing on this short list of things Paul argued against was pride in sense perception. I have suggested that this was a kind of hypersensitivity or superior discernment that may have been thought to have been related to the gospel. Certainly, Christ is to be perceived, to be comprehended. And discernment is required of faithfulness, but what is to be cast aside is pride and superiority.

Seeing Christ, understanding Christ is not a function of human ability, but of God's grace alone. It is not that Christians are superior to others because they are faithful. But rather, that people are so dense that they cannot even see the kingdom, cannot even see God or Christ apart from God giving them eyes to see (Deuteronomy 29:4, Ezekiel 12:2) and ears to hear (Mark 4:9). God doesn't save people because they have the sense to be faithful. Rather, people are so dumb and blind to God that He has to give people new eyes and new hearts just so they can be cognizant of Him! The wonder isn't that all people are not saved. The wonder is that any are saved.

Paul went on in verse 19 saying that faithful Christians need to hold "fast to the Head (*kephalē*), from whom the whole body, nourished and knit together through its joints and ligaments, grows with a growth that is from God." First, said Paul, we need to hold fast. The Greek is one word (*krateō*) and literally means to seize or retain. It is the action of faithfulness. It is a kind of grip.

HEADSHIP

What are we to hold fast to? The head (*kephalē*). This is a reference to Christ, but does not indicate Christ by name. It refers to Him by function or purpose. *Kephalē* is the same word that Paul used in 1 Corinthians 11 in his discussion of headship. We are to hold fast, not just to Christ as a Person, nor simply to the teachings of Christ, but to the structure of biblical authority that acknowledges Christ as the Head of all authority. The structure of authority that Paul had in mind is representative authority where the authority of the head—Christ—is acknowledged and honored (obeyed) through His various representatives as if those representatives were Christ Himself.

The next phrase, "from whom the whole body, nourished and knit together through its joints and ligaments" suggests that the whole body of the church, including each and every member, is connected to the Head (Christ) directly, though through Christ's various representatives. The representatives are real and have real authority. And at the same time, each part of the body, each gifted member, is knit together with other members as various body parts are knit together through joints and ligaments. Whatever else this description is, the body or church is described here as an organic whole, an organic unit, an organism, as distinguished from a mere organization.

An organism is different than an organization in that an organism is alive and an organization is an abstraction, an abstract entity, a mental construct. This is important because, while an organization is made up of members, officers, committees and regulations, an organism is a living being. I don't want to make too much of this, but neither do I want to give it short shrift. The difference is important. One is an intellectual pattern of relationships, the other is an actual being. One is an abstraction or idea, and one is actually alive.

The fact that Paul calls attention to this difference suggests that the difference is important in regard to Paul's larger point here. And what was that point? It had to do with the reality of Christ's forgiveness. It had to do with shadow and substance, with Old Testament ideas and New Testament realities. Paul was suggesting that it is possible to understand Christ from the different trinitarian perspectives.

DIVISIONS

The first division is between those who openly believe the gospel and those who openly and consciously don't. We are not dealing with that here. A second division exists within the category of self-conscious believers, and is under consideration here. It is a further refinement of those who acknowledge and believe in Jesus Christ as the Messiah of God. It suggests that there are two opposing ways to believe in Christ, a right way and a wrong way, a true way and a false way, a real way and an imaginary way.

Sure enough, Paul's larger argument in First Corinthians was about false belief, about believing wrongly in the right thing, about misunderstanding Christ, about believing, but believing wrongly, falsely. Apparently, Paul was aware that some of the Colossian believers had confessed Christ, had believed in Christ and even taught about Christ, but they did not treat Christ as the reality that He actually is. Rather, they treated Him like an abstraction.

They were caught up in the knowledge game and treated the Lord of Glory like a piece of a knowledge puzzle, as if the goal of Christianity was getting the knowledge puzzle right, as if an abstract, speculative understanding of the Bible and Christ's role in it was itself the salvation of which Christ spoke. It was a head game for the Gnostics, and Paul was here arguing against the head game approach to Christianity, against what we would call an academic approach or an academic understanding of the gospel.

While correct analysis is important, Christianity is more than correct analysis. It is a matter of being in correct or real relationship with Christ, and with His various representatives. Christ cannot be separated from His representatives, from the church, because Christ is the Head of the organism. To separate the Head from the body is to kill the organism. And apart from that living relationship Christianity was nothing more than an organization, an empty shell, devoid of actual life.

Paul spoke of the whole body being nourished, and in keeping with this body analogy the nourishment of the body comes from outside of itself. Bodies consume food for nourishment. The nourishment alluded to here can only be the bread and wine of the Sacrament. The bread represents the body, broken on the cross and healed—unified—by the grace of God through participation in the church, by grace through faith. The cup represents the covenant in the blood of Christ, poured out on the cross and shared by the members of the church. The New Covenant, given through Christ's blood, is a shared covenant in the church. It is shared among the members and the various representatives of the Head. It is both a God-and-me covenant and a God-and-us covenant because it is a covenant in, with and through the body of Christ.

The function and purpose of the church is to represent, to present again, the reality of Jesus Christ to a dying world, not as an idea but as an actual community, a body, that functions in Christ, not a mere organization, but a living entity. The sharing of the gospel of Jesus Christ is not mere talk, but being—existence. Talking is involved, of course. That is how people communicate. But it is not mere talk.

People get so caught up in talk, in abstract ideas, in thinking that we begin to think that the thought is the reality. But it isn't. We get so distracted by our talking that we neglect the bodily reality that is the context of our communication. The point is that Christ is the context of the actual lives of Christians. Yes, Christ is also the intellectual context of our thinking about life. We do think about Christ as an idea, but Christ is much more than an idea. More importantly, Christ is that in which we "live and move and have our being" (Act 17:28).

GROWTH

The result of all of this is that the body, the church, "grows with a growth that is from God" (v.19). But because God is perfect, He does not Himself grow or increase. God is perfect and does not change (Malachi 3:6). So, Paul was not speaking about God's personal growth, but the growth of the body, the growth of the church. Paul was describing how the church grows.

There are two measures of growth. We can call them quantitative and qualitative, size and maturity, physical and spiritual. Each pair suggests the same difference, and Paul was speaking here of both measures. The church grows quantitatively and qualitatively. What is the difference? Quantitative growth involves gaining new members through conversion. Qualitative growth involves growing improved members through sanctification. The two are related, or should be related. Healthy churches should be increasing in both measures.

If we use biology as an analogy because biology is about living beings, we see that biological growth involves feeding and cell division. Nourishment is consumed and the various cells of the body increase through a process of cell division. They grow from the inside out.

Biological growth can also occur through a process of grafting, which Paul discussed in Romans 11:17-24. Grafting is a process of adding different cells to a body from the outside. Paul used the grape vine as an analogy. Here different kinds of vines can be grafted or integrated together. But the grafting process is not accomplished by the vines themselves, it is imposed upon them by the farmer. Paul spoke of God pruning off unproductive branches and grafting in new branches. Pruning the vine increases its growth and its fruit. Pruning, cutting off, is also a kind of division, and is the usual method of increasing the fruit yield of a vine.

How does this apply to church growth? The normal method of church growth would be cell division, or growing from the inside out. It would be a matter of reproduction and of Christian families. The normal method of church growth would be, then, familial or cultural, where the family is a unit or cell of covenantal identity and grows by cell division. Christian children grow up and establish new covenantal units, new Christian families. That is how the biological analogy applies to church growth, and is the normal method of biological growth.

The other method involves grafting in other branches. And that is what God did with the Gentiles, He grafted them into the vine by establishing them in Christ. Here outside members are united with the vine. But grafting is something that God does. Of course, God ordinarily works through people. So, it isn't anything mystical, though it is miraculous. God grafts individuals and families to the body of Christ through evangelism.

But it's not grafting in the same sense as grafting was initially done in Acts. The grafting done in Acts integrated Jews and Gentiles into a universal church, with regard to races or cultures. The Jew/Gentile graft created Christ's church by destroying the racial and/or cultural differences between Jews and Gentiles. From that point on we can say that no one was grafted in anymore. Or we can say that everyone is grafted in. The point is that everyone is treated the same regarding God's grace for salvation. Today Christ's church simply grows by conversion and assimilation.

What Happened?

What is the point I'm making? The growth of Western churches in the past 50 years or so has not kept up with raw biological population growth. And this suggests that something has interfered with the normal cell division kind of church growth over this time period. The increase of divorce also indicates that the covenantal nature of marriage and family have seriously deteriorated, which will have an detrimental effect on the church. The fact that too many children from Christian homes have not established Christian homes themselves indicates that covenantal transmission from one generation to the next has broken down.

The covenantal model of Christianity, or growth through generational or familial transfer of the covenant that happens within the body of Christ, has given way to growth through bringing in new members to the church from outside the body of Christ, from outside of existing local church families. Rather than growing from the inside out, churches began growing from the outside in, by bringing non-Christians into fellowship, people unrelated to existing church families. This was done unconsciously as a result of abandoning the demands and practices of covenantal Christianity by church members and by discounting the value and effectiveness of the idea and practice of generational transfer. Over the past 50 years or so Christians have failed to adequately disciple their own children.

At the same time, churches have responded to this crisis by developing programs of evangelism that try to reproduce the great revivals of former times rather than focusing on covenantal development, membership maturity and generational transmission of the gospel among members. At the same time that churches have focused on reaching outside of the church through evangelism and revival, the covenantal integrity within the churches and families has deteriorated. It seems that as churches have given increasing attention to the idea of evangelism and revival, they have not been paying attention to the body of Christ, to the actual, immediate covenantal relationships within the church. And this focus on evangelism has only come up because, for the most part Christian churches are in crisis. People are looking for a solution. But genuine revivals are very rare, and they always have been. They are not the norm.

The actual growth of Christianity in the West has plateaued or declined over many decades because covenantal transmission has been failing, which deteriorates the quality of the church community. And the lack of covenantal families in the churches have made the culture of the church less attractive because there are plenty of broken covenant relationships among non-Christians. The attraction of the church community isn't there because the quality of the church community differs little from its surroundings.

Could it be that churches have neglected the biological model of growth through cell division (covenantal transmission within families) and greedily focused on the idea of becoming a "great" church through revival and outreach? Could it be that churches have neglected the hard work of family discipleship, of body development, while dreaming up new thoughts and ideas about church growth? Has the church been compromised by thoughts and ideas—dreams, even pipe-dreams—of its own success? Are churches lusting for worldly success? Are you?

ﻼ૦౮

Christians and their churches have an inadequate sense of their own identity. They don't know who they actually are because they have an inadequate understanding of the Trinity. Here's who Jesus said Christians are: "I (Jesus) in them and you (God) in me, that they (Christians) may become perfectly one, so that the world may know that you sent me and loved them even as you loved me" (John 17:23). God is in Jesus and Jesus is in us and we are the body of Christ. *Christos Singularis!*

13

WHY INDEED?

If with Christ you died to the elemental spirits of the world, why, as if you were still alive in the world, do you submit to regulations— "Do not handle, Do not taste, Do not touch" (referring to things that all perish as they are used)— according to human precepts and teachings? These have indeed an appearance of wisdom in promoting self-made religion and asceticism and severity to the body, but they are of no value in stopping the indulgence of the flesh.
—Colossians 2:20-23 (ESV)

At verse 20 Paul came to the rub. He put his finger on the sore spot and identified the problem. If you have been born-again, if you have been saved by the blood of Christ, why don't you behave like a Christian? Paul had argued that Christians have died to the world. He wrote to the Romans (6:10-11), "For the death he died he died to sin, once for all, but the life he lives he lives to God. So you also must consider yourselves dead to sin and alive to God in Christ Jesus." To be dead to sin means to be unresponsive to the temptations of sin. There is no greater contrast than life and death. The two things are utterly divergent, disparate, different.

To be dead to sin is equivalent to having "died to the elemental spirits of the world" (v. 20). The Greek word translated *elemental spirits (stoicheion)* is also translated as *rudiments* or *principles* of the world. The elemental spirits are the underlying assumptions or presuppositions of worldliness. They are not ghosts, but are thoughts, ideas, principles or worldviews that have a kind of animated coherence and produce various social consequences.

Scripture makes a clear distinction between worldliness and godliness, between the ways of the world and the ways of the Lord, between a biblical Christian, trinitarian worldview and all other worldviews. Paul suggested that this difference was comparable to the difference between life and death. They are opposites. They oppose one another. There is an unbridgeable gulf between them. To mix these two ideas of worldliness and godliness together in a kind of syncretistic fusion is like mixing poison with food. To introduce corruption to purity only serves to spread a kind of contagious and life threatening disease.

The ideal process of salvation is to make a clean break from our old ways of thinking and behaving to new life in Christ, to new ways of thinking and behaving in the Lord. To embrace life is to reject death. Here Paul called the Colossians on the carpet for not making a clean break, for falling back into their old habits before the ink was dry on their newly signed covenant with Christ, so to speak.

The situation in Colossae was similar to the situation Moses faced when he had come down from the mountain with the Ten Commandments from God and found Aaron, his trusted servant, and the Israelites dancing before a golden calf (Exodus 32:8). Though the ancient Israelites had promised to follow God, they immediately reverted to their old Pagan ways of thinking and habits. They did this before they even knew what the Ten Commandments were, before they had any understanding of what God had provided through Moses. They rejected God before they understood Him. This might sound odd, but it is actually quite common.

Paul was similarly disappointed with the Colossians, as Moses had been with the Israelites. Aren't we all like that? Aren't old habits difficult to break? They are, of course. But break them we must. Of course, the truth is that we cannot. Our habits have a way of capturing and dominating our intentions, apart from our understanding. We cannot pull ourselves up by our own bootstraps in order to get ourselves out of our foxholes, if I may mix metaphors. It just can't be done. Newton's First Law of Motion states that a body at rest will remain at rest unless an outside force acts on it. That's why it was necessary for Christ to come and die on the cross, and demonstrate the power of God through His resurrection and to send the Holy Spirit to provide for us what we cannot provide for ourselves. Humanity needed outside help.

We are creatures of habit, and the habits we adopt early in our lives tend to stay with us all our lives. "Train up a child in the way he should go; even when he is old he will not depart from it" (Proverbs 22:6). Whatever we learn in our youth tends to stay with us all our lives. So, the better, more effective way to accomplish the evangelization mandate is to first disciple our own children, and then and only then reach out to others. Paul insisted on this (1 Timothy 3:4-12). Once bad habits are established, it is a hundred times more difficult to break them. So, Scripture teaches us to learn, model and then teach good habits, godly habits. This must be the foundation upon which evangelism rests.

CONVERSION REVERSION

Colossae provided a case study. The Colossians had been converted as adults, as had been most everyone during Paul's ministry because for the most part they were all first generation Christians. Though the Colossians had been converted to Christ, some of them had been reverting to their old habits while at the same time retaining an outward profession of faith in Christ. That surprised Paul, probably because his own conversion had been so complete, so stark, so definite. Paul had made a very clean break from Judaism to Christ, from death to life, and he expected others to make a similar clean break. But the truth was that some did and some didn't. For some the process of conversion[40] took longer, and for some it proved to be a mirage (Matthew 7:21-ff). Those who could not abandon their old habits and ways of thinking would be pulled back into the whirlpool of death. Well, they weren't actually pulled *back* into it. Rather, they had never actually been extracted from it.

So, Paul asked why, if they had died with Christ to worldliness, died to the spirits, the rudiments, principles, ways or habits of worldliness, why were they voluntarily submitting to various rules and regulations that were not of Christ? Why had they not made a clean break with their past? The fact that he asked the question means that some of them were in fact doing exactly that. Yet, such people had not left the Colossian church or denied their conversion. Rather, they had turned their backs on Christ. And they did it in the very name of Christ! There was a disconnect between their words and their behavior, between their profession of belief and their actions of unbelief.

Paul cited some of those man-made rules in verse 21: "Do not handle, Do not taste, Do not touch." They remind me of Eve in the garden. God had said "you shall not eat" (Genesis 2:17). But Eve

---

40 In the same way that babies are human beings but not adults, so born again Christians are fully Christian but not fully converted or mature.

replied to the Serpent, when he asked her what God had said, "You shall not eat of the fruit of the tree that is in the midst of the garden, neither shall you touch it, lest you die" (Genesis 3:3). God said *don't eat it*, and Eve said *don't touch it*. Eve's added restrictions were more severe than God's. And that's the way it usually is. Our own man made religious rules are usually stricter, more narrow, than God's.

Sure enough, the Colossians, like the Pharisees before them, had expanded on the discipline of faithfulness to Christ by reverting to various old habits of diet and various forms of constricted behavior. They thought that they were being spiritual by doing these things. So they did them in the name of Christ, thinking that doing so was a good thing, thinking that Christ was another deity like the other deities they had worshiped, like a deity of the Roman or Greek pantheons, perhaps stronger than the others. Rather than understanding that Christ was utterly unique among the so-called deities of the world, they understood Christ to be a new manifestation of the same old thing, a new name for an old religious perspective. No other religion has ever or since understood or expressed God as trinitarian.

The trinitarianism of God could not be understood or expressed until Christ had manifested in the flesh as the Son of God. So, the advent of Christ in the world was, in fact, a new and unique thing in the history of humanity. Because He is the second Person of the Trinity, Christ revealed the trinitarian character of God, and the reflected trinitarian character of humanity, who has been created in the image of God.[41]

THE PROBLEM

The problem that Paul found in Colossae was that the assumptions and expectations that the Colossians had about God, about worship, about life, before they came to know Christ continued with them after they confessed Christ. Paul found that it was easier to get the people out of Judaism or Paganism than it was to get the Judaism or Paganism out of the people. The stubbornness of false belief and old habits surprised Paul, but it didn't surprise God. God had wrestled with this problem from the Fall. God knew that people

---

41 The allusion to the plurality of God in Genesis 1:26 points to the corporate character of the Trinity. Man (humanity) had been created in the image of that trinitarian character, which is both individual and corporate.

were stubborn and stiff necked.[42]

Today, too, people continue in their unbiblical assumptions and expectations about themselves, about life in general, about the church and about a lot of things. These unbiblical assumptions and expectations then provide a kind of barrier against the gospel of Jesus Christ. The wrong assumptions keep the truth out.

It is curious and interesting how this works. These unbiblical assumptions and expectations keep people from even seeing Christ, much less thinking about Him as He actually is. John understood that apart from regeneration and the new way of thinking and see-ing that accompanies it, God cannot be seen (John 3:3). The actual biblical, Christian issues of life and death, of sin and salvation, of Heaven and Hell, of faithfulness and faithlessness simply never naturally occur to people. And when they do, people tend to think of them not in terms of Christian trinitarianism, but in whatever old ways of thinking and believing they grew up with. Jews think of them in Jewish terms, Pagans in Pagan terms. The issues and con-cerns of trinitarianism are so fundamental, so basic, so much a part of our assumptions about reality, that they are below consciousness for most people. They are part of our common presuppositional substructure or meta-narrative that is learned and "mastered" in our early childhood. Once it is mastered, it is not usually con-sidered again. And even when it is, its is very difficult to question or evaluate its reality or accuracy.

It is not that people have well defined and defended religious or philosophical positions against the gospel or the Trinity. It's that people don't really think about it. The truth is suppressed, sub-merged, hidden by unrighteous thoughts and behaviors (Romans 1:18). People are distracted away from biblical considerations by the simple momentum of old habits. It's too hard to rethink everything.

We could ask where these unbiblical assumptions and expecta-tions come from, but it doesn't matter. They are everywhere avail-able, and always have been. Faithlessness is the natural condition of humanity since the Fall. The better question to ask is why Chris-tian parents stopped teaching and inculcating biblical assumptions and expectations to their children. The problem is not that people

---

42 This is a major theme of Scripture. Note Deuteronomy 9:6, 9:13, 10:16, 31:27; Judges 2:19, 2 Kings 17:14, Nehemiah 9:29, Psalm 78:8, 81:12; Isaiah 30:1, 46:12, Jeremiah 5:23, 16:12; Ezekiel 2:4, 3:7; Hosea 4:16, Zechariah 7:11, Acts 19:9.

have acquired godless, unbiblical assumptions and expectations—though they have. The problem is that people have not been taught godly and biblical habits, assumptions and expectations when they were children by their parents, and by their churches. These things were traditionally understood as covenantal expectations. We can also call them Christian hopes. Christians seem to have abandoned their actual hope for a spiritual hope, abandoned the biblical hope for this world for a spiritual hope regarding heaven.

Once godless, unbiblical assumptions and expectations have been allowed to proliferate in the hearts and minds of people, any arguments or movements toward genuine consideration of the gospel, of the biblical truth, must first overcome the godless and unbiblical assumptions and expectations that have blossomed and produced the fruit of godless thinking and behavior. Godless and unbiblical assumptions and expectations simply crowd out any thoughts or considerations of the truth of the gospel in the same way that the demands of life tend to crowd out idealistic hopes for something better. The real actual trumps the imagined spiritual.

The idea of the gospel is dismissed before it can be intelligently conceived as people cling to their old habits and patterns of thought. The old and the new cannot coexist. True and false biblical assumptions cannot coexist over time in one mind. Evangelism and the advancement of Christian culture would be much easier if people began with at least neutral assumptions and expectations about God, Jesus and the Bible. But that is not where people are. No one is neutral. We live in a society and at a time when the popular social norm is godlessness, when the norm is an assumed devaluation of everything biblical. People assume that the Bible is just a bunch of myths, old stories, wives' tales and superstitions.

THE CHILDREN

The common Christian response to this situation is to think that we must reach the children before they get habituated and/or indoctrinated against the teachings of the Bible. And there is a measure of truth in this response, but not enough to actually make the needed difference. If there were a cadre of adults who were sufficiently free of their own godless indoctrination, and who were in social positions to actually and consistently teach genuine biblical truth to a sufficient number of children, I might agree.

But the truth is that churches today don't have sufficient adult members who are themselves adequately clear of unbiblical assumptions and expectations, or who are in significant teaching positions to reach and teach sufficient numbers of children to turn the tide. The churches themselves are so compromised by the doctrines of the world that the truth of Scripture is obscured in the beliefs and behaviors of their own members, and in too many cases even in their own formal statements of faith and theological positions. So, before we can reach the children with the unvarnished biblical truth of the trinitarian character of God and the reflected trinitarian character of human beings, much less the hope of the gospel, we need to reach and reteach the adults. Lord, have mercy.

But neither should we expect that someone else will be able to teach biblical Christianity to our own children when God has given that responsibility to parents. The kind of teaching, the consistency and comprehensiveness of the teaching that is required, cannot happen in Sunday School. An hour or two a week is not sufficient, and the Sunday School teachers do not have the authority or the position to counter the godless rebellion from authority that is taught in our society at large.

Teaching the faith requires a consistent and sustained effort to counter and correct unbiblical thinking and behavior whenever and wherever it arises. Moses insisted: "You shall teach them diligently to your children, and shall talk of them when you sit in your house, and when you walk by the way, and when you lie down, and when you rise" (Deuteronomy 6:7). The need is for regularity and consistency.

There is no better situation for such teaching than the first 10-12 years of a child's life, and the earlier the better. It is something that only parents can accomplish. Not only is such a practice beneficial for the children, but it is beneficial for the parents as well. No one learns more than the teacher (Matthew 10:24). Teaching requires learning first. So, if everyone needs to learn a thing, everyone needs to teach it. By placing this responsibility in the family, upon the parents, God has insured maximum social saturation of His doctrine.

No Idea

Christ came to save the world, and His primary instrument of salvation is the church. People are to be saved *out of* the world and *into* the church, where they are to be nurtured and trained in biblical thinking and behavior, so they can go back into the world to reach others with the message of salvation. However, the church as an institution of Christ has been decimated by a sustained attack on it from many sides over many generations, through public education, mass media, the legal establishment and the arts. The churches are at the point today that professing Christians generally have no idea what the church is supposed to be or how it is supposed to function.

We ourselves have never seen or experienced the church actually functioning as it was conceived and inaugurated by Christ to function. What do I mean? I mean that there is no actual, comprehensive, fully supporting biblical culture to be saved into in our day. We see churches, but not a comprehensive biblical culture where family, church and state actually function biblically, through genuinely biblical representation through civil, church, family and individual moral structures that have limited authority through a biblical balance of power. Properly understood, Christian trinitarianism insures the distribution and limitation of human authority and power throughout society. God is the author of the idea of checks and balances of the various human authorities and political powers.

The reality of sin mandates such checks and balances. But, where sin is belittled, denounced and/or denied these checks and balances are belittled, denounced and/or denied by the natural propensities, desires, habits, preferences and inclinations of human beings. Where sin is denied it cannot be limited and will therefore come to dominate human beings. Sinners are like alcoholics who deny their alcoholism and drink themselves to death.

All we can do is talk about the ideal biblical structure for church and society because there is no actual Christian culture in our day, where culture is defined as the whole of a society. Our culture today is dominated by godlessness and worldliness. And in all likelihood, this has always been the case with regard to various nations. By this I simply mean that there has never actually been an extant Christian nation, one actually governed according to biblical trinitarian principles of government—not completely, not comprehensively.

Today there is no respite from sin, not even in the traditional sanctity of our own homes. For the most part our homes are plugged into godlessness and rebellion through the modern media outlets—literature, TV, radio, the Internet, etc. In addition, what we call churches today are mostly empty husks, organizations that have a form of godliness, but which deny the power of God (2 Timothy 3:5) by holding unbiblical assumptions and expectations in the name of Christ!

Christians are today like the ancient Israelites dancing before various idols of our own choosing. We are like the Colossians of Paul's day proclaiming Christ, but holding on to the various vestiges of sin that have accrued throughout history. We have grasped the form of godliness, but deny in a thousand different ways the function and therefore the power of the gospel. And what is worse, we don't even know it.

WHAT WENT WRONG?

The church was supposed to influence the world with the doctrines of godliness, but throughout history and in an increasingly accelerated way, the world has influenced the church with the doctrines of godlessness. The wholeness or unity of the churches was supposed be a leaven for the wholeness and unity of society at large. But the compartmentalization of the Christian faith, and of the churches, has created a compartmentalized society.

We understand human society, not in terms of organic growth but in terms of a modern factory production line, not in terms of holistic integration but as components that are assembled to make a finished product. The difference is that one is alive, living, and one is manufactured, dead. Churches have either been laid waste by their less than trinitarian presuppositions and are in a state of serious decline in terms of membership, authority and social effectiveness, or have been turned into manufactured and popularly successful, dynamic synagogues of Satan (Revelation 2:9). Not all of them, of course, but far too many of them.

Anyone who has ever tried to share a new idea with someone knows how hard it is for people think new thoughts or to change (Jeremiah 13:23). For the most part people don't like change, not really. People like consistency and continuity, regardless of what they may say. People want change when they are unhappy with their current circumstances, but at the same time we quickly adapt to whatever circumstances we are in. People are creatures of habit. We live in habitats, and for the most part our very lives depend upon the habitual patterns of life, i.e., night and day, breathing, eating, waking/sleeping, etc.

There is an advantage to having an habitual nature when it comes to having good habits. Develop good habits when you are young and they will stay with you all your life. But when we have bad habits, our habitual nature is problematic. Bad habits are hard to overcome, and this was Paul's concern.

"If with Christ you died to the elemental spirits of the world, why, as if you were still alive in the world, do you submit to regulations—'Do not handle, Do not taste, Do not touch' (referring to things that all perish as they are used)—according to human precepts and teachings?" (vs. 20-22). *Why,* asked Paul, *are you doing these things when I taught you better? Why are you listening to man rather than to God? Why are you living according to human precepts and teachings? Have you not heard the gospel?*

What are these human precepts and teachings? Anything other than Scripture. While this applies directly to Paul's concern about the foolishness of the Greek academicians, it also has a wider application because human foolishness is more broadly conceived than can be contained within academia. This isn't to say that all of academia is useless, only that for the most part it is godless. Paul's allusion to teaching means that this insight has application to education in general. But the actual Greek word here is *didaskalia*, and literally means doctrine, those teachings that are accepted as authentic or authoritative by some group or school, in this case, worldly doctrines. The usage indicates education in the general sense of unbiblical godlessness or any form of education that is not Christian.

SEEMS OKAY

In contrast, Paul said in verse 23 that worldly teachings or doctrines have the appearance or reputation of being ideas that issue from wisdom. Rules like don't handle, don't taste, don't touch, etc., seem wise. They seem like good and helpful ideas. But, said Paul, they actually aren't. They only seem that way to people who don't know Christ, who don't know Scripture. People entertain these kinds of rules because they seem like good and helpful things to do, but in fact they retard Christianity.

They are not good ideas, nor are they good things to do. They are godless and worldly things. They are the foolish traditions of men. They issue from the human brain and not from the Word of God. They encourage false religion because they are falsely religious. They are self-made religious practices that have nothing to do with Jesus Christ. Whether these Colossians had come out of Judaism or Paganism they had been reverting to their old habits of thinking and acting. They had been falling back on old rules, old habits, old disciplines and diets that had nothing to do with Christ.

Such things were "of no value in stopping the indulgence of the flesh" (v. 23). This is a curious verse because for the most part ascetic disciplines are usually understood to deny the flesh. Ascetic disciplines usually deny access to particular foods rather than indulgence in food. They usually require sexual abstinence rather than sexual indulgence. So, why does Paul call them indulgences of the flesh? Because they are body-centered, body-focused, rather than Christ-centered disciplines. They are of the body, from the body, and for the body. They are not of Christ, from Christ or for Christ. They are expressions of humanism, the idea that the chief and highest purpose of humanity is to serve human welfare. They are not of Christianity, which teaches that "man's chief and highest end is to glorify God, and fully to enjoy him forever."[43]

Please understand that this traditional teaching is not opposed to human welfare. Rather, the difference between these two doctrines (humanism and Christianity) is a matter of emphasis. Humanism is primarily interested in human welfare at the expense of interest in God by its denial of sin, whereas Christianity is primarily interested in God, whose trinitarian character provides the only actual way to safeguard human welfare by providing the only way to overcome the disastrous consequences of sin. Thus, humanism, by denying sin, actually allows sin to run free. And Christianity, by acknowledging sin, actually provides a way to keep sin in check until such time as God eliminates it entirely (John 1:29).

Where Christ has called people to new life, to regeneration, and demonstrated the reality of new life through His own resurrection from death, Paul found that some who had gathered with the faithful were actually zombies—the walking dead. Where Christians walk in the newness of life in Christ, zombies are dead men walking apart from Christ. Zombies mimic life, but are actually dead. They are animated by the principles of death, by whatever is not of Christ, whereas Christians are born again to life from zombie death.

Christ rose *from* the dead (Matthew 28:7), whereas zombies are

---

43 *Westminster Confession, Larger Catechism,* Question one.

the arising *of* the dead. Christ's resurrection and our regeneration in Christ are functions of life. Christ has conquered sin and death. Paul knew this. The Colossians knew this. And yet, Paul asked them why, if they knew this, had they slipped back into their old habits and behaviors of godlessness. Why indeed? The question points to the relationship between belief and behavior. Belief that does not manifest in godly behavior is, of necessity, false belief. Thus godly behavior cannot be divorced from orthodox belief.

Getting the gospel right results in genuinely godly culture. And culture is always a multi-generational reality. While it is built on individual faithfulness, it requires more than individual faithfulness because the sum of the gospel is greater than the sum of its parts. Thus for a society to actually be Christian the people need to be Christian, at least the majority of them. But that's not all! The corporate aspect of society must also be Christian. The social or cultural aspects of society must contribute positively to the development of Christian character, as well. At a minimum, the culture should not undermine Christianity.

CR8D

Christians are individuals, but Christianity is holistic. It is humanity centric. And the holistic aspects of Christianity are central to the character of individual Christians. This interpenetration or porosity between parts and whole is essential. Where this interpenetration breaks down, Christianity breaks down. Christianity requires the whole and the part, the culture and the individual to be mutually supportive of the gospel. Jesus said that He dwells with or among those who gather in His name. Thus, the presence of Jesus is the "more" that makes the whole of Christianity greater than the sum of its parts. *Christos Singularis!*

14

IDOLATRY DEFINED

If then you have been raised with Christ, seek the things that are above, where Christ is, seated at the right hand of God. Set your minds on things that are above, not on things that are on earth. For you have died, and your life is hidden with Christ in God. When Christ who is your life appears, then you also will appear with him in glory. Put to death therefore what is earthly in you: sexual immorality, impurity, passion, evil desire, and covetousness, which is idolatry.   *—Colossians 3:1-5 (ESV)*

Paul begins with a conditional clause, "If then you have been raised with Christ" (v. 1). *If* means maybe or perhaps. *Then* means accordingly or therefore. The word *if* is conditional, but the word *then* is definite and implies explicit conclusion. If the one thing is true, then the other follows. So, this sentence must be read in two ways. The first way is: 1) if then you have been raised in Christ, 2) you have been raised in fact. It states both the condition and the conclusion as a way of saying that you can't have one without the other. Because Christ has raised you, you are raised indeed.

The other way to approach this would be to separate the phrase "if then" and put the word *if* in the first clause and the word *then* in the second clause: *If* you have been raised with Christ, *then* seek the things that are above. *If* you have been raised with Christ, *then* act like it, because if you don't act like it, then the condition may not be true. Paul was chastising them, criticizing them, criticizing their faithlessness as a method of encouragement. It is a good thing to criticize a bad thing. Paul's criticism was a comfort to the saints. How on earth was Paul's chastisement an act of encouragement? Paul's chastisement was directed at faithlessness, at the act of faithlessness.

He was not chastising individuals. He was chastising behaviors, not people.

The unsaved among them would have been incensed at Paul's audacity to suggest that they—members in good standing of the Colossian church—might not actually have been saved. However, the saints among them would have been glad to hear Paul's critique on two counts. First, they would have appreciated Paul's prodding because, had they themselves missed the mark of faithfulness, they would have wanted to do better. An athlete in training appreciates his coach's goading because he knows that it is for his own good.

Second, the saints want the purity of the church. So, if Paul's chastisement offended those who would not repent, those who would draw the fellowship back from making corporate progress in faithfulness because of their willful, stubborn resistance to God's grace of salvation, then the fellowship of the saints would be blessed by the departure of the unrepentant. A measure of unity would have been restored by their departure.

We forget that Christ came not just to gather the lambs, but to separate them from the goats (Matthew 25:32). Christ came to gather the wheat into the barn, and to burn the chaff (Luke 3:17). Both the gathering and the burning, the separating, are of benefit to the saints. Both further the cause of Christian unity. I know that this seems like a hard message for people to hear. But the hardness of the message is not a reflection on me. It's not *my* message, I'm just the messenger. The message belongs to Christ, to the Bible. To see the message as hardness is also a reflection of confusion because it fails to hear the voice of the Shepherd. (John 10:27).

So, if you don't like the message, blame its Author. The perception of the hardness of the message is actually a reflection of the condition of the people who find it offensive. It is a message that offends faithlessness. And it is supposed to offend faithlessness! It is a challenge for self-reflection. The offense will then either draw the people into better compliance, into faithfulness, or repel the faithless who refuse to repent of their ongoing sin.

BOTH WAYS

Paul goes on to say that if the faithful want to follow Christ or to keep their eyes on Christ, they need to seek the things above because that is "where Christ is, seated at the right hand of God" (v.

1). Furthermore, they could not seek both the things above (heavenly things) and the things below (earthly things) at the same time. They would need to hang on to the one and let go of the other (2 Corinthians 6:15).

One of the problems that plague Christians is that they want to hold on to both heavenly things and earthly things, and so they do. Because Christians live between the almost and the not yet, because sin continues to dog people (Romans 7:15), because sin has not yet been completely eradicated, nor has the kingdom of God been established on earth, Christians have a foot in both camps, so to speak.

Christians think that they can have it both ways, that they can serve both God and mammon. The problem with this idea is that some of the people who do this will end up being saved, and some won't. In addition, we saints have a very hard time telling the difference between sheep who are clinging to old worldly habits and goats who are pretending to heavenly bliss. Regardless, this dual clinging corrupts the purity of the church on both counts. It either tolerates the habits of immature believers, which encourages immature faithfulness, or it tolerates willful godlessness and false faithfulness among the saints, and corrupts the purity of the church.

Paul nailed it in verse 2, "Set your minds on things that are above, not on things that are on earth." Note the clear division and the lack of tolerance for doing both. Do the one and don't do the other! The contemporary churches must deal with this issue if they are to grow in faithfulness. Such growth will likely produce a decrease in church membership numbers as the false believers get offended and weed themselves out of fellowship. But weeding will be done one way or another because, if we don't do it now, Christ will do it at judgment when He returns. And as any kid knows, it's better to clean the mess up before dad gets home. We may still get a lickin', but if we 'fess up and clean up before dad gets home, it won't be nearly as bad.

NEWS

So, how might this actually play out in our lives today? Well, first, too many Christians today are news focused, world focused. With the advent of television, computers, the Internet and mobile phones people have become news junkies. The news media loves it because our interest in and attention to the news builds and grows the news industry.[44] That's what they do for a living, so the more our eyes and ears are glued to the news, the more the news industry grows. In case you haven't noticed, the news is all about the "things that are on earth" (v. 2). In case you didn't make the connection, this is precisely what Paul said *not* to set our minds on.

Of course, we are not to ignore or deny the news, either. We still live in the world and we need to know what is happening in the world. But we don't need to understand it from the perspective of the world, and this is the problem. Even the conservative news analysts do not present or analyze the news from a Christian or biblical perspective. Of course, neither do the liberals. Consequently, the news reports in the media are not actually Christian.

Furthermore, Christian media outlets usually only summarize events. They simply pass along what they have received from the Associated Press or other non-Christian news agencies. They choose to report news that is of special interest to Christians, of course, but hardly ever will we hear a Christian evaluation of the news. Why not? Because the Christians themselves are so divided that any perspective or analysis brought forth will offend one Christian group or another. So in the interest of not offending anyone, a Christian or biblical perspective is excluded from news analysis. The news industry, including the Christian news industry, does not want to offend its audience because such offense will produce a loss of market-share. This is a huge problem because it contributes to the immaturity of contemporary Christians on the one hand, and fails to allow biblical chastisement on the airwaves. The kind of prodding that Paul did in Colossae to encourage the saints to grow in faithfulness is simply disallowed in the media.

"Set your minds" (v. 2) said Paul. Faithfulness is a mindset, a mental attitude that determines how to interpret and respond to situations. It's a worldview, a dynamic and comprehensive view of the world and human life. Maybe it would be better to call faithfulness a heavenview rather than a worldview because of the admonition to set our minds on things that are above, and not on the world. Nonetheless, it is not something static, but something that grows over time. And it must grow and continue growing. The only option to growth is death.

The other problem is that too many people tend to read the

<hr/>

44 Richard M. Weaver provides a discussion of this concern in his book, *Ideas Have Consequences*, University Of Chicago Press, 1984.

Bible through the lens of the news rather than reading the news through the lens of the Bible. People tend to apply the news events of the day to the Bible, so that they understand the Bible in the light of the news, rather than applying the Bible to the news events of the day in order to understand the news in the light of Scripture. Much of the current end times mania of dispensationalism and its variants issues from this error. It's a mindset or worldview (heaven-view) issue.

What does this mean at a practical level? First of all, we are tempted to believe that the news tells us what is actually happening in the world. However, the news attempts to be objective by omitting all references to God, and particularly all analysis from a biblical perspective. And this is precisely what Paul has warned against. An ungodly, unbiblical, unChristian selection of, presentation of and/or analysis of human events will always fall far short of the truth from a biblical perspective. Exposing ourselves to the news media saturates our minds with various kinds of ungodliness including gossip, lust, greed, lying and covetousness. These sins are news media staples.

Paul went on to say that Christians have died. He meant that we have died to sin (Romans 6:2), died to the world (Colossians 2:20). When people are dead they do not respond. So, being dead to a thing means not responding to it. It doesn't mean that we are not exposed to it, but that we do not respond to it.

WITH CHRIST

Paul also provided a way to realize Heaven. He said, "your life is hidden with Christ in God. When Christ who is your life appears, then you also will appear with him in glory" (vs. 3-4). The first phrase is an allusion to the trinitarian nature of God, and of God's trinitarian image in us. To be hidden in Christ is an allusion to our unity in or with Christ.

We often teach little children that Jesus lives in our hearts. And, while this is true from a certain perspective, it would be better to teach that we live with Christ in God's heart. In truth, we are in each other—Christ and us—much like Christ and God are in each other. This mutual "inness" is not an ordinary kind of being in something. But neither is it purely mystical. For instance, if I go swimming in a lake and swallow some of the water, it could be said that I am in the lake and that the lake (or at least some of it) is in me. Clearly because God is infinite, He could not possibly be entirely in anything. This is why it is better to talk about us being in God rather than God being in us.

Of course there is a certain amount of mystery in this idea of being hidden with Christ in God. It does mean that neither our lives nor Christ are obviously accessible to view. They're hidden. It also means that this unity in Christ has been designed to elude detection, it is difficult to see. These are some of the various meanings of the word *hidden*. Our hiddenness with Christ in God also has some implications regarding evangelism. At the very least it means that showing people something that is hidden may be more difficult than we first imagine. The point here is that Christianity is a perception thing, a mindset thing, a heavenview thing, a trinitarian thing, and our evangelism methods must acknowledge this.

Have you ever seen one of those perspective puzzles like the faces or the vase?[45] We've seen it so often that we know to look for the other image, but the first time a person sees it, he will see it only one way. The mind sees it as one thing, defines it, categorizes it and files it away as whatever we think it is without further consideration. Well, it is the further consideration that is the stuff of Christianity and evangelism.

Paul then gives us a vision of Heaven: "When Christ who is your life appears, then you also will appear with him in glory" (v. 4). Did you see it? Consider it again. Paul said that our lives are hidden with Christ in God. Think of Russian nesting dolls, you in Christ in God. But that is not the image Paul gave. Here Paul said that Christ *is* your life, nothing about *in*. He did not say you *are* Christ or Christ is *in* you, but Christ *is* your life. Here Paul said that it's not that Christ will be revealed in your life, or through your life, but that Christ will be revealed *as* your life, as you live and move and have your being in Him (Acts 17:28). Christ is revealed through the lives of Christians.

There's more. When Christ appears as your life, "then you also will appear with him in glory" (v. 4). As Christ, who is hidden in your life with God, appears as your life, as you live in Him, then you will also appear with Christ in glory. This is a very trinitarian idea. Paul was not blending identities. You are still you and Christ is still Christ and God is still God. But there is a porosity or an overlapping of the boundaries of identity, of Christ's identity in you, and as your

45 See Appendix for an example, p. 252. Don't just look at it. Get someone across the room to hold it, and then watch it as you walk toward it.

personal life—not as Christ, but as a Christian, as a person who is of Christ, or an image of God in Christ, not *in* you but *as* you. I am speaking analogously, as was Paul.

If you like thinking about the beauty and complexity of things, these are great thoughts. But if you don't care about the beauty and complexity of God, this might seem confusing. It is not actually confusing at all, but it is complex like a flower or the structure of a crystal. The thing that confuses people is not the biblical doctrine of the Trinity, but the false, unbiblical ideas about it and everything else that we have come to accept as individuals and as a society. These false ideas, idolatries of ever sort, keep us from seeing the truth of the Trinity. Everything that does not reference or reflect the trinitarian character of God is potentially idolatrous. God's truth is always present and is always trinitarian, but people usually build up a perspective that hides or veils it (2 Corinthians 3:16) because it threatens the identities they have grown used to. God's truth threatens the simplicities we comfort ourselves with because the complexity of reality is overwhelming.

CLEAN BREAK

Finally, Paul draws a conclusion, a *therefore*: "Put to death therefore what is earthly in you" (v. 5). Even though we have already died to what is earthly, as Paul mentioned in verse 3, he further instructs the saints to finish the job by putting to death any remaining vestiges of earthly worldliness that might remain. Here Paul argued for a clean break from our old lives, our old habits, while at the same time he acknowledged the reality that there is often some overlap of godliness and worldliness.

Both of these ideas are encouraging. First, we should be relieved that Paul recognized the reality that believers will have a period of time in their lives when they are drawn in opposing directions, when they have been called to holiness by God in Christ, but have not completely let go of their old ways and habits. Because there is such a drastic change involved in conversion, it is a relief to know that struggling with old ideas and habits is a normal part of it.

However, the fact that Paul then told the Colossians to put those old habits and ideas to death at some point following their conversion demonstrates that conversion is a process that continues (Philippians 2:12). The distinctions between conversion and sanctification are not as clear as we sometimes like to make them.

Nonetheless, living in perpetual Christian immaturity is not an option. We must at some point grow up. And what does it mean to grow up, to put worldliness to death? Paul tells us that we must put an end to five things—sexual immorality, impurity, passion, evil desire, and covetousness.

The first is sexual immorality (*porneia*), also translated as *fornication* (Authorized Version) and *whoredom* (Young's Literal Version). This simply indicates sexual relations with anyone other than your spouse. Listening to the news or engaging the entertainment media in our day makes us voyeurs of this sin. The violation of this sin is so common today that it isn't even noticed—even by Christians! We have all become almost completely callous to it. Nonetheless, Paul has drawn a clean, clear and straight line making this, not a gray moral issue, but a black and white moral issue. We must not allow the shades of gray that so color our own practice of biblical morality influence the clarity God's black and white distinctions.

Next Paul listed impurity (*akatharsia*), also translated as *uncleanness* (Authorized Version). This has to do with both the purity of one's soul and the purity of the church, both individual and corporate purity. To be pure is to be unmixed, which can only mean the cessation of the commingling of godliness and worldliness, both in one's own life and in the fellowship of the church. Each Christian must continue to grow in personal purity, and the corporate church must also grow in purity by weeding out the impure. We must take care not to weed out the less pure who are growing in purity, but only remove those who are not growing at all or who are growing less pure (James 1:27).

Passion (*pathos*) is third on Paul's list. It is also translated as *inordinate affection* (Authorized Version) and *lust* (Holman Christian Standard Bible). Paul mentioned the same thing in his letter to Titus, saying that a person "must be blameless, as a steward of God, not self-willed, not full of passion" (Titus 1:7). Strong's says that the word refers especially to concupiscence (the desire for sexual intimacy), also defined as lust. More broadly conceived, it means not being led or directed by our desires and feelings. Rather, we are to be led and directed by Christ through Scripture.

Evil desire is the only term on the list that uses two Greek words: *kakos*, which means worthless, depraved, wicked and evil, and *epithumia*, also translated as *concupiscence* (Authorized Version) and *desire* (Young's Literal Version). Together they suggest the idea of wanting what is worthless, depraved, wicked and evil.

What is worthless comes to nothing. What is depraved is sinfully indulgent. What is wicked is enthusiastically sinful. And what is evil contradicts the righteousness of God. The focus is again on our wants and desires and not merely our actions.

The fifth item on the list is covetousness (*pleonexia*) and means avarice or greed, and all of the things that lead to and/or promote greed. Strong's includes fraud and extortion. To be fraudulent is to make deceitful pretenses. Usually it involves money, but it could also include deceitful pretenses regarding sex or social standing as well. Extortion covers whatever fraud misses. Extortion involves any kind of overcharging, price gouging, unjust or felonious exaction of money. Piracy comes to mind, and all sorts of pirates exist today, on and off the high seas.

IDOLATRY

So, Paul said that Christians must stop doing these five things. He grouped these five things together and equated the last one with idolatry (*eidōlolatreia*—v. 5), commonly understood as image worship or the worship of images. So, covetousness and idolatry are the same thing, which means that idolatry is a matter of wanting the wrong things. It is a matter of desire and imagination. Idolatry is a matter of not wanting God, or of failing to correctly understand and worship God. Anything other than biblical worship of the triune God is idolatry. And it is a very serious, misunderstood and yet common sin, even among people who identify themselves as Christians.[46]

The Greek word translated as *idolatry* is a combination of two words: *eidōlon* (image) and *latreia* (worship or service). The first word is of special interest because the same Greek spelling exists as the English word *eidolon*, which is defined as an unsubstantial image or an ideal, something not real. The fact that it has been transliterated into English suggests that a comparable English word does not exist, which means that defining *eidōlon* as image is at best inadequate. While the idea of image is related to the definition of idolatry, it falls short.

The definition of the English word *eidolon* puts us right in the middle of Greek philosophy, Platonic philosophy in particular, in

---

46 God also complained a lot about the idolatry of the Old Testament Jews, which means that idolatry is a common and persistent sin. And while it is true that Jesus Christ is the cure for idolatry, the application of the cure is not yet complete because the application is progressive.

the sense that Socrates, Plato's teacher, is commonly identified as the originator of the idea of the ideal. Greek and Western language, thinking, categories, interpretations and analysis all tend toward the abstract, toward ideas and essence, etc. What is this difference?

Hebrew language, thinking, categories, interpretations and analysis, on the other hand, tend toward concrete, specific particulars, and avoid abstract generalization. This can be seen in the way that the Greeks discuss and define God versus the way that Scripture (the Hebrew culture) discusses and defines God.

Consider the Zen koan, "What is the sound of one hand clapping?" Westerners are usually amazed and confused by the simplicity of the accepted answer, which is to swing one hand forward as if to clap. There are two points to notice: 1) there is no sound, and 2) the answer demonstrates rather than explains. The demonstration is an instance of concrete thinking. Abstract thinkers tend to ask "why" and "how" questions that require a reasoned answer. The two perspectives have difficulty understanding one another.

Concrete thinkers tend to ask "when" and "where" questions that don't require reasons. These different kinds of thinking tend to talk past one another. Reasons are abstractions that require speculation. Another difference is that concrete thinking tends to be personal or specific and abstract thinking tends to be general or universal. But the primary difference between idolatry and biblical understanding is that idolatry is not grounded in the Bible. Biblical reasoning issues from Scripture, whereas idolatrous reasoning does not.

This issue, this difference is at the heart of the definition of idolatry in the sense that idolatry involves a misunderstanding, misuse or faulty worship of God. Scripture (Hebrew thought forms) refers to and discusses God in concrete, particular and specific ways, while the Greeks (Western thought forms) refer to and discuss God in abstract, universal and general ways. These different approaches or different thought forms suggest that the two things that are indicated, which both go by the name of *God*, are actually quite different. It implies not just different understandings of God, but different Gods.

God, as approached by the Western mind, is quite different than God, as approached by the biblical mind. One is abstract, categorical, general, an idea. The other is concrete, particular, individual, unique and actual, something real. For example, it suggests the difference between the idea of a particular person versus the actual reality of a particular person. One is a concept and one is a reality. While the idea or concept of a person may or may not be accurate, it is never more than an abstract idea. But the actual reality of a person is always much more than an idea. Similarly, the reality of God is always much more than the mere idea of God.

Idolatry, then, as Paul was using it here has a specific application to Greek philosophy, and more than Greek philosophy really, because the idea of ideals is virtually everywhere in human history. Plato taught that there was an abstract world of ideals or universal forms, a kind of spiritual world. Aristotle taught that there is no actual world of ideals or universal forms but that specific, concrete things had within them an ideal or universal essence as opposed the material substance of the thing.

But Scripture teaches that both of these are mere abstractions. They are copies of, or images of, or imaginations about God, and are therefore functions of idolatry. They fail to do justice to God and therefore are false gods. In the modern world, because of the universality of Western culture and technology, this kind of idolatry can be found wherever things are understood or explained without reference to the trinitarian God of the Bible.

TAXONOMY

Adam was involved in taxonomy, the study and application of the general principles of classification. Adam's job in the Garden was naming things, categorizing things, plants, animals, etc. And what is a name? It is a word that is substituted for a thing in thought and communication. He was developing a linguistic inventory of the world's assets. And from this inventory, from this list of available assets in the world, literature, culture, art, science and technology would eventually be developed in history. These kinds of abstract, intellectual, artificial, Greek thought-forms are themselves the fruit of the Fall.

Originally, all of the things that Adam named, his inventory of things in the world, were related to God and through God. God was indigenous to them all. But Satan challenged the integrity of the relationship between God and the taxonomy of the world by getting Eve to doubt the integrity of God's Word. The Serpent "said to the woman, 'Did God actually say...'" (Genesis 3:1). Can God be trusted?

That doubt didn't actually break God's integrity or the reality of

God's relationship with the world He had created. God's truth continues to be true, but it did break the simple, naïve trust or faith
that Adam and Eve had regarding God's integrity. It broke Adam
and Eve's trust in the direct relationship between God and the
things that Adam had named by introducing the abstract idea that
God had deceived Adam and Eve. This idea of deception, then,
brought into question the integrity of God, and by extension the
integrity between the name or sign of a thing and the thing itself.[47]
If God was untrustworthy, then Adam's taxonomy was equally
untrustworthy, and the only remaining way to determine truth was
human experience. This is the heart of Original Sin.

So, what is idolatry as Paul was using the word? It is the worship of ideals, the worship of abstractions or abstract ideas. It is in
a sense the worship of Greek philosophy, or the worship of abstract
thinking, or the indulgence of abstract thinking. It is turning
abstract thinking into a god. It is thinking that one's own or the
cumulative thinking of humanity is a kind of absolute, that it is
more important or more honest than God's Word. It is serving
human thought as if it were a god or were the voice of a god. It is
the divination of human thinking, of taxonomy or reasoning apart
from God. It is the failure to value God as the ultimate value of
being human, and replacing God with some other ideal, some other
idea.

This is actually quite important because it is about the integrity
of language itself. How so? If truth requires reference to God
because God provides the ultimate context, framing and meta-narrative for everything in His creation, then omitting, denying or neglecting God's role and position regarding a thing obscures the very
thing (God) that clarifies its truth. The omission or denial of God
always hides the truth.

---

47 According to the Enlightenment philosopher, Immanuel Kant (1724-1804),
humans can make sense out of phenomena in various ways, but can never directly know the "things-in-themselves," the actual objects and dynamics of the
natural world. Kant's Critiques or methods were an attempt to correlate in useful ways, perhaps even accurate ways, the structure and order of the various
aspects of the actual universe. Nonetheless, said Kant, we cannot know "things-
in-themselves" (*noumena*) directly. Rather, we must infer the extent to which
thoughts correspond with things-in-themselves by our observations of the manifestations of those things that can be seen, heard, touched, smelled and/or
tasted, that is, of *phenomena*. "Enlightenment is man's emergence from his self-
imposed nonage. Nonage is the inability to use one's own understanding without
another's guidance" (*What is Enlightenment?* (Immanuel Kant). The point of
this footnote is to suggest the deep reality of sin and its continuing influence in
the world.

All five of the things that Paul listed are forms of idolatry—sexual immorality, impurity, passion, evil desire, and covetousness. Each of them requires displacing God's Word, God's commands against them, with the idea that they are okay. Paul's list is not a comprehensive list of idolatries, but it is significant. The thing that makes these things idolatrous is that they are forbidden by God. So, doing them requires the devaluation of God as the ultimate authority in one's life, and replacing God's sanction against them with some idea that grants permission to engage them. Idolatry, then, involves the attempt to dethrone or replace God. It is anything and everything that denies, discounts, disavows or discourages the authority of God, both individually and socially or culturally.

CS&C

The most common form of idolatry is the denial or ignorance of God as Trinity. The actual denial of God is impossible in the same way that the denial of gravity is impossible. Sure, people can say that they deny gravity, but doing so doesn't make gravity stop working. Such a denial simply changes the description of it. Paul said that sinners naturally transfer the function(s) of God to various elements of nature (Romans 1:23). Ultimately, there is only one fix for the problem of idolatry—the trinitarianism of *Christos Singularis!*

15

IN CHRIST ALONE

*On account of these the wrath of God is coming. In these
you too once walked, when you were living in them. But
now you must put them all away: anger, wrath, malice,
slander, and obscene talk from your mouth. Do not lie to
one another, seeing that you have put off the old self with its
practices and have put on the new self, which is being
renewed in knowledge after the image of its creator. Here
there is not Greek and Jew, circumcised and uncircumcised,
barbarian, Scythian, slave, free; but Christ is all, and in all.*
—Colossians 3:6-11 (ESV)

In verse 6 we find a Greek text issue that presents an important
theological concern. The English Standard Version, along with a
host of modern manuscripts, leaves out the last phrase of verse 6
because some Greek manuscripts omitted it. It is included in the
Authorized Version, which means that the omitted phrase was
included in the Received or Majority Greek Text. The phrase has
been in use for about 1900 of the 2000 years of Christian history. It
seems to me that rather than clarifying the issue, it produces doubt
about the integrity of the Bible. The Authorized Version translates
this verse as, "for which things' sake the wrath of God cometh *on the
children of disobedience*" (v. 6, italics added). Other versions leave
out the italicized phrase.

There are two concerns in this verse. First, that the wrath of God
is coming because of the failure to make a clean break with the past,
because of disobedience, as Paul discussed in the first few verses of
this chapter. And secondly, upon whom does God's wrath come?
Does it come upon everyone, unbelievers and believers alike? Or only
upon the disobedient, only upon unbelievers? The issue is whether

God's wrath comes to those who have embraced the gospel of Jesus Christ. The question is whether those who believe escape all vestiges of God's wrath.

It is a troubling issue. The common view, that unbelievers receive God's wrath and believers receive God's mercy, is not completely wrong, but neither is it completely right. The reality is not quite so neat. The omitted phrase hides the fact that God's wrath sometimes leaches into the church in the sense of what we might call collateral damage. However, from God's perspective it is neither accidental nor unintentional, but may be more a matter of pruning (John 15:2). I suspect that Paul intended this issue to be troubling in order to stir up renewed study and commitment to Christ. I understand why people would want to omit the phrase. But I also understand why God would want to include it.

The idea provided by the missing phrase is that God's wrath may come, not merely to people who have rejected Jesus Christ, but to some who have ostensibly accepted Him, who have nominally accepted Him and His gospel, but have done so in a halfhearted manner. Too many Christians have met Christ only halfway, but have refused to give Him their all. According to the parable of the sower (Matthew 13:3-ff), the gospel seed sown by the Lord in a variety of situations encounters various conditions and comes to various ends. Different contexts produce different experiences and bring about different results. It's not that God doesn't save all of His people, He does. The problem is that all those who claim God do not actually belong to Him. In addition, we must consider that those who belong to Him are not always spared difficulties in this life, not even usually.

We must also consider the reality of the faithful martyrs, who were saved and completely dedicated and faithful to Christ, but who lost their lives, families, livelihoods, property, etc., *because* of their faith. Were the difficulties they experienced the result of God's wrath? This is a difficult and disturbing question, and requires us to understand Christianity from both an individual and corporate perspective. We know that God was not angry at the martyrs personally, but used them in a way that is difficult to distinguish from His wrath against others. I'm unable to solve this problem. All I can do is raise it. It's resolution may require some other term than God's wrath, or some distinctions within it.

Again, the issue in this verse concerns whether God's wrath comes only to non-members or whether it leaches into church membership as well. Remember, in the churches there are both disobedient Christians and unbelievers who have the form of godliness, but deny its power (2 Timothy 3:5). So, can people avoid God's wrath by simply being members in good standing of a local 501(c)(3) organization that calls itself a church? Is that the church that God intends to save? Will a simple confession of Jesus Christ as Savior keep people from experiencing difficulties in this life, from tasting a measure of God's wrath? Exactly what is the church of Jesus Christ that will ultimately be saved? Has God provided this issue to show us that believers and unbelievers are connected in some very fundamental ways?

The normal way of defining a church today is legal. Churches are usually defined according to Internal Revenue Service (IRS) law. But Paul didn't have the IRS and was founding churches in opposition to both Roman and Jerusalem authorities, which means that Paul was founding them in opposition to the official legal structures of his day. The Romans would tolerate any religion that would put itself under Caesar. Christians would not, and that was what got them in trouble with the Roman authorities. Paul was not concerned with getting the proper paperwork in order. As I have said before, the earliest Christian churches were not like our contemporary churches of any denomination.

DISTRIBUTED OWNERSHIP

If we can use Jesus as a model, or Paul, or Peter, or James, or John, or the Martyrs, etc., then Christians can expect to share in the wrath of God to come (Amos 4:11). Again, it is not that Christians will not be saved. We most certainly will be! But the process of salvation may well include some painful and unsettling experiences this side of glory. God has not promised anyone that life or salvation will be pain free, in fact quite the opposite (John 15:19). This world is a difficult place. Faithfulness to Jesus Christ can mitigate the difficulties, but until sin is completely eradicated difficulty and hardship will remain in varying degrees, even among God's people.

The issue of including the last phrase of verse 6 is the question of whether Christians experience God's wrath, or whether only the unsaved experience it. The biblical answer, taking into consideration the whole counsel of God and of the trinitarian character of reality, is that Christ's church will be exposed to the wrath of God to the same extent that she as a whole remains unfaithful to her calling. Note the corporate character of the church. The church is a corporate entity. Stated positively, faithfulness will reduce our exposure to God's wrath to the extent that faithfulness is practiced by everyone in the church. This issue illustrates the simultaneous individual and corporate character of salvation. The lives of believers and unbelievers are intertwined because of God's covenant with humanity.

This idea continues in verse 7, "In these you too once walked, when you were living in them." We need to be careful here because unclear pronouns and referents can cause a lot of confusion. The speaker or writer always knows clearly who or what he is referring to. But the listener or reader can often be confused by an unspoken assumption or an unclear referent. In *what* did *who* once walk, when *who* was living in *what* (v. 7)? Paul was saying that the faithful Colossians had themselves once walked in the sins that he had listed in verse 5—sexual immorality, impurity, passion, evil desire, covetousness, and idolatry.

Those who had been saved, those who had confessed Christ as Lord and Savior, those who had been baptized into the church, had themselves once been sinners. In fact, everyone in Colossae had once walked in these sins. But by the grace of God and the faithfulness of Jesus Christ some of the Colossians had been saved out of these sins—and other sins, by being saved into Christ's church.

But the rub is that to the extent that people hang on to their old sins, they are liable to the wrath of God. Again, God will ultimately save all of His people. But the faithlessness and disobedience of some of the Colossians exposed the faithful, not to God's wrath, but to the discipline of His love. "For the Lord disciplines the one he loves, and chastises every son whom he receives" (Hebrews 12:6). And speaking to the church at Laodicea, the risen Lord said in Revelation (3:19), "Those whom I love, I reprove and discipline, so be zealous and repent." The difficulty people have is that it is often hard to tell the difference between God's wrath and His discipline in the heat of the experience of it.

Consider Job. Did Job experience God's wrath? The destination of believers and unbelievers are different, but the life experiences are often remarkably similar. The primary difference is in how people handle it. In the face of difficulties (God's wrath), the faithless flee God, while the faithful turn to God. George Buttrick said, "The same sun that hardens the clay melts the wax."

So, does God's wrath come to all people or only to those who are disobedient? We know that God's full wrath comes to the faith-less, and that it is mitigated by the faithfulness of Jesus Christ on the cross for the faithful. The half-faithless/half-faithful are some-where between God's wrath and His loving chastisement. Is there such a critter? Not really. Such people are simply undecided. Those who don't make a clean break with their old thoughts and habits remain exposed to God's wrath. Scripture has made a clear call to faithfulness, both a clean break from our old habits and thoughts and a full embrace of the disciplines and thoughtfulness of faithful-ness. The call, the ideal model, is going from death to life. But the transition is not as smooth and easy as people usually hope.

ABANDON THESE

Paul repeated that call for a clean break in verse 8, "But now you must put them all away: anger, wrath, malice, slander, and obscene talk from your mouth." He expanded the list of sins that we are to leave behind (v. 5) in order to make the contrast more clear.

Anger (*orgē*) points to both human wrath and indignation, and is used to indicate punishment itself. To engage *orgē* is itself a pun-ishment. It's painful, disconcerting and usually has bad con-sequences. The command to not be angry is much like Scripture's command to love God and neighbor in that it demands control of human feelings. How can anger and love be commanded? Don't they just happen? Don't they just well up? Aren't people at the mercy of love and anger? *No*, said Paul, and God. *Get a grip on your emotions! Get over it!* said Paul. *Let it go! Don't engage it. Don't do these things.*

Emphasizing this point, Paul added wrath (*thumos*) to the list. The Greek word literally means passion and evokes the idea of breathing hard. The idea is to avoid fierceness and indignation, as well.

The addition of malice (*kakia*) includes the various forms of depravity, naughtiness, wickedness, and the like. Slander (*blas-phēmia*) is translated as *blasphemy* in the Authorized Version, and while it means especially blasphemy against God, it includes all sorts of evil speaking and railing against this or that, including rail-ing against other people about most anything.

You'd think that *blasphēmia* would cover it, but Paul added obscene talk (*aischrologia*), which includes vile conversation or filthy communication, dirty talk, potty talk, or talking about vile things. In contrast, Paul counseled the Philippians to focus on "whatever is true, whatever is honorable, whatever is just, whatever is pure, whatever is lovely, whatever is commendable, if there is any excellence, if there is anything worthy of praise, think about these things" (Philippians 4:8).

Did Paul or God want only church members to cease and desist from these behaviors? No, of course not. Because God's wrath comes in response to these things, it is better for everyone, members and nonmembers alike, to not invite God's wrath because everyone will be effected by it when it comes. In addition, avoiding these things is not only good for Christians, but such avoidance is good for everyone. It makes our shared society a better, kinder and more gentle place to live.

Nonetheless, God uses natural disasters and wars as vehicles of His wrath and whole communities are effected, some more and some less. Consequently, the church is to model godly behavior as a positive influence to improve the moral behavior of everyone, believers and unbelievers alike. And the better the church does at modeling godly morality, the more effective it is in the community at large, the more God's wrath will be kept at bay from the community at large. Or when it comes, the community will fare better because of the kinder social practices shared by all.

Emphasizing this point, the conjunction *but* that leads verse 8 implies a stark contrast. Paul said to the church: *that was then, when you also engaged all these things. But this is now when you must stop those old habits and ways.* The *now* stands in stark contrast to the *then*.

NOT

The difference between unfaithfulness and faithfulness, between unbelief and belief is like the Boolean logic operator known as "not." Boolean logic is used in math and on the Internet when we search for things. The common Boolean operators are "and," "or," and "not." Using the "not" means that there is no overlap between two sets of things. None of set A is contained in set B. For instance, I'm looking for sweaters, definitely blue, but not red. Paul was drawing a sharp distinction between unfaithfulness and faithfulness. *You all used to do these kinds of things before you were saved, but not anymore, not now, not in Christ.*

The human reality, of course, is that there is an overlap of time between unfaithfulness and faithfulness. There is a period of transition, of adjustment, of change when people become less unfaithful and more faithful until they are completely overwhelmed by the Holy Spirit, who is ultimately and perfectly faithful. Paul was not denying the reality of this overlap, this process of conversion.[48] Rather, he simply noted that at some point that transition would be complete, and the sooner the better. Paul longed for the day that God would put an end to sin in this world. But that day was not here yet.

By adding to the list of sins to overcome in Christ, Paul testified that the transition period would likely be longer than we might want, certainly longer than he wanted. Paul hoped for the end of sin to come quickly, the end of sin being the coming and/or return of Christ, the Day of Judgment (Romans 6:1-2, 2 Corinthians 5:2-4). Because the process of human sanctification does not end in this life, but continues into glory,[49] the list of sins and the reality of incomplete sanctification in this life insure that Christ's church will experience a measure of God's wrath. God's wrath is directed against sin, so as long as there is sin in the world, we will have to contend with God's wrath. It cannot be avoided because the birth of God's kingdom is a bloody, painful process, as history witnesses.

QUIT LYING

Yes, this is a hard teaching. But, counseled Paul, "do not lie to one another, seeing that you have put off the old self with its practices and have put on the new self, which is being renewed in knowledge after the image of its creator" (vs. 9-10). Lie about what? About everything, including this truth. Don't explain it away.

He had spoken of deceit in the previous chapter. "See to it that no one takes you captive by philosophy and empty deceit, according to human tradition, according to the elemental spirits of the world, and not according to Christ" (Colossians 2:8). This is the lying, the deceit, that Paul wanted them to avoid. And to avoid this lie, the empty deceit of godlessness, means putting Christ first in everything. It means understanding and analyzing things in terms of Christ's trinitarian character. It means understanding that Jesus

---

48 Conversion is not justification. Justification involves a decision that God makes, and while God also is the cause and power of sanctification, sanctification takes time.

49 Eternal life is not a static state but a sustainable condition of ongoing improvement. It begins with regeneration and continues into sanctification and even glory. Eternity for growing creatures means growing forever.

Christ is the context of all human being, of all human experience, including history, science, technology, literature, art—everything. In Christ we live and move and have our being, and apart from Christ there is only deceit and lies—empty philosophy, empty explanations, empty traditions.

The phrase, "seeing that you have put off" (v. 9) is one word in the Greek (*apekduomai*). It means to completely divest a thing, and it is in the past tense (middle voice). It is past in that the process of divestment has already begun, and it is present or continuing in that it has not yet been completed. Paul was telling them to complete what they had begun, to complete their divestment of sin. Paul wanted them to make progress in that direction.

Similarly, the phrase, "have put on" (v. 10) is one word that means invested or engaged. And what is it that is put on? The new self that has been renewed by the knowledge of God as creator, that is God as Trinity. Christians are to put on the knowledge of the Trinity, to see things as God sees them, through trinitarian eyes.

We see here the contrast between the old self and the new self. The new self, which is in Christ, "is being renewed in knowledge after the image of its creator" (v. 10). This is an interesting phrase. Because the human self of the saints, of Christians, lives and moves and has its being in Christ, Paul was speaking of an identity issue. The death of the old self and the birth of the new self refers, not to the death and birth of the individual, physical body, but to the death of the old identity and the birth and/or renewal of a new identity in Christ (Romans 6:1-18). It comes about through the knowledge of the image of God, the Creator in whose image we have been created. Because the original is trinitarian, so is the image.[50]

TRIUNE

This allusion to the trinitarian character of God should not be missed. It is an allusion to the knowledge that we have been created in God's image, which is trinitarian. It is an important statement about the character of the saints. Not only has the character of the new self been created in the image of the trinitarian God, but this new identity in Christ trumps all other descriptions of human identity. In this new self "there is not Greek and Jew, circumcised and

---

50 See *Arsy Varsy—Reclaiming the Gospel in First Corinthians*, by Phillip A. Ross, Pilgrim Platform, 2009, particularly the sections that deal with the body of Christ.

uncircumcised, barbarian, Scythian, slave, free; but Christ is all, and in all" (v. 11).

Each of these nouns provides a description of human character. People are normally identified as Greek or Jewish or Sythian or American whatever. Men are identified as circumcised or uncircumcised, which is an reference to circumcision as a religious identity issue. People are identified as barbarian (Scythian), slave or free. These are all characteristics of identity and character. Each noun points to a different human classification or grouping, to the old way of identifying people, to race or religion, to nationality or legal standing before civil law. It should also be noted that identity pertains to both individuals and to groups (religions, towns, races, nations, etc.).

But, said Paul, *being in Christ puts an end to all of that old way of human classification.* That was the old way, and it identified the old self. But the new self is now identified as being *in Christ*. And in Christ there is unity—the unity of the Godhead, and the reflected unity of the image of God in the trinitarian character of the saints. Our being in Christ also pertains to both individuals and groups (churches).

It is not only a statement about the trinitarian character of Christians, but is a statement of Christian unity in the light of God's trinitarian character. Christian unity, which is about the character and identity of Christians being *in Christ*, is also trinitarian. Christians are both one and many in that we are each unique individuals and yet we are all one, corporately in Christ. In Christ we are one in Christian unity. Being in Christian unity is part of being in Christ. The only unity available is this unity in Christ.

Christian unity is not something that we do or accomplish. It is a given because it is a function of the trinitarian Godhead. God is one, and Christ is one with God, and with the Holy Spirit, and with those who are in Christ. The only thing that we have to do regarding our Christian unity is to be faithful in Christ, both individually and corporately. It is more a matter of being than doing, more a matter of being in relationship than doing the right things. The definition of being faithful is actually being in Christ.

Again, our Christian identity is a reflection or image of God, who is trinitarian. We have an individual identity in Christ, a spiritual identity in Christ and a corporate identity in Christ. But these identities are not different. They are one in Christ. Christians belong to Christ individually, spiritually and corporately as the church. God is one, yet three. And in a similar way, Christian unity, Christian identity, which is in the image of God, is one, yet three, diverse in us, and unified in Christ.

Human beings are complex. Our identity is complex. We are individuals, yet no single individual can exist in this world for very long. Individuals are born as the result of procreation, which does not involve self-effort. It takes a man and a woman to produce a child. Yet, the individual is not the couple, nor is the couple the family or the group. And neither is the family or group identical to the individual.

Individuals and groups are mutually dependent. Individual human beings cannot exist apart from groups, nor can groups exist apart from individuals. People necessarily exist in groups, in families, clans, neighborhoods and nations. The individual and the group exist in a mutually dependent relationship. Apart from one another they are abstractions, but together they comprise something real. And with the advent of Christ we have come to see that our primary dependence is always upon God in Christ. As God is in Christ and we are in Christ, we are all together one in Christ.

COMMON DENOMINATOR

Not only are we in Christ, but "Christ is all, and in all" (v. 11). To say that Christ is all is to say that Christ is the common denominator of the largest possible human group—humanity. And a group is always identified in the singular as a unit. A group is a kind of singularity, or perhaps we should call it a plurality. Humanity or the human race is one *kind* in the biblical sense (Genesis 1:11).

The Greek word translated *all* (*pas*) includes all the forms of declension. It is a primary word that means all, any, every, and especially the whole. Christ is the whole. The whole of what? Well, because Christ is a member of the trinitarian Godhead, He is co-equal with God. But with the advent of Christ, He became a human being. Yet He retained his divinity, the trinitarian character of the Godhead. But with His incarnation His wholeness became focused or localized in His humanity. Thus, Christ is the whole of—or better yet, the wholeness of—humanity as a type (Romans 5:14). In Christ humanity best experiences, expresses and is identified as its wholeness. Or, the wholeness of humanity is a wholeness that is in Christ alone by faith alone through Scripture alone to the glory of God alone. The word *alone* (the Latin *sola*) here is not a description of solitude, but of singularity, of wholeness and unity.

Here, the word *alone* must also be understood in a trinitarian sense because God is trinitarian and we have been created in God's image, and Christ is a member of the trinitarian Godhead. Therefore, the word *alone* must be understood in both an individual sense and a corporate sense, in the sense of wholeness and without division. In the same way that Paul said, "Christ is all" (v. 11), we must also say *Christ alone is all*. But if Christ is all, then Christ's aloneness, His singularity, His wholeness, His unity must also be His all.

This idea is confusing because time intercedes between the death of the old self and the birth/renewal of the new self. God's purpose and Christ's function in the world is the establishment of the kingdom of God. In the fullness of the kingdom "every knee shall bow..., and every tongue shall confess to God" (Romans 14:11). Eventually, the whole world will acknowledge its identity as being in Christ.

As the hymnist wrote:

For lo! the days are hastening on,
By prophets seen of old,
When with the ever-circling years
Shall come the time foretold,
When the new heaven and earth shall own
The Prince of Peace their King,
And the whole world send back the song
Which now the angels sing.

(*It Came Upon The Midnight Clear*, by Edmund H. Sears, 1810-1876)

CB&ED

The ultimate fulfillment of God's mission on earth is the conversion of every extant person to Christ,[51] because Christ is Truth itself. Eventually Truth will reign over the whole earth. The kingdom of God will be fully established on earth when every person will be self-identified as being in Christ, with all of the various trinitarian subtleties thereof. On that day Christ will truly be all in all. That will be a glorious day. *Christos Singularis!*

---

51 See the James Jordan footnote, p. 11

16

THE GREAT PUT ONS

Put on then, as God's chosen ones, holy and beloved, compassionate hearts, kindness, humility, meekness, and patience, bearing with one another and, if one has a complaint against another, forgiving each other; as the Lord has forgiven you, so you also must forgive. And above all these put on love, which binds everything together in perfect harmony. And let the peace of Christ rule in your hearts, to which indeed you were called in one body. And be thankful.   —Colossians 3:12-15 (ESV)

Based upon what Paul has said to this point, he now draws another conclusion. He had warned them about being deceived by their own assumptions and presuppositions at the end of the previous chapter. So, it should not surprise us that our own expectations can mislead us as well. If it could happen to them, it could happen to us. No one is immune to this.

Given all that Scripture has said about the tenacity of falsehood and deceit in the human heart, and the human propensity for sin and self-delusion, we must be willing to consider the possibility that many Christians today have some of the most central elements of the gospel incorrect, that the false gospel that had infected the early churches has not yet been defeated within the larger body of Christianity, that the wheat and the tares have been growing together for centuries. It is not simply that earlier Christians got things wrong, but that they got them inadequately for our needs, from our perspective. Every generation must come to this conclusion because it will always be true. Time marches onward, as Christ continues to reveal Himself in His fullness. I'm simply pointing to the persistent character of sin, and the reliability of Christ's Word.

The gospel of grace as it was taught by Paul is so foreign to humanity that, though people think they have understood it, such understanding often continues to issue from an assumed pride in our own human ability to understand and master the intellectual subtleties of Scripture and the eternal doctrines of grace. That pride has often cloaked itself in a false or inadequate conception of the doctrine of election or the doctrine of God's sovereignty, or others. How does this false understanding of election, for instance, work?

People today continue to rationalize God's choices regarding salvation on the basis of human behavior, human character and/or human potential. Myriads of people continue to think that God chooses those whom He knows will eventually choose Him, that God's choice in election is predicated on the human free will of unregenerate people. This line of thinking is almost true, but it gets the truth backwards at the crucial point.

While it is true that those who are saved do eventually choose to answer God's call in the affirmative, it is not true that God chooses people because He knows that they will eventually agree with Him. Rather, those whom God has chosen eventually do freely choose God, but they come to agree with God because of God's prior actions, because of God's election. It is not that God comes to agree with the free will choice of unregenerate sinners, but that sinners regenerated by the election of God come to agree with the free will choice of God in election.

People come to agree with God through His saving action in their lives. God does not save people because they will come to agree with Him, though they do. To get this wrong is to reverse cause and effect. Apart from God's election, no one would ever choose to be saved by the God of Scripture. God's motivation is not to save those who will eventually agree with Him. That's not how it works. Rather, those whom God saves eventually come to agree with God's truth as a consequence of their having been saved. Having been saved themselves, they come to see how it works. Prior to that they have no idea how salvation could possibly work—and don't believe it. God's election is the cause of human belief, human belief is not the cause of God's election.

GOD LEADS

For those with eyes to see, all of what I have just said has been given by Paul in verse 12. In the first half of this verse Paul identified the Colossian church without qualification as "the elect of God" (Authorized Version), "God's chosen ones" (English Standard Version). Though Paul clearly recognized that some or all of these church members had not yet "put on ... compassionate hearts, kindness, humility, meekness, and patience" (v. 12), he identified them as elect. The fact that Paul told them to put these things on means that they had not yet put them on sufficiently. Had they already been exercising these virtues, Paul would not have needed to tell them to do so. But he did, which means that these virtues were not in evidence, at least not to the degree that they should have been. The Greek word translated as *put on* literally means to settle into.

That's one line of argument, but there's another line of thinking that breaks open our narrow conception of the doctrine of election even further. Do we think that Paul wanted only church members in good standing to practice these virtues? Of course not! He wanted everyone everywhere to be filled with the love of Christ and to practice Christian virtue. I don't mean that Paul was writing to everyone at Colossae. That's not what I'm saying. I'm saying that Paul wanted everyone at Colossae to be a Christian. And there is no evidence for this because it is a speculation based on Paul's understanding of the gospel. Christians want everyone to be Christian because the gospel is universal.

Paul's comment was most certainly directed to all of the Colossians. Certainly Paul wanted all of the Colossian church members to practice these virtues, but given Paul's emphasis on evangelism beyond the traditional confines of Jewish fellowship, Paul was calling the nations to exercise these Christian virtues, as well. Nations (*ethnos*) refers to Gentiles, heathens, everyone other than Jews. Paul both expected and hoped that God's election that had been planted in the Jewish nation was flowering in and through Christ. And because it was flowering it would reach into the nations, increasingly over time, until the whole world would be caught up in Christ.

The practice of virtue is not like salvation in that there is eventually a clear demarcation between the saved and the not saved (lost). The more time one spends in the saved camp, the greater the difference becomes. Eventually there will be a judgment that will forever divide these two groups from each other. But with regard to the exercise of Christian virtue in the meantime, there is a continuum of conformity to the model of perfection. While it is either true or false that we have been saved by the Lord because justification is instantaneous, our practice of Christian virtue grows and develops over time. The saved get better at it with practice, and the lost get worse at it. And sometimes someone who thought he was saved realizes that he isn't, and someone who thought he wasn't realizes that he is.

However, it must be understood that the doctrines of grace insist that God does not save people *because* they are virtuous. Rather, He saves people *so that they can be* virtuous. People can be genuinely virtuous only because of Christ, only because they have been regenerated by the power and presence of the Holy Spirit, chosen and equipped for salvation by God first and foremost. Genuine virtue issues from genuine salvation, whereas virtue that is not genuine does not. What is not genuine issues from pretense and deceit—hypocrisy.

It is only later that people come to a conscious and willing acceptance of the Lord and of all He has in mind for them as a result of their justification. Nonetheless, Paul calls all people without regard to any of our human classifications of race, religion or nationality. Paul called all of the *ethnos* to the exercise of common Christian morality. That is the basis of Western Civilization, not the Enlightenment. The Enlightenment was an historic aberration that moved culture away from God, and we are still in the midst of recovery from it.

Paul's call was a method of sanctification and evangelism, not a method of personal salvation. It was/is a way to bring people everywhere into a personal awareness of the reality of the kingdom of God. Not all will come, of course. Paul did not have the insight or authority to know who would and who wouldn't respond to the gospel—nor do any human beings. That decision is a matter of the election or choice of God.

IN CHRIST

It is because God's chosen people are holy and beloved in the Lord, in Christ, that they can exercise genuine compassion, kindness, humility, meekness, and patience. Apart from Christ there is only a false or inadequate understanding of Scripture and the gospel, and a less than full practice of Christian virtues. Apart from Christ these virtues are exercised out of the wrong motivations. Apart from Christ people can only fake these virtues at worst, or only partially practice them at best. Apart from Christ the human motivations of pride, greed and covetousness infect all human behavior. Apart from Christ the effort toward compassion is self-serving. Apart from Christ human kindness is self-seeking. Apart from Christ displays of humility are self-aggrandizing. Apart from Christ people are proud of their meekness, boastful of their faithfulness and cunning in their patience.

And yet, it is better for unregenerate sinners to pretend or to only partially practice these virtues than it is for them to completely ignore them. It is better for them, and it is better for the saints because God's purpose and God's goodness spills out of the church into the larger human society. Of course, it is only because of Christ, it is only in Christ, it is only through Christ and the power and presence of the Holy Spirit through regeneration that people can genuinely practice compassion, kindness, humility, meekness, and patience. It is only because of the trinitarian character of God and of those who have been created in His image, that we can imitate Jesus or Paul with any degree of success. And because conformity to Christ is not uniformly distributed throughout humanity, the mastery of Christian virtues is not uniformly manifested either.

As I have noted before, the only-ness of Christ is not a function of His solitude or His social isolation, as if His church can be isolated and ghettoized, neatly and completely separated from the larger society. Rather the only-ness of Christ pertains to the singularity of the Godhead, to the absolute uniqueness of the trinitarian God of Scripture and the incorporation of that uniqueness into the corporate unity of the plurality of the body of Christ.

It is only because Christians are in Christ together, in unity or union with Christ, that we can bear with one another. To bear with someone means to endure, support or sustain them. Emotional or psychological endurance is often necessary, but ultimate philosophical agreement is not even possible because often the two philosophical positions are mutually exclusive.

Believers cannot bear with unbelievers, nor can unbelievers bear with believers, not ultimately. The differences between believers and unbelievers are too great, too disparate, too different. The opposition between them is too stark, too complete, too thorough, too comprehensive. Ultimately, one or the other, believers or unbelievers, must have dominion (Genesis 1:26). At the final judgment believers and unbelievers will be separated, divided.

COMMON GROUND

So, the only common ground that exists between believers and unbelievers belongs to God. It is defined and upheld by God. This understanding and use of the common ground argument is the opposite of the more common usage. It builds on the teachings of Cornelius Van Til and is therefore presuppositional rather than evidential in this regard.[52]

The suggestion that God is not the ground of being for unbelievers feeds their delusion and denies the sovereignty of God and the common creation of all humanity in Genesis. The argument between believers and unbelievers is about the reality and character of our common human ground of being. Faith is all about the ground of being. By suggesting that the ground of being for all of humanity is not the same ground capitulates to the unbelief of unbelievers before any discussion of the matter begins.

Unbelievers insist that religious discussion about faith take place on their ground, on the ground of their supposed objective and unbiased assumptions that God is not real. This puts the burden of proof upon believers and stacks the deck against them because objectivity is defined as godlessness. However, if God is real and everything testifies to God's reality as the Bible teaches, then objectivity comes only from God, which puts the burden on unbelievers to disprove God. Van Til demonstrated that their assumptions of objectivity and supposed absence of bias are neither objective nor true. They are not objective nor unbiased regarding God because these assumptions deny God's reality at the outset.

Van Til taught that both believers and unbelievers are actually biased. Believers are biased toward God and unbelievers are biased against God. Being faithful means being biased toward God, loving God and believing Scripture. Van Til demonstrated that biblical arguments cannot succeed on the basis of unbiblical assumptions

---

52 The origins of presuppositional apologetics are in the work of Dutch theologian Cornelius Van Til, whose effort was focused primarily on the preeminence of the Bible as the ultimate criterion for truth. His student, Greg Bahnsen, furthered the development of Van Tillian Presuppositionalism. John Frame, another student of Van Til, also continues to advocate a presuppositional approach. By 1952, presuppositional apologetics had acquired a new advocate in Gordon Clark. His approach to apologetics, following his Platonic epistemology, was more closely concerned with the logical order of assumptions than was Van Til's. The differences between the two views on presuppositionalism caused a significant rift between the two men. Presuppositional apologetics has established itself securely as a legitimate perspective on apologetics, and Van Til's approach is far more popular and widespread than Clark's.

about God because unbiblical assumptions are not true. Rather, the argument between believers and unbelievers is an argument about differing assumptions, vying biases. Romans 1 declares that God provides common ground for all humanity, and that unbelievers deny it and "by their unrighteousness suppress the truth" (Romans 1:18). So, to agree with unbelievers that God is not their ground of being feeds their delusion.

We are all creatures of God's creation, living together on God's created earth—and like it or not, aware of it or not—ultimately serving God's purposes. God uses all things to accomplish His purposes (Hebrews 3:4). Unbelievers deny God, and by denying God they deny any and all common ground that exists between themselves and believers. It is not that I as a Christian deny the reality of common grace, but that unbelievers as unbelievers deny the only common ground or common grace there is between believers and unbelievers. They do so by their denial of God and of the reality of God's grace. The denial of God constitutes a denial of common grace because it denies grace itself. The denial of God is the denial of God's grace, and the denial of God's grace is the denial of common ground.

It is only by God's grace that people can bear with one another, as Paul counseled in verse 13. Consequently, to agree with an unbeliever in his denial of God's grace is itself a denial of the only real common ground believers and unbelievers have. God's grace is itself our only common ground. But when unbelievers deny God and His grace, they cut themselves off from the only vehicle of commonality with and toleration of others. The denial of God robs people of the ability to bear with one another. The denial of God makes life with others ultimately unbearable. And that is the definition of Hell.

So, how can people bear with one another? It is hard enough for believers to bear with one another, but how can believers and unbelievers bear with one another? Well, unbelievers cannot bear with believers because of their denial of God. God has promised that unbelievers will end up in Hell, in eternal torment. This idea is so offensive and so unacceptable to unbelievers that they categorically dismiss it, and will not take seriously anyone who believes or proclaims it. To accept the idea is to contemplate the reality of their own demise, and such an idea is simply unthinkable. It is intolerable because of their natural instinct for self-preservation and the avoidance of pain.

So, the burden of bearing falls to believers. Note that Paul did not say that believers were to bear with only other believers. He made no such limited application of these dictates. Believers understand that unbelievers can become believers, as they themselves have done. Nothing stands in the way except the unbelief of the unbeliever. Some people will make the transition from unbeliever to believer, and some won't. And we can't know who will until they do. So, we must bear with all unbelievers, and attend them as a midwife attending a woman who might be pregnant. Believers must care for unbelievers with care and concern, love and patience, wisdom and instruction in the hope that some of them will eventually believe.

FORGIVENESS

Paul continued, "if one has a complaint against another, forgiving each other" (v. 13). Forgiveness is the key to bearing with one another. But we can only forgive people after they have offended us. If there is no offense, there is no need or occasion for forgiveness. Forgiveness is predicated upon there having been an offense. So, being offended should be a signal that forgiveness is needed. The call to forgiveness is universal. Everyone needs to practice forgiveness because everyone is guilty of causing offenses of various sorts.

When our children were young, we taught them about forgiveness. When one of them hurt or offended another, the offending party was required to ask for forgiveness from the party they had offended. This scenario went something like this:

Someone would get hurt and complain about it. *He hurt me!*

We would then instruct the offender to apologize. This would often take some coaxing. Sometimes we would have to separate them for a while. But we'd stay with it until the apology came, often under parental duress. *I'm sorry.*

At the point that the apology was given, the natural inclination was to forget the infraction and go back to playing. But we couldn't let that happen. There was another step in the process. Forgiveness needed to be acknowledged. This would also take some coaxing. We insisted on it, so it was eventually given, again often uttered under parental duress. *I forgive you.* Only at that point was the process completed.

There was the acknowledgment of the hurt or offense. There was the apology. And then came the declaration of forgiveness.

Both the apology and the forgiveness were hard to express, while the injury or offense was easily incurred and easily expressed. It is easy to offend someone because people are easily offended. But apology and forgiveness are harder.

However, this is not what Paul taught the Colossians here. Paul was not teaching people to wait for the offender to apologize. He insisted that the offended party take the lead and exercise forgiveness first, without waiting for an apology. Paul was saying that the forgiveness would itself eventually coax out an apology.

Christian forgiveness was based upon the model of Christ's sacrifice. Here's how it works: Christ suffered the cross as a public apology to God in order to provide God's forgiveness for an as yet unrepentant people. God's forgiveness, given as a result of Christ's apology on the cross, would then coax people to acknowledge their own offense, their sin. And out of the realization of their own sin people will individually and collectively give God a belated apology in Christ, a confession of sin, a personal confession of error. That confession, acknowledging both one's own sin and Christ's propitiation on the cross, then in turn leads to personal repentance.

OFFENSE

Offended people get locked into a behavioral pattern of anger and revenge. One person's offense leads to another person's hurt and anger, which triggers revenge, which increases the harm and further aggravates the offended person. And round and round she goes in a self-perpetuating cycle of offense, anger, revenge, offense, anger, revenge, ad infinitum. The only escape from this treadmill of offense and revenge is for someone to break the pattern. That's what Christ did. He broke the pattern on behalf of humanity's sin against God.

People are always willing for the other guy to break the pattern by apologizing. But pride and fear keep people from taking such an initiative themselves. So, Christ took the initiative by making a public apology to God by suffering the punishment for our sin on the cross. That, then, broke the pattern and opened the door to reconciliation, to apology and forgiveness. Paul emphasized this in the last phrase of verse 13, "as the Lord has forgiven you, so you also must forgive." We must, of course, take care not to trivialize the offense by using our forgiveness as a dodge to serious consideration of the issues, or by owning a "holier than thou" attitude.

As important as all these things are, and they are very important, said Paul, "above all these put on love, which binds everything together in perfect harmony" (v. 14). Again, note that we don't tell people to put on a coat if they are already wearing one. Paul knew that this was a timeless command that all Christians would always need to heed. Love can always be put on.

The words *put on* in verse 14 are not in the Greek. They have been added to the English. Without them verse 14 is a sentence fragment in English. The action of putting on, mentioned earlier in verse 12 is assumed, and rightly so. Paul was simply extending the list of things to put on—compassion, kindness, humility, meekness, patience and now, love.

The Greek word is *agapē, charity* in the Authorized Version, but is almost always translated in the more current versions as *love.* Today, love is a misunderstood and over-used word that has been hijacked by the Romantic, sexually indulgent culture in which we live. Christians would do well to return to the older renditions of the Greek by using *charity* or *beneficence* in order to purge the idea of any amorous and/or sexual overtones that are associated with it.

The fact that Paul has elevated Christian love to the top of his list is reminiscent of 1 Corinthians 13, the great love chapter, where Paul put *agapē* above all the other spiritual gifts. Doing so also reminds us that *agapē* is first and foremost a gift from God, and not something that we have to work up in our own effort. Yet again, we must not neglect the fact that the gift of God's love both demands and engenders a response.

The human failure to respond negates God's love by making nothing of it. The same is true of human love. When someone's love is not returned, nothing comes of it. It's like trying to make an omelet without eggs. It can't be done. Even powdered eggs are eggs. There are no omelets apart from eggs. Nor is there such a thing as Christianity without love, without *agapē,* without charity or beneficence reciprocally practiced.

Interestingly, eggs are often used in cooking as a binding agent. Eggs in a cake mix hold the flour and other ingredients together. Similarly, Paul said that love "binds everything together in perfect harmony" (v. 14). Love is the "bond of perfectness" (*teleiotēs,* Authorized Version) or completeness, wholeness. The only other place in Scripture that uses this particular Greek word is in Hebrews, where it is translated as *maturity* in the English Standard Version. "Therefore let us leave the elementary doctrine of Christ and go on to maturity, not laying again a foundation of repentance from dead works and of faith toward God" (Hebrews 6:1). Here in Christian maturity is the harmony and perfection of the faith, the goal toward which Christians are racing.

Paul was not finished. He had another thing to add to his list— peace. "And let the peace of Christ rule in your hearts, to which indeed you were called in one body." (v. 15). On Paul's list were compassion, kindness, humility, meekness, patience, love and now, peace. The Greek word (*eirēnē*) conveys a sense of prosperity, in that hunger and destitution do not engender a sense of peace. Peace among human beings requires sufficient resources to keep people comfortable, to keep one group of people from feeling the need to liberate resources from another group. Peace requires a measure of security from both danger and desire. A hungry person is not a peaceful person, and neither is a greedy person.

Completing Paul's list, he added thankfulness, not as an after- thought, but more as a capstone, the crowning achievement that marks the maturity of Christian faithfulness. "And be thankful" (v. 15). Yet, it was a kind of afterthought because thankfulness cannot lead the list. It must come at the end, at the conclusion. We cannot be thankful until we have something to be thankful for. Only when we actually have something real do we have something to be thank- ful for. Engaging Paul's list of human character qualities—compas- sion, kindness, humility, meekness, patience, love and peace—- provides a quality of life for which people can truly be thankful. Conversely, apart from these things, people will have little to be thankful for.

Thankfulness is at the heart of God's covenantal relationship with His people. Note that in the Lord's Supper Jesus took bread and wine, and only after He gave thanks, did He give it to His dis- ciples (Luke 22:17-19). Paul complained about the godless, saying that "although they knew God, they did not honor him as God or give thanks to him, but they became futile in their thinking, and their foolish hearts were darkened" (Romans 1:21). It was the lack of honor and thankfulness toward God that made or enhanced the darkness of godlessness. Indeed, being thankful is at the heart of Christian faithfulness.

In the fullness of the kingdom of God, thankfulness will play a central role. John of Patmos prophesied that "whenever the living creatures give glory and honor and thanks to him who is seated on the throne, who lives forever and ever, the twenty-four elders fall down before him who is seated on the throne and worship him who lives forever and ever" (Revelation 4:9-10). Their worship issues out of glory, honor and thanks. Thus, giving God glory, honor and thanks is at the very heart of worship and faithfulness.

Paul's list of Christian character qualities show us what a faithful response to the gospel looks like. Conversely, people who do not manifest these qualities cannot be among God's elect. People never manifest them perfectly, but we need to engage them genuinely, heart-fully.

This, however, does not mean that only God's elect will benefit from the exercise of these qualities. Indeed, even the most hardened atheistic, unrepentant sinners will personally benefit from the practice of these Christian qualities—compassion, kindness, humility, meekness, patience, love and thankfulness. And the more people in any society or culture who actually engage these virtues, the more prosperous that society will become because these qualities are the foundation for human cooperation, for genuine social peace, progress, and long-term cultural development that is actually sustainable. Science, technology and business will flourish in an environment of these characteristics because these characteristics serve righteousness and justice, honesty and integrity. And apart from these characteristics, the foundations of honesty and integrity that are necessary for science and technology to develop will crumble.

CS&O

These virtues provide the foundation for the kingdom of the trinitarian God of the Bible, and have been imposed upon human history by Jesus Christ, by His willing death on the cross. Christ has broken the cycle of offense, anger and revenge between God and humanity and between people of every race, religion and nationality. He has done it for us all. *Christos Singularis!*

17

THE END BEFORE THE BEGINNING

Let the word of Christ dwell in you richly, teaching and admonishing one another in all wisdom, singing psalms and hymns and spiritual songs, with thankfulness in your hearts to God. And whatever you do, in word or deed, do everything in the name of the Lord Jesus, giving thanks to God the Father through him. —*Colossians 3:16-17 (ESV)*

I'm not familiar enough with Greek to understand why the translators have added the word *let* to verse 16. In the Greek the sentence begins with a definite article, which is usually translated as *the, this, that, one, he, she,* or *it.* While it is important to cooperate with the word of Christ that dwells in Christians, the suggestion that we *let* (or allow) Christ's word dwell in us makes it sound as if we give God permission to do so. If that is the case it inverts the authority and sovereignty of God by suggesting that God functions on the basis of our permission.

It might be better to translate the first phrase of verse 16 as, *the word of Christ dwells in you richly,* and drop the word *let.* The difficulty, of course, has to do with Paul making a statement that might be too broad by suggesting that the word of Christ actually dwelt with all of the Colossians. Was Paul making an unqualified presumption about the Colossian congregation? Did Paul mean that the word of Christ actually dwelt richly with all of the Colossians? Of course he didn't because he was writing in order to correct them. He was well aware that there were false believers in their midst.

What was the word of Christ doing in their midst? The word of Christ was "teaching and admonishing (them) in all wisdom" (v. 16). Paul was encouraging them to teach and admonish one another in the wisdom of Christ's Word. Just as Paul had been teaching and admonishing them, they were to teach and admonish (*noutheteō*) one another. The idea of admonishment involves warning, putting people on guard or taking people to task. These are all related to the idea of counseling, and counseling better expresses Paul's intent here. Biblical counseling (sometimes called Nouthetic Counseling by Jay Adams and others)[53] uses Scripture as the counseling model or foundation rather than relying upon the secular foundation of psychology as taught today.

So, the kind of admonishment Paul had in mind was a matter of corporate Bible study as a means of finding direction and providing correction for church members. This does not mean sitting around and engaging in morose self-introspection, nor of setting up a court for the chastisement of others. Rather, it means engaging in the process of learning and understanding Scripture among Christians in order to help one another assimilate the biblical perspective in all that they say and do. While encouragement is an important element of the process, we must not Romanticize the process of learning to the point that all chastisement is banished. Correcting the wrong answer is as important as praising the right answer.

DWELLING

To suggest that the word of Christ can dwell is to suggest that it is alive, and that is exactly what Paul believed. He knew that the word of Christ could dwell in people, that it was alive, because it dwelt in him. The word of Christ had taken up residence in Paul's heart and mind, and was living.

One definition of life suggests that living organisms are capable of growth and reproduction. Being alive is not simply a chemical reaction, nor is it a matter of independent existence. Rather, all living things grow and reproduce. Anything that does not grow or reproduce is not alive. Thus, Paul was suggesting, not that Christ was alive and dwelt in the hearts and minds of His people—which He does, but that "the word of Christ" (v. 16) does so. Indeed, Christ's church, the corporate body of Christ, is alive because it grows and reproduces.

Paul's word was *logos*, the *logos* of Christ, which means more than the words of Scripture. *Logos* indicates the mental faculty of reasoning, or a controlling motive, and by extension a kind of com-

---

53 National Association of Nouthetic Counselors, 3600 W. 96th Street, Indianapolis, Indiana 46268, www.nanc.org.

putation or calculation, such as the application of logical rules that determine a procedural outcome. The Word (*logos* in John 1:1) of Christ points to a living dynamic or power (*dunamis*) that functions in, as, and through the Spirit of Christ (Romans 8:9). It is not the words of Christ, nor the words of Paul or Peter, James or John, etc., but the Word (singular) of Christ. The Word of Christ is the controlling motive of the body of Christ, the trinitarian church in all of her various manifestations, combinations and permeations, individually and collectively.

This *logos* of Christ, alive in and as the body of Christ, was not just a vague mysterious notion that lacked definition or connection with other thoughts and ideas, but it dwelt richly, said Paul. Was it already dwelling richly or was it to dwell richly in the future? The answer is *yes* in both cases! It dwelt richly from the very beginning because it was the trinitarian Spirit of Christ. The Spirit of Christ is infinitely rich and wise, and yet as He dwells in God's people, He grows.

Of course, God doesn't actually grow because God is perfect and does not change. Nonetheless, the Word of Christ grows in the people of Christ as the people grow in the Word of Christ. How does this growth happen? First, it is growth in both love and understanding of God's Word. And second, it involves the progressive or unfolding revelation of Jesus Christ as the second Person of the Trinity. Scripture reveals Jesus Christ as the central character of the Bible, and over time more and more truth regarding this comes to light.

This *logos* of Christ serves two related functions. It teaches and it admonishes. It teaches and counsels nouthetically or biblically. First, the Word of Christ teaches. It imparts both skill and knowledge. About what? About Jesus Christ, about His role in Scripture, His role in the lives of Christians and His role in the world. Secondly, the Word of Christ admonishes or counsels. Jay Adams said that the word *noutheteo* "always implies a problem, and presupposes an obstacle that must be overcome; something is wrong in the life of the one who is confronted."[54] Nouthetic counseling is the art of correcting that problem or presumed obstacle, and doing so through the application of Scripture. Scripture, correctly understood and taught, removes all obstacles that stand in the way of faithfulness, and faithfulness provides the correction to the prob-

---

54 *Competent to Counsel*, by Jay Adams, Zondervan, 1986, p. 44.

lem or presumed obstacle. Such a presumed obstacle can also be a false or unbiblical presupposition, a false or half-formed doctrine that the counseling or correction confronts by teaching correct or complete Christian theology and doctrine.

Thus, the counselor/admonisher should not tell the person what to do or how to respond or behave. Part of the counseling process requires the individual to figure out what is needed and do it of his own accord. This way the new behavior belongs to the individual and not to the counselor. The counselor should simply provide correct theology, correct doctrine, correct interpretation and an explanation of that theology in a context that relates to the problem. The correct explanation of the theology will itself imply ideal behaviors or responses appropriate to the theological principles involved.

In this way the counselee is guided to compare his or her response with the correct explanation of the doctrine without being told specifically what to do. The person being counseled is encouraged to respond in the light of Christ. Again, the counselor does not tell the counselee what to do, which avoids some of the problems and temptations associated with abuses related to authoritarian relationships. Personal autonomy remains intact throughout the process. The point is to make Scripture the authority, not the counselor.

The counselee is directed to prayer and Bible study regarding particular issues that impact the problematic obstacle or the false presupposition that has mislead him into difficulties and problems. Reliance on God's Holy Spirit through Bible study and prayer lead to increased faithfulness and Christian maturity through reliance upon Christ, not reliance upon the counselor. The oppressive and dangerous situation of one person telling another person what to do or how to behave is avoided as people study God's Word and come to their own conclusions in the light of Christ and the fellowship of other mature believers. The ideal is for them to do this, not by themselves, not in isolation from others or from the body of Christ, but in the midst of experienced teachers and counselors who are themselves in the service of Jesus Christ and His people.

Paul intended that the Colossians, and all Christians by implication, engage in mutual teaching and admonishment (nouthetic counseling), and to do so with wisdom (*sophia*). Paul did not mean that Christians should be engaged in sophistry, nor should they extol the wisdom of Greek philosophy. Rather, Paul likely had in mind more of what Daniel Webster understood as the definition of wisdom: "In Scripture theology, wisdom is true religion; godliness; piety; the knowledge and fear of God, and sincere and uniform obedience to his commands. This is the wisdom which is from above (Psalm 90, Job 28)."

SACRED SONG

Paul then spoke of "singing psalms and hymns and spiritual songs" (v. 16). At first glance it may seem odd that Paul mentions music at this point, but there it is. That's what he did, so we need to understand the role of music in this issue. What has singing to do with teaching and counseling?

Hymns and the music of the church have always been a primary means of instruction and consolation. Singing helps memory retention. The classic hymns are veritable compendiums of Christian theology and doctrine (not all are good, so care must be taken). In addition, at the time that Paul wrote this, books and reading were not as prevalent as they are now, and people made their own music. So, music was very much a part of the church and the family. It was practiced regularly and functioned pedagogically.

Some scholars believe that Paul's use of these three terms was synonymous, that he was not differentiating between musical genres but emphasizing a point through repetition. Others believe that Paul recognized three different musical genres, "psalms and hymns and spiritual songs" (v. 16). Let's assume that both of these things are true, that Paul was emphasizing the importance of music, and that he differentiated three musical genres in use at the time.

We will assume that Paul was familiar with each of these genres. Psalm singing was as old at the Psalms themselves. Many, maybe even most, of the people Paul was with would have had some familiarity with psalm singing, at least among the Samaritans and others with whom ancient Jews of the diaspora would have mixed.

Known as the *diaspora,* there were many former Jews who, for a variety of reasons, had been dispersed among the Gentiles at various times in history. Most of those to whom Paul had written would have been familiar with Psalm singing. So, by citing Psalm singing Paul struck a note of familiarity among people.

Hymns in Paul's day were probably not much different than

hymns today. They were probably popular (not to be confused with secular) renditions or translations of some biblical passage, story or idea, set to music and intended for congregational singing. The advent of Jesus Christ created an outpouring of worship and praise by all sorts of people. It would be hard to imagine that people would not have been writing and singing hymns during Paul's day. Of course, at some point all music and all lyrics were new. Nonetheless, the beauty of tradition is that it works to preserve the best and/or the most popular pieces over time. Paul probably had in mind some body of beloved hymns that were in common usage among the churches.

His mention of spiritual songs suggests a musical genre different from Psalms and hymns. Exactly what it refers to is lost to antiquity. It was a meaningful term to the Colossians that served to group certain songs or tunes together. I imagine it to have been some sort of folk music category.

Was Paul recommending exclusive Psalm singing? Unlikely. Paul's ministry was evangelical. He focused on Christ's ministry to the Gentiles and Pagans in the area. So, it is unlikely that Paul would have narrowed the effectiveness of musical ministry. Was Paul then recommending only Psalms and hymns to be sung? Again, for the same reasons, I don't think so.

Paul was not focused on any particular musical genre. The three terms he used suggest a spirit of inclusiveness. Nor was he engaged in a discourse on music. His concern was not the music, but the hearts that sang. Paul was focused on the propagation of the gospel, not the means of propagation. Obviously, some means are better than others. And some means undermine various values and aesthetics of the gospel. But to take Paul's conversation about music in that direction is to take it where Paul was not going.

More likely, Paul mentioned music because of the joy of singing that he knew as a believer himself, and because of the power that music had when it was harnessed to the Lord. Picking up a previous point, Paul mentioned that whatever singing people did they should do it "with thankfulness in (their) hearts to God" (v. 16). Because thankfulness was at the very heart of worship, and because congregational singing plays an important role in worship, Paul brought these themes together as he instructed believers to sing with thankfulness to God.

Note also that Paul did not have in mind a generic thankfulness, but that Christian thankfulness always has a specific source and a specific object toward which our thankfulness must be directed—Jesus Christ. While the English Standard Version cites this combined source and object as God, the Greek word is actually *kurios* and is usually translated as *Lord*. Because of Paul's Christological emphasis, it is more likely that he intended that the thankfulness be directed toward Jesus Christ and definitely not some unidentified or amorphous idea of god that so often comes to mind among contemporary people.

NAME & REALITY

Capitalizing on this Christological emphasis, Paul continued, "And whatever you do, in word or deed, do everything in the name of the Lord Jesus, giving thanks to God the Father through him" (v. 17). Christians often speak of this, of doing everything in the name of Jesus, yet too often fail to actually do it. Simply parroting this verse provides a display of piety that sounds faithful but, apart from actually engaging the intent of Paul's words, results in a very common sin.

Jesus spoke of this sin, "This people honors me with their lips, but their heart is far from me" (Matthew 15:8). Apparently, the integration of words and actual beliefs is a common problem. Isaiah noted the same problem centuries earlier: "Because this people draw near with their mouth and honor me with their lips, while their hearts are far from me, and their fear of me is a commandment taught by men" (Isaiah 29:13). Jeremiah also noted the problem: "This is the nation that did not obey the voice of the Lord their God, and did not accept discipline; truth has perished; it is cut off from their lips" (Jeremiah 7:28).

The lack of integrity between words and reality is a serious and persistent problem. A major purpose of language is to provide a way to describe reality in order to manipulate it for the benefit of humanity. Such description and manipulation are the activities of science and technology. Science is the art of accurately describing the various elements of reality to discover the consistencies that can be technologically manipulated for some purpose. But when the integrity between language and reality fails, the enterprises of science and technology become threatened, as well as the modern human culture that depend upon them. Science and technology are only possible if language provides a reliable description of reality. The breakdown between language and reality, between words and actions, between the sign and the thing signified undermines the reliability of the cognitive tools that make science and technology possible.

Paul said that we must do everything in the name of the Lord Jesus. Why? Because Jesus Christ, the second Person of the Trinity, is actively involved in everything. God, the first Person of the Trinity, actually holds the world together (Psalm 89:11, Jeremiah 10:12, John 9:5, Colossians 1:17) in conjunction with the work of the other members of the Trinity. The Trinity always functions both individually and collectively.

God has provided a biblical framework for analyzing and understanding the world in which we live. Adam began a taxonomy of the world by naming the various animals in the Garden. That was the job God gave him. In the Garden God mediated reality to Adam by creating language as a way to describe the world. Language and the reality of the trinitarian character of God is at the very heart of the scientific and technological enterprises because these enterprises are built upon the reliability of truth itself, where truth requires integrity between words and reality.

In our day, Postmodernism[55] strikes a blow at the integrity of language and undermines its reliability and dominates our universities. To see this more clearly, we can think of mathematics as a form of language. Science and technology depend upon the integrity of the language of math. So, inasmuch as math doesn't work or isn't understood or is taught improperly, the development of science and technology suffer the consequences. Postmodernism, by undermining objective truth, undermines the reliability of math because math depends upon objective measures of truth.

Is there a connection between language, including math, and God? Yes. God created language. He created the world and everything in it. Consequently, everything in the world is foundationally or fundamentally grounded in God. God is the unifying principle of the world. God is the prime source of all meaning. God is the universal context of the world, and God is trinitarian in character. Consequently, God's trinitarianism is at the heart of

55 Postmodern philosophy is often particularly skeptical about binary oppositions characteristic of structuralism, emphasizing the problem of distinguishing knowledge from ignorance, social progress from reversion, dominance from submission, and presence from absence. Postmodernism has attacked and undermined the traditional values and language of the West, of Christianity, and has flowered and gone to seed in the recent academic discipline known as Queer Theory (www.queertheory.com).

everything and of our understanding of the world. To dismiss God or fail to properly understand God's trinitarian character hamstrings our understanding of the world, including science and technology.

Plato preceded Christ by some 600 years. Nonetheless, Plato's quest to understand the philosophical problem of the "one and the many"[56] has proven to be fruitless because Plato was not acquainted with the God of Scripture, who is the One and only trinitarian God in whom the world adheres. Plato's Paganism did not resolve the dilemma of the one and the many because he did not have access to the doctrine of the Trinity, nor to regeneration. So, he constructed his philosophical system without it, and thereby provided Western Civilization with an unsolvable philosophical problem that served to retard the development of science and technology until Christians saw the doctrine of the Trinity at work in Christ and His church, and proceeded to assume it. That assumption (or faith) then provided sufficient resolution of the one and the many dilemma for science to take root. Science needed the trinitarian

---

56 Philosophers try to account for the myriad of objects and phenomena in the world. But there is fundamental problem. We live in a world of things that are constantly changing, yet there seems to be an underlying unity and stability to them in spite of the changes. For instance, every human being begins as an infant and then grows into an adult. Every adult is radically different than they were as an infant. We change so much that we are, in fact, unrecognizable as being the same thing. Yet we recognize that they are the same person, the consistency of the person has remained the same even though the infant has changed into something that is almost completely other than its original state. Similarly, a corpse is nothing like the original living human being, but we still recognize that something has remained constant. This same stability and constancy exists in everything. There are many kinds of trees, yet there is still some constancy and stability to "treeness" which never changes.

This observation of the world of phenomena leads many cultures to believe that the infinity of things and their changes can ultimately be related back to a single object, material, or idea. The problem of finding the one thing that lies behind all things in the universe is called the problem of "the one and the many." This problem begins with the unity of personal experience. Because our experience coheres, we believe that there is one, unifying "something" behind everything. It could be material, such as water, or air, or atoms. It could be an idea, such as number, or mind. It could be divine, such as the Christian concept of God or the Chinese concept of Shang-ti, the "Lord on High." The problem, of course, is figuring out what that one, unifying idea is. The Bible teaches that the one thing is God, and Christianity posits that the changes are a function of the Trinity and the trinitarian character of reality.

Philosophy in the Western world began with this question; the earliest Greek philosophers mainly concerned themselves with this question. As a result, the problem of the one and the many still dominates Western concepts of the universe, including modern physics, which has set for itself the goal of finding the theory that will unify the laws of physics.

understanding regarding change and consistency to make sense of the world.

Paul said, "whatever you do, in word or deed, do everything in the name of the Lord Jesus, giving thanks to God the Father through him" (v. 17). Paul intended that all human thought and activity acknowledge its objective reference to the God of the Bible in the name of Jesus Christ.

What did Paul mean by "in the name (*onoma*) of the Lord Jesus" (v. 17)? The Greek word (*onoma*) literally and figuratively refers to authority and character. We are to do everything in the authority and character of the Lord Jesus. Why? Because all authority has been given to Jesus by God (Matthew 28:18). To do something in the character of the Lord Jesus is to call attention to the combination of qualities or features that distinguish the Lord Jesus from all others. It is to highlight the uniqueness of Jesus Christ, which involves His role in the uniqueness of the trinitarian Godhead. The trinitarian character of Jesus Christ is the Lord's most unique quality. It differentiates Him from all others, which is the function of naming. To name Jesus Christ is to call forth the uniqueness of His character. Thus, Paul's admonition to "do everything in the name of the Lord Jesus" (v. 17) is a call to relate the uniqueness of Christ's trinitarian character to everything.

SINGULARITY

By designating the name in which to do this as "the Lord Jesus" (v. 17) Paul pointed to both the Lordship of Christ and the Person of Jesus. Christ's Lordship emphasizes His divinity and the name Jesus emphasizes His humanity. Paul's use of this particular phrase, then, points to the trinitarian character of the Lord Jesus, to the singularity, to the simultaneous unity and multiplicity of the Godhead that was manifest in the particularity of the individual known as Jesus Christ.

Again, my intention here is not to wax mysterious by referring to the mystery of the trinitarian Godhead, but to demonstrate the philosophical depth, breadth and extent of Paul's intention that whatever we do, in word or deed, we need to do everything in the name, in the authority and character of the Lord Jesus. My intention is to suggest that the Trinity is the original singularity.[57] Everything already and actually reflects the trinitarian quality of

---

57 Where *many* collapse into *one* without losing particularity or uniqueness.

God's character because we human beings have been created in God's image. And so, the integrity of language itself requires that our words and deeds acknowledge this objective reality or fact of God's trinitarianism and the implications of God's trinitarianism on the activity of human thinking, being and doing.

To take Paul's admonition to "do everything in the name of the Lord Jesus" (v. 17) seriously requires taking God's trinitarian character seriously, and the reflected trinitarianism of the character of human beings. This means that relating to God from a monotheistic perspective such as that of both Judaism and Islam is simply inadequate. The universalism of a monotheistic philosophical perspective tends to flatten out the topography of reality by imposing a one-eyed myopic absolutism upon the complex texture of trinitarian reality. Wrong also is the pantheistic Paganism that locates God in the multiplicity of particularity, which ignores the inherent unity of all things under the ultimately unique singularity of God.

Only the trinitarianism of Christianity reveals and accounts for both the unity and the diversity of the actual world in which we live, first by seeing the delicate and interrelated topography of reality through a two-eyed stereoptic[58] perspective that reveals the three-dimensional subtleties that more accurately represent the complexities of the reality of the actual world. Such a perspective is foundational for the development of science and technology.

All of this is to say that Paul's call to do everything in the name of the Lord Jesus is much more than making reference to Jesus Christ as some sort of talisman. Rather, it was a call to take up the trinitarian perspective of Jesus Christ, to see things through the eyes of the Lord Jesus, to re-envision in the light of Christ everything that the Old Testament had taught about God. Paul called the world to see Jesus Christ in the light of the Trinity. Paul taught that the advent of Christ put an end to the Old Man, to the old way of understanding God. The advent of Christ put an end to the Old Testament and its doctrine of monotheism, and revealed the richer trinitarian character of God as Father, Son and Holy Spirit.[59]

---

58 Stereoptic vision: The perception of depth and three dimensions accompanying binocular vision resulting from differences in parallax producing different images on the retina of each eye. Two eyes produce vision in three dimensions.

59 Most people still classify Christianity as monotheistic, but the doctrine of the Trinity has redefined the inherent complexity of Christian monotheism. The acknowledgment of this reality will go a long way toward solving the world's religious problems by setting biblical Truth on its proper axis.

The consequence of the advent of Christ, which brought God's actual trinitarian character into view, cannot be understated. The importance of Paul's insight regarding God's trinitarian character has hardly been noticed in the history of the world to date. Trinitarianism has remained shrouded in the fog of mystery, even in the theological history of Christianity itself. Few scholars have successfully addressed the doctrine of the Trinity. And though the Trinity has provided for the development of modern science, science itself has yet to acknowledge its philosophical debt to Jesus Christ.

Even so, the development of modern science and technology, built upon the reliability and increasing complexity of language itself, upon Jesus Christ who is the trinitarian Word of God, has provided a sufficiently sustained experience of reality (over many generations) to demonstrate the philosophical implications and the practical and concrete aspects of the doctrine of the Trinity. Recent studies of Christian trinitarianism, grounded in the philosophical work of Cornelius Van Til, have brought new clarity regarding the ultimate uniqueness of the Person and role of Jesus Christ, who is the very Word of God.[60]

This central aspect of Christianity has recently set the stage for human cultural development and maturity in Christ to a heretofore unknown degree. The doctrine of the Trinity distinguishes Christianity from all other religions, theologies and/or philosophies, and has contributed significantly to the development of science and technology.[61] Science and technology have revealed a significantly greater degree of complexity regarding the world than previously known. What we accept as ordinary, people from previous generations would consider to be nothing less than magic. For instance, the reality of local, geographic transcendence through the mediums

---

60 I am employing the work of Cornelius Van Til, who has made a significant contribution to Christian theology. His work is a must read. Also see, *The One And The Many*, by R.J. Rushdoony, Ross House Books. Subtitled *Studies in the Philosophy of Order and Ultimacy*, this work, building on Van Til, discusses the problem of understanding unity vs. particularity, oneness vs. individuality. "Whether recognized or not, every argument and every theological, philosophical, political, or any other exposition is based on a presupposition about man, God and society—about reality. This presupposition rules and determines the conclusion; the effect is the result of a cause. And one such basic presupposition is with reference to the one and the many." The author finds the answer in the Biblical doctrine of the Trinity. Ralph Smith has also provided a helpful treatment of this issue in his books, *Paradox And Truth*, Canon Press, Moscow, ID, 2002, and *Trinity and Reality*, Canon Press, Moscow, ID, 2004.

61 There are many Christians contributors to science, http://en.wikipedia.org/wiki/List_of_Christian_thinkers_in_science.

of modern communication and travel were unimaginable in previous generations. Today, humanity stands at the beginning of a new chapter in history, grounded in the cross of Christ alone, that has the potential to forward Christ's cause of sustainable human development in unprecedented ways.

This is only to say, "Repent, for the kingdom of heaven is at hand" (Matthew 3:2), and as the kingdom continues to unfold in the world, it becomes increasingly at hand—immediate. The Greek word translated *at hand* (*eggizō*) simply means near in the dual sense that we are approaching it and it is approaching us. The prelude to the kingdom, which has been playing in human history since the resurrection of Jesus Christ, is the judgment of God. God's judgment, which cannot be avoided, increases in tempo and crescendo as it plays out in history, as it approaches its climatic purpose. God's judgment is the fulcrum of history that divides the old from the new. And while this most certainly means the end of the old, it simultaneously and with equal certainty means the beginning of the new.

"Is a lamp brought in to be put under a basket, or under a bed, and not on a stand? For nothing is hidden except to be made manifest; nor is anything secret except to come to light. If anyone has ears to hear, let him hear" (Mark 4:21-23).

Upon the announcement of the birth of Jesus Christ an angel appeared to the shepherds who watched over their flocks by night. "And the angel said to them, 'Fear not, for behold, I bring you good news of great joy that will be for all the people. For unto you is born this day in the city of David a Savior, who is Christ the Lord" (Luke 2:10-11).

Jesus spoke to those who were afraid of the coming judgment. "Are not five sparrows sold for two pennies? And not one of them is forgotten before God. Why, even the hairs of your head are all numbered. Fear not; you are of more value than many sparrows. And I tell you, everyone who acknowledges me before men, the Son of Man also will acknowledge before the angels of God, but the one who denies me before men will be denied before the angels of God" (Luke 12:6-9). "Fear not, little flock, for it is your Father's good pleasure to give you the kingdom" (Luke 12:32).

Fear not, but "be ready, for the Son of Man is coming at an hour you do not expect" (Matthew 24:44), and, I might add, in a manner that is beyond our ability to expect. But it is not beyond God's ability to anticipate it. This anticipation of the kingdom of

God is the main subject of the Bible, a subject that is overlooked or denied at great peril in the light of current historical developments.

CʒEᴑ

Roosevelt was wrong. During his inauguration on March 4, 1933, which occurred in the middle of a bank panic, he said, "The only thing we have to fear is fear itself." Not true! Because "The fear of the LORD is the beginning of wisdom" (Psalm 111:10) those who do not fear the Lord have no wisdom. "When will we ever learn?" (a line from the folksong, "Where Have All The Flowers Gone?" by Pete Seger, 1955). *Christos Singularis!*

18

FAMILY FUNCTION

Wives, be subject to your own husbands, as is becoming in the Lord. Husbands, love your wives, and do not be bitter against them. Children, obey your parents in all things, for this is well-pleasing to the Lord. Fathers, do not provoke your children, lest they be discouraged. Slaves, obey your masters according to the flesh in all things; not with eye-service, as men-pleasers, but in singleness of heart, fearing God. —Colossians 3:18-22 (ESV)

In order to understand Paul's injunctions about Christian families we need to see them in the larger context of the chapter at hand. Paul has been discussing the new self that manifests in Christ through regeneration. He has spoken of the death of the old self (Colossians 3:3) and the need to abandon those human tendencies and characteristics that have accumulated throughout history and have attached themselves to people in ways that seem to be natural —"sexual immorality, impurity, passion, evil desire, and covetousness, which is idolatry" (Colossians 3:5). He then adds anger, wrath, malice, slander, obscene talk and lying to the list (Colossians 3:8-9). These are aspects of the old self that must be abandoned when the new self in Christ is embraced.

The characteristics of the two self identities, the old and the new, are ultimately mutually exclusive, which means that there needs to be a clean break between them inasmuch as that is possible. Of course, if they are mutually exclusive we might be tempted to think that they cannot coexist by definition, which is true. However, they only coexist during the war between them. At the conclusion of the war, which is a total war because of God's claims on the totality of human being, one side or the other wins and the fact of their mutual exclusiveness manifests in full.

The failure to make a clean break brings troubles and difficulties because of the failure to abandon sin and corruption, which are the actual source of our troubles and difficulties. The failure to make a clean break is the cause of the war. And yet, the break is never perfectly clean. It takes time and practice to rid ourselves of our old habits and values. Conversion is always a process. Whether or not the war is necessary is unknown. What is known is that the war is raging right now, and sides must be taken.

The break between the old self and the new self is not made by simply abandoning the old. Something cannot be replaced with nothing. So, Paul lists the new characteristics that are to replace the old—compassion, kindness, humility, meekness, patience, forbearance and forgiveness (Colossians 3:13, Ephesians 4:20-32). And above and beyond all of these qualities, Paul commends Christians to "put on love" (Colossians 3:14). The old characteristics are replaced, not by the emptiness of asceticism, but by the fullness of faithfulness, by living in Christ.

Out Goes The Old

Having, then, mentioned that love is the penultimate Christian characteristic (see also Ephesians 5:21-22), Paul turned his attention to marriage and family life. Christian family relationships were not to be like Pagan and unregenerate marriages and families. From time immemorial unregenerate people have sought and used power and control by any and all means available to impose their selfish, unregenerate wills upon others, in the family and out. Apart from Christ, the world is a proverbial dog-eat-dog world which is shaped by the characteristics of the old self that were to be abandoned in Christ.

The means of the control and domination of others by unregenerate people are and continue to be anger, wrath, malice, slander, obscene talk and lying (Colossians 3:8). These are the things that lead to intimidation, extortion, revenge, violence and murder. So, rather than dealing with such behaviors directly, Paul taught Christians to abandon the thoughts and characteristics that motivate such behaviors. History has adequately proven that such behaviors cannot be controlled externally by laws or social conventions that are imposed upon people, much like family values and behaviors are imposed upon children. Such imposition is always seen by the immature and unfaithful as a constraint against personal freedom, and only fans the flames of resentment which eventually lead to revenge, which in turn exacerbate the old habits and behaviors.

The external behaviors of violence, intimidation, extortion, revenge and murder inflicted upon this or that person or population are resented. Eventually that resentment builds until it returns like for like, sin begets sin. The various reciprocal revolutions explode and political power shifts from one person or group to another, but nothing really changes because the means by which the power is changed—intimidation, violence and extortion—are the means by which power is kept. So, the players change roles but the structure and substance of the social patterns remain the same, and keep the world and its people in patterns of revolution and domination that impede the development of genuine social progress. Progress requires building on history, not continually revamping it. Revolution always impedes progress. Jesus was not a revolutionary. He submitted Himself to Roman law. In fact, His submission to it increased the legitimacy of His case. Progress requires breaking the cycle of sin and revenge.

Jesus Christ broke that pattern of sin, revenge, and revolution, and is in the process of replacing it with a godly, heavenly or biblical culture based upon the positive character attributes Paul described. The world is still in the process of this cultural change. At the center of this change is the human family and its various relationships. This focus on the family does not deny the central role of the church, but rather suggests that family and church are related concerns. In the larger scheme of things church and family are mutually interdependent.

FAMILY

Paul's first concern is the place and role of authority in the family because Christ's first concern is the place and role of authority in the world. The central element of the ministry of Jesus Christ is the announcement of the reality and nearness of the kingdom of God. This reality establishes the fact that God is king of everything, and the king is the highest authority within his kingdom. Thus, God's kingship establishes a hierarchy of authority because all authority is necessarily hierarchical by definition.

Paul knew that family relationships are always foundational for character development. What we learn in our families we carry with us all our lives. It has long been held that the family is the cradle of human culture. Paul knew this, as did Jesus. The Bible has always placed much importance upon families and family relationships. So, it is no surprise that Paul addressed family relationships.

Because the family is a major training and educational center for human beings, the family is a model for general human relationships and interactions. The family is the crucible for the character development of the children and the character of the grown children provides the foundation of culture. At the same time culture reciprocally shapes the character of adults and the character of adults provides the foundational elements for family relationships. As an example, contrast the character of the parents who weathered the Great Depression and World War II with their children who became Hippies, and the respective cultural effects of each. By and large, what the parents built up, their children have torn down.

Thus, there is a mutual interdependence and interrelatedness between family and culture, where the qualities and characteristics of each help shape the qualities and characteristics of the other. The character of the individual impacts the character of the group, and the character of the group impacts the character of the individual.

The trinitarian God provides the only foundational reality in which both the individual and the group actually exist simultaneously as actual entities. Because of the Trinity, an individual (or in philosophical terms a particular) can be considered in distinction from a group (or universal), and visa versa. But the actual existence of a particular necessarily requires the actual existence of the universal in the same way that the actual existence of the universal necessarily requires the actual existence of a particular.

For instance, groups (families) produce individuals (children), and individuals constitute groups (families, churches, nations). The singularity of God, His unity, His wholeness, is trinitarian. God is simultaneously one and many. God is both simple and complex. Yet, his unity does not detract from His multiplicity, nor does His multiplicity detract from His unity. Rather, they require and enhance one another. Like the three dimensional reality in which the world exists, each dimension can be considered and measured apart from the others, but no single dimension ever actually exists apart from the others. Reality, like God, is dimensionally holistic (complete, perfect—*tâmîym* in Hebrew, *teleios* in Greek).

This trinitarian character of God has everything to do with families because "God created man in his own image, in the image of

God he created him; male and female he created them" (Genesis 1:27). Individual human beings, which are the necessary parts that comprise humanity as a whole, as a race, as a kind, issue from the relationship between a man and a woman. The individual issues from a group that functions as a unit. A baby is produced by the group effort of the husband and wife in unity. The unit is the marriage—male and female, husband and wife. The unity of humanity as a whole, as a kind, as a race that endures over time, is complex. Unity, the idea of being united into one, oneness, the quality of being united, wholeness, is complex. Wholeness is always composed of parts, yet the whole is greater (or other) than the sum of the parts.

COVENANT OATH

What is it that holds things together in unity? The power that causes a man and a woman (husband and wife), for instance, to become a unit, to become united, is a covenant or promise of faithfulness. This covenant, however, is not simply a legal contract. More than a legal contract, it is also and foremost an oath of allegiance that involves heart, mind and soul. The mention of heart, mind and soul is not to suggest a tripartite division of the human being, but rather, that covenants involve more than words.

However, the marriage covenant and the unity it authorizes and creates is not simply between an individual man and an individual woman, but because it provides the foundation for a larger society through child bearing and culture through child maturing, it calls for the witness and support (acknowledgment) of the larger society. The commitment to fidelity between the husband and wife must be recognized and honored by the larger society in order to provide for the care of children and reduce the natural competitions and conflicts that are associated with sex.[62]

The man and woman, having become husband and wife by the authority of a mutual oath of allegiance, agree to function as a unit (in unity) in the larger society and/or community in which they live, and to contain their sexual activities to the marriage relationship. Because the fruit of this unity (Genesis 2:24) produces additional human beings, which are created by God, God is also a party

---

62 God's covenant applies to all humanity ("Behold, I establish my covenant with you and your offspring after you" (Genesis 9:9), but it does not apply in the same way to all. Deuteronomy 15 tells about the difference between covenant keepers and covenant breakers.

of the covenant. In fact, the covenant itself is issued by the authority of God through Christ because only God has the authority and ability to create human beings, and God has given all authority regarding this world to Christ (Matthew 28:18). All of this simply acknowledges that human beings are creatures of God, and that God has authority over them (us) because He is the Creator of humanity.

Paul has discussed and established the hierarchical authority of the family elsewhere (1 Corinthians 11, Ephesians 5 & 6).[63] The issue of submission to authority is essential for the well-being and longevity of human individuals and societies. Those societies that don't master the art of submission to authority devolve into chaos and destruction over time. Why? Because the more people included in a society or culture (*oikonomia*) the more complex the society or culture becomes. Additional complexity requires a greater sensitivity and a more delicate compliance with the authority of social order. The greater the population the greater the complexity of the order required for cultural sustainability. Small populations require less social order than large populations.

Human freedom and compliance to social order have usually been set in opposition to one another in our contemporary Western society. Most people think that the greater the freedom the less compliance to social order. Conversely, the increase of compliance with social order is usually thought to be an infringement on personal freedom.

Apart from Christ, these things are true because apart from Christ the reality of the Trinity is disregarded. And where the Trinity is disregarded, the individual and the group are in a kind of philosophical conflict rather than in harmony. It is only in the midst of the multidimensional trinitarian reality that the complexity of being human is able to manifest simultaneously in both its particularity and its corporality.[64] In Christ, or through an increase in conformity to the trinitarian character of Christ, through the imitation of Christ, which is ours by grace through faith (Ephesians 2:8), people find an actual increase of personal freedom through participation in a group. Freedom increases through participation

63 For more on this see *Arsy Varsy—Reclaiming the Gospel in First Corinthians*, Phillip A. Ross, Pilgrim Platform, Marietta, Ohio, 2008, pgs 183-197.

64 *Corporality*: of or related to body. See the ideas of *body* and *body of Christ* that are found throughout *Arsy Varsy—Reclaiming the Gospel in First Corinthians*, ibid.

in the unity of the church or body of Christ.

ADMONITIONS

Paul began here by addressing wives. It is important to see that Paul was speaking to wives and not to women generally. He said, "Wives, submit to your husbands" (v. 18), not women, submit to men. The authority that was to be submitted to was covenantal, not sexual. The source of covenantal authority is the trinitarian God, not husbands. The wife is to submit to the covenant authority of her husband, who is himself to be submitted to the covenant authority of God. How do we know this? Because of the second clause, "as is fitting in the Lord" (v. 18). The idea of being fitting or proper in the Lord pertains to fitting into the array of God's trinitarian character, of being *in Christ*. This phrase, then, means that Paul set this injunction in the light of the whole fabric of God's covenant and applied it to the context of believers in Christ.

This injunction was not given to men (males), and must not be used by men generally or promiscuously. It must not be used by men as a license to impose themselves upon their wives. Too often the unsanctified co-opt God's Word as a means to bully their own will upon others. It is not for the husband to misread these verses and demand submission, but for the wife to give it willingly as an expression of her love and respect for her husband. Authority works best when it is honored. The husband must live honorably if he expects his wife to honor him willingly. Demanding it usually produces conflict, not harmony. We must guard against the temptation to Lord over others through a fruitful reading, a holistic understanding and a careful application of God's Word to ourselves first, foremost and primarily.

Thus, the husband's job is not to earn the honor of his wife, but is to simply love her as Christ loved the church (Ephesians 5:25). Paul also spoke to this issue: "Husbands, love your wives, and do not be harsh with them" (v. 19). Remember that love is the penultimate characteristic of faithfulness. So, Paul's call for husbands to love their wives is a call to faithfulness in the most intimate human relationship—marriage. Marriage can only thrive in the midst of genuine honesty, compassion, kindness, humility, meekness, patience, forbearance and forgiveness (Colossians 3:13). Marriage is the primary theater in which faithfulness is manifest, or not. This is not to suggest that only married people can be saved, but only that marriage is the most common and most valuable relationship with regard to personal sanctification and covenant faithfulness.

Because children are the natural fruit of marriage and are fully vested in the family, Paul then turned his attention to them. "Children, obey your parents in everything, for this pleases the Lord" (v. 20). Paul was here speaking to those who are under the care and jurisdiction of the family, to those who are unmarried, who are not responsible adults (who are able to care for themselves). While children are directed to simple compliance with their parents' instructions, the justification for their compliance has little to do with the parents. Rather, the reason that children are to be obedient to their parents is because it pleases the Lord. The children are not to comply in order to please their parents, but to please the Lord. The parents are simply a cog in God's chain of command.

Parents are not to demand compliance to their own whims, but are to bring their children up "in the nurture and admonition of the Lord" (Ephesians 6:4—Authorized Version), endeavoring to teach respect and honor, through their own obedience to the Lord, and thereby earning respect and honor from their children. Again, the source of the authority in the family is not the family, nor the father, but the Lord. Families are God's idea. Families are not necessary for human life or culture. Children can be born and raised without families. But God's plan is for children to be raised in Christian families. Why Christian families and not Pagan, Hindu, Buddhist, Jewish, Islamic or secular families? Because only Christianity provides the whole truth regarding the Trinity, which allows human culture to bloom into its full potential through the development of science and technology.[65] The failure to understand and teach the fullness and intricacies of God's trinitarian character tends to flatten out the full potential for the development of human character, both the character of individuals and the character of cultures.

But why refer to civil government in this context? Because the family is the cradle of civilization. It is the model for the church, for human culture and society, and civil government is a necessary element of human culture. The success and longevity of human culture requires representative government with the distribution of

---

65 See The *Victory of Reason: How Christianity Led to Freedom, Capitalism, and Western Success*, by Rodney Stark, New York: Random House, 2005; also *Rock Mountain Creed—Jesus' Sermon on the Mount*, by Phillip A. Ross, Pilgrim Platform, 2010; and *Christos Promptus—Peter's Vision*, by Phillip A. Ross, 2011.

power, as the American Founders understood. Such a system mitigates the dangers of sinful people abusing power.

How so? Monotheism tends toward totalitarianism, and polytheism tends toward anarchy. Monotheism fails to account for the ultimate texture and particularity of reality, and polytheism fails to account for the ultimate unity of enduring things (kinds, species) and the interdependence of all things. Whereas trinitarianism tends toward representative government. Representative government alone respects the biblical reality of the hierarchy of all authority, and apart from respect for the hierarchy, authority cannot function. Totalitarianism abuses authority by amassing it at the top of the chain, and ultimately abusing it. Anarchy ignores authority, which destroys it.

Paul continued, "Fathers, provoke not your children to anger, lest they be discouraged" (v. 21). This is Paul's second admonition to men, given first to husbands and now to fathers. No other family member has received this much attention in this section of Scripture. Apparently, fathers are easily tempted to provoke their children, and such provocation easily discourages children. The word provoke (*erethizō*) in this context suggests contention, debate, and strife. In addition, the discouragement (*athumeō*) that Paul mentions leaves the children spiritless and disheartened.

Given the massive defection of Christian children from the faith, from Christian churches and homes, it appears that we are currently in the midst of an epidemic of provocation and discouragement. It also appears that, because fathers have the negative responsibility to *not* provoke their children into what is essentially faithlessness, fathers also have the positive responsibility to encourage their children into faithfulness. The responsibility of passing the Christian faith to the children belongs to the father. This is the father's primary responsibility. And it is this failure on a large scale that has allowed the acidic culture of godlessness to thrive in our day.[66]

SERVICE

Paul's instructions regarding family authority were not limited to the nuclear family, but included the extended family—even slaves or servants. "Slaves, obey in everything those who are your

---

66 For resources on Christian family recovery see www.VisionForum.com and other materials on the family integrated church model.

earthly masters, not by way of eye-service, as people-pleasers, but with sincerity of heart, fearing the Lord" (v. 22). Interestingly, the Authorized Version translates *doulos* as *servants*, where the contemporary English Standard Version translates it as *slaves*. The root of the Greek word is *deō*, which literally means to bind.

The idea is that the ideal Christian is a servant leader, which in the ancient world was an oxymoron. Ancient leaders did not understand themselves to be servants. Nonetheless, Christian service was to take the lead regarding the promotion of Christ in the midst of all circumstances. That is to be the calling of all Christians. But it was an oxymoron in the ancient world because servants didn't lead and leaders didn't serve. Nonetheless, the kingdom of God reverses the values of the world—the first will be last and the last will be first (Matthew 19:30).

There is a sense, then, that all Christians should live in obedience to this verse, even though it is directed toward servants. We should all "obey in everything those who are (our) earthly masters, not by way of eye-service, as people-pleasers, but with sincerity of heart, fearing the Lord" (v. 22). We are all to honor the hierarchical nature of authority.

The allusion to eye-service and people-pleasers refers to the same thing, to doing a job, not on the basis of the work required to do a good job but on the basis of making it seem as if a good job has been done when it hasn't. It is a caution against the shallowness of "looking good" and "glad handing," rather than sincerely applying one's self to the work at hand. This verse gives directions to workers, to slaves and servants. It is a work-oriented admonition.

Work should be done with "sincerity of heart, fearing the Lord" (v. 22). To work sincerely (*haplotēs*) is to work with a single focused heart and mind. It is to work without dissimulation or self-seeking, and to do so generously. It means keeping your attention on the work at hand. Working in the fear of the Lord is an allusion to working with wisdom because fear is the beginning of wisdom. It is wise to work in the fear of the Lord.

However, Paul doesn't mean that people should cower in dreadful fear of being hammered by God. Rather, he means working in such a way as to avoid God's judgment by doing the job right. If you are an engineer, it means correct analysis, measurements, procedures, etc., so that what you build is built correctly. It means using righteous weights and measures. It means applying honesty and integrity to one's work.

Paul has been showing how regeneration in Christ by the power and presence of the Holy Spirit, who is a member of the Trinity, provides for the longevity and sustainability of human culture through covenant obedience. Covenantal fidelity is the glue or unity of human culture. It binds together husbands and wives, parents and children, churches and members, workers and bosses, governments and citizens, individuals and God. God's covenant holds everything human together. All human agreements are held together in or on the basis of God's covenant. God shows us how to keep our agreements.

CƺƑƆ

Human culture or society is actually held together by promises. All legal agreements, contracts, debts—even money itself—are nothing but promises. Some promises are more important than others because of their centrality to human life. The two central promises that hold human societies together are 1) God's promise, His covenant with humanity through Jesus Christ, and 2) marriage, our covenant with God. Yes, marriage is a trinitarian partnership. To leave God out of marriage is like trying to sit on a two-legged stool. *Christos Singularis!*

19

CALLING, CLAIMING, COMPLETING

*And whatever you do, do it heartily, as to the Lord and not
to men; knowing that from the Lord you shall receive the
reward of the inheritance. For you serve the Lord Christ.
But he who does wrong shall receive justice for the wrong
which he did, and there is no respect of persons.*
                                        —*Colossians 3:23-25 (ESV)*

P aul now suggested that all he has been talking about applies to
work, employment, occupation and calling. Regeneration, the
death of the old self and the birth of the new, abandoning the
characteristics of sin and taking up the characteristics of love, and
the biblical structures of authority all apply to work. This chapter
calls men, women, children and servants[67] to engage everything
("whatever you do") heartily or with "singleness of heart" (v. 23,
Authorized Version). To do a thing heartily is to do it with all one's
heart. And because men were the primary workers it applied mostly
to men.

The Greek that is translated as *heartily* is composed of two
words, *ek* and *psuchē*. It is an allusion to the physical, bodily experience of breathing hard, of being heart-pounding-out-of-breath. It is a
symbol of exertion, of hard work and of passion that is the result of a
single-minded focus on the accomplishment of something. Paul has
provided the internal, subjective tools for working in the kingdom of
God.

God is a worker. Creation itself is a fruit of God's work, God's
labor. The Sabbath was established as a reminder of God's commitment to work. God's rest, and ours, provides the opportunity to eval-

---

67 Including extended family members, which for our purposes here includes one's
Christian brothers and sisters.

uate and reflect upon our work. Having been created in God's image, we too are workers. So, God gives us work to do as our primary objective, both as individuals and as a whole, as a family, as business, as a church and culture. In Christ we understand our work Christologically and trinitarianally (if I may coin a word). The majority of our week is given to work. Our work as Christians, both individually and culturally, is to be God-centered or Trinity-center-ed, which means that there are three centers corresponding to the Father, the Son and the Holy Spirit, to the universal, the particular and the actual, to use a philosophical analogy. Therefore, a man's calling or purpose for work is universal, particular and actual. Whatever work we engage in, we are to engage it with these three coequal, independent but overlapping emphases.[68]

HEY YOU!

Paul has issued a call to Christian ministry that is universal, particular and actual, but not in the sense that most people have thought of it historically. It is not simply a call to the pastorate. People are not equally gifted. Rather, "there are varieties of gifts, but the same Spirit" (1 Corinthians 12:4). The universal aspect of this call applies to everyone and is a call to work for the Lord in one way or another. The particular aspect of this call applies to each individual in different ways as individuals exercise their unique gifts. And the actual aspect of the call points to the reality of the call and the reality of the work.

Hard work apart from compulsion was not the norm for ancient cultures or peoples. It is not that such people did not work hard, they most certainly did. But they didn't appreciate it. Work was a necessity, not an endeavor of love. For the most part, people worked hard in order to escape the necessity for hard work. Leisure was the goal, not purposeful work in the service of the kingdom of God. The world has yet to rise above this godless attitude.

It was not until the Protestant Reformation that all forms of work began to be understood as a calling, and even then only a few people actually practiced this biblical ideal. Nonetheless, Luther rightly honored it and provided theological and biblical justification for it in his book, *The Babylonian Captivity of the Church* (1520). Someday Christ's church will escape from this captivity, and the kingdom of God will begin to flower on earth as it flowers in

---

68 Be careful about putting too much stock in analogies. They are useful, but only to a point.

Heaven. Paul emphasized this by calling people to "work heartily, as for the Lord and not for men" (v. 23). This work that Paul referred to is the central purpose of man, male and female, individually and culturally. We are called to work for God in Christ through the Holy Spirit, and to do so heartily. "For God is not unjust so as to overlook your work and the love that you have shown for his name in serving the saints, as you still do" (Hebrews 6:10).

Our work, our labor, is to be "for the Lord and not for men" (v. 23). Here Paul called attention to the universal, eternal and divine aspects of human labor that are to be engaged in the midst of particular, time oriented (secular)[69] and human tasks. In Christ universality and particularity are held together in creative tension through the Holy Spirit in actuality.

Paul was not saying that Christians should not be employees, that Christians should only work for themselves and not for other people—not at all. Rather, Paul's point was that we should strive to please God in all things, to please God in the little things, to work as if God is the boss, as if God Himself will inspect our work. We are not to disrespect or disregard those we work for, nor those who work for us. Rather, we are to respect and regard God in everything, not just the spiritual things, not just in the church things or the religious things, but in everything.

God does not expect people to work for nothing. There are many reasons that people need to work and one of them is to provide sustenance. The Psalmist said, "Blessed is everyone who fears the Lord, who walks in his ways! You shall eat the fruit of the labor of your hands; you shall be blessed, and it shall be well with you" (Psalm 128:2). Jesus said that "the laborer deserves his wages" (Luke 10:7). Money is essential for the accomplishment of work. Money is not a bad or evil thing. It is, in fact, a godly thing. It is a thing that has been created by God for our benefit. It is a blessing when used correctly, according to God's principles. And it is a curse when it is abused.

INHERITANCE

Paul continued, "knowing that from the Lord you will receive the inheritance as your reward" (v. 24). Inheritance is a common

---

69 *Secular*: Characteristic of or devoted to the temporal world as opposed to the spiritual world. Secularism abandons the ideal, spiritual and universal elements of trinitarian reality usually associated with God by focusing on the practical, physical and particular aspects.

biblical theme. It is mentioned almost two hundred times and it almost always refers to the transfer of the estate of a decedent. Hebrews speaks of an "eternal inheritance" (Hebrews 9:15) and Peter speaks of "an inheritance that is imperishable" (1 Peter 1:4); the Authorized Version translated it as *incorruptible* (*aphthartos*).

Christianity has spiritualized the idea of eternal inheritance, and rightly so because of the biblical emphasis upon resurrection and eternal life with God in Heaven. However, given the trinitarian nature of reality, Heaven is not the only dimension in which this inheritance will manifest in Christ. The kingdom of God brings Heaven and earth together. Not only do people go to Heaven, but Christ has inaugurated Heaven on earth. Heaven is in Heaven and not currently on earth because that is where God's will is done perfectly. Heaven is coming to earth and we anticipate it as we pray that God's will be done on earth as it is in Heaven (Matthew 6:10). All of this is to suggest that this inheritance, as it has been used by Paul, is not merely heavenly, but is also earthly. There is an earthly element to it. "The earth is the Lord's and the fullness thereof" (Psalm 24:1).

The original inheritance idea from the Old Testament was about inheriting the land of milk and honey, a land that was occupied by others. "And you shall not walk in the customs of the nation that I am driving out before you, for they did all these things, and therefore I detested them. But I have said to you, 'You shall inherit their land, and I will give it to you to possess, a land flowing with milk and honey.' I am the Lord your God, who has separated you from the peoples" (Leviticus 20:23-24).

The long story of the Bible is that the estate of the Lord has been bequeathed to God's children in Christ. In Christ, the meek shall inherit the earth (Matthew 5:5). In Christ, people who leave their estates in the service of Jesus Christ "will inherit eternal life" (Matthew 19:29). Capitalizing on this theme, Jesus told the rich young ruler when he asked how to inherit eternal life, "Do not murder, Do not commit adultery, Do not steal, Do not bear false witness, Do not defraud. Honor your father and mother." But the rich young ruler lacked "one thing," said Jesus: "go, sell all that you have and give to the poor, and you will have treasure in heaven; and come, follow me" (Mark 10:19-21). The rich young ruler had been blinded by his wealth. So, the log in his eye that had to be removed to cure his blindness was his wealth, his preoccupation with money. Pray that you are not like the rich young ruler.

So, what is the eternal inheritance that does not perish that God gives to His children in Christ? It's not a thing. It's not land. It's not wealth or crops or intelligence. Nor is it earned wages for services performed. Peter got it right when he wrote:

> As obedient children, do not be conformed to the passions of your former ignorance, but as he who called you is holy, you also be holy in all your conduct, since it is written, 'You shall be holy, for I am holy.' And if you call on him as Father who judges impartially according to each one's deeds, conduct yourselves with fear throughout the time of your exile, knowing that you were ransomed from the futile ways inherited from your forefathers, not with perishable things such as silver or gold, but with the precious blood of Christ, like that of a lamb without blemish or spot (1 Peter 1:14-19).

While it may appear that Peter was writing to Jewish Christians, perhaps converts from the *diaspora*, and there were certainly many such Christians to whom Peter was undoubtedly writing, there are also strong indications that most of the Christians to whom Peter wrote were former Pagans, not Jews. So, to interpret Peter to have been speaking of another Jewish exile is to miss the main point, that point being that Peter was speaking to those who were in Christ. Judaism was a thing of the past for Peter. The Spirit of God was gathering people up in Christ through regeneration.

Nonetheless, Peter did mean to say that Christianity would exist in exile because Christianity, like Christ Himself, "has nowhere to lay his (the church's) head" (Matthew 8:20). Jesus told Pilate, "My kingdom is not of this world" (John 18:36), which means that Christ's kingdom does not originate in this world, nor is it like the kingdoms of this world. The contrast that Jesus provided concerned kingdom defense. "If my kingdom were of this world, my servants would have been fighting, that I might not be delivered over to the Jews" (John 18:36). God's kingdom is trinitarian. It is coming into the world through Christ, but it is not of the world.

KINGDOM

Worldly kingdoms are created and defended by arms and military might, by courts and laws, by flags and finances. The kingdom of God is different. It is of a different order, a different kind. Most Christians believe that God's kingdom is heavenly and has no actual presence or application on earth. But because of the trinitarian nature of God, of His kingdom, of His covenant and of His world—this world—not only is the kingdom near (Luke 10:9, 21:31), but the kingdom is also here in Christ (Luke 17:21). The kingdom has been growing like a mustard seed (Matthew 13:31-32) for a long time now.

What does it mean to have the kingdom of God manifest in the world in Christ? It's hard to say, which means that it is not impossible to say, but that saying it and hearing it in such a way as to understand it is demanding. It's hard. God's kingdom is a big deal. It is a big idea, an ultimate concern. So, it requires big thoughts and complex explanations because truth is big, complex and ultimate. Truth is not suited to sound bites and photo ops. It cannot be reduced to slogans or political campaigns. Rather, it requires study and discipline, concentration and patience, practice and perseverance.

"For the gate is narrow and the way is hard (*thlibō*) that leads to life, and those who find it are few" (Matthew 7:14), unlike the other gate, which "is wide and the way is easy that leads to destruction, and those who enter by it are many" (Matthew 7:13). Contrary to popular opinion, this does not mean that only a few people can find the way or that only a few people actually go to heaven. Both verses 13 and 14 contain the Greek word *autos*, which has a self-contained or self-reflective sense. The comparison that Jesus was making was about the inherent problem of self-dependence that must be overcome in order to enter heaven or to do God's will.

The context of these verses is a discussion of God's gift of grace. The Father only gives good gifts to His children (Matthew 7:11). His point was that many people find the broad way all by themselves because people who are self-dependent cannot escape the constraints of sin. Heaven is closed to the self-dependent. In contrast, those who find the narrow gate that leads to eternal life on their own, without God's help, are small minded. They have limited sight and limited light because of their self-dependence. The gate that leads to eternal life cannot be found apart from God's gifts. So, the self-dependent cannot find it. And those who claim to have done so are false prophets. Indeed, Jesus went on to talk about false prophets in this context.

A better translation of these verses might be something like: *Enter by the narrow gate. For the gate is wide and the way is easy that leads to destruction, and those who enter by it on their own are many. For the gate is narrow and the way is hard that leads to life, and those who find it on their own are self-limited.* Indeed, they are false prophets.

The Greek word translated *hard* (*thlibō*), which is also translated as straightened, narrow, confined, constricted and compressed, literally suggests being crowded together. The kingdom is not limited by the idea of size because the kingdom of God is not merely physical. It is not confined to the physical idea of size. The gate, of course, is narrow because Jesus is the only way. It is only by the gift of God's grace through the propitiation of Jesus Christ on the cross that opens heaven. And self-dependence or self-justification, even though it may seem like the right thing for people to do, actually closes the gate.

Rather, the kingdom of God is trinitarian because God is trinitarian and it is His kingdom. The character of the kingdom reflects the character of the King. The kingdom of God touches on physical space but is not limited by it. It is heavenly in the sense of being ultimate, of being furthest or highest in degree or order. It's a quality, state or condition of being, not merely a place. The idea of heaven suggests a degree or grade of excellence or worth. The idea of Heaven being a place above the sky, for instance, is a statement of degree as well as location. Heaven is above, superior, and primary in relationship to the earth.

The idea that heaven is simply a place above the sky involves the wrong assumptions that produce a flawed reading and understanding of Scripture that results in what Alfred North Whitehead called, the fallacy of misplaced concreteness.[70] The popular idea of Heaven is more a product of Greek philosophy than biblical theology. And as long as the academy controls the categories of biblical analysis for the church, Christians will continue in the errors of abstract analysis (Greek, Western, Modern, Postmodern, etc.). Only when the categories of biblical analysis are grounded in and generated from the trinitarian character of God and His Christ through the power and presence of the Holy Spirit will the church and her people be free in Christ to see what God is revealing in Scripture, to understand what God has given, and to be what God has created

---

70 Alfred North Whitehead, *An Enquiry Concerning the Principles of Natural Knowledge,* 1919; and *Science and the Modern World,* 1925. Whitehead was not a Christian philosopher, nor did he argue from a biblical perspective. Nonetheless, unbelievers also live in the world that God created, and this insight is helpful.

His people to be.

Heaven (the kingdom of God) exists, not in abstraction, but in actuality. However the actuality in which Heaven exists is the trinitarian actuality of God in Christ, and simultaneously at the ultimacy of God's trinitarian being. It permeates the dimensions of God's trinitarian reality, and God's reality is trinitarian. It reflects His character. That is to say that philosophically reality has three dimensions: universality, particularity and time, where the prototype (kind or species) is universal, every instance of the prototype (individuals) is particular, and time is a measurement of motion in space.

Reality can only be understood as the ultimate final or concluding state or condition of the universe, of time and history, because reality is the totality of being which can only be perceived in terms of its own end or conclusion. The process of arriving at the conclusion of the ultimate purpose of reality (or God) is too complex, too large, too much for mere humans to conceive, perceive or process. The kingdom of God is the final goal, purpose, perfection and end of history.

Heaven is the abode or kingdom of God that has come to earth through and in Jesus Christ, and is growing through Christ. Its establishment is the means of Christ's return, Christ's manifestation. The establishment and maintenance of the kingdom is the work of God's Holy Spirit through God's people. This trinitarian reality is the only reality that actually exists. Other explanations of reality are just that—explanations, merely "waterless clouds, swept along by winds; fruitless trees in late autumn" (Jude 12).

Of course, Heaven or the kingdom of God is ultimately mysterious in that it cannot be fully known or understood by our finite minds. However, its ultimate mystery does not mean that it is completely unknown or unknowable. For *in Christ* the kingdom is both near and here. It is both already and not yet. "Repent," said Jesus, "for the kingdom of heaven is at hand" (Matthew 4:17). It is past, present and future at the same time because it is both outside of and inside of time and space. It is apart from time and space, different than time and space, and yet within time and space. And the time to realize the reality of God's kingdom is now (2 Corinthians 6:2)! Now is time in motion. The kingdom is in the world like Christ is us who are in God: "that they may all be one, just as you, Father, are in me, and I in you, that they also may be in us, so that the world may believe that you have sent me" (John 17:21).

Inasmuch as you are engaged in this work, implied Paul, "You are serving the Lord Christ" (v. 24). This whole thing, what Paul has described in chapter three comprehensively, is what it means to be engaged in the service of Christ.

JUDGMENT

The final verse of this chapter appears to be an odd addition. "For the wrongdoer will be paid back for the wrong he has done, and there is no partiality" (v. 25). The general idea of the verse is that doing wrong brings or results in injustice. The accumulation of injustice in history will eventually bring God's judgment. Now add to this the idea that God is no respecter of persons. No individual or group of people have immunity from God's judgment. As Paul discussed the manifestation of Jesus Christ, the necessity of dealing with God's judgment came to mind.

What does this final verse have to do with the rest of the chapter? Paul has been arguing that regeneration, the death of the old self and the birth of the new self in Christ, is ground zero for the Christian faith. He lists the character traits that must be abandoned in Christ—sexual immorality, impurity, passion, evil desire, and covetousness, which is idolatry (Colossians 3:5), anger, wrath, malice, slander, and obscene talk (Colossians 3:8). Then Paul lists those characteristics that need to be put on—compassion, kindness, humility, meekness, patience, forbearance, forgiveness and love (vs. 12-14).

To indicate that these are not mere abstractions or characteristics that awaited God's people in some distant Heaven, Paul put them in the context of ordinary family and work experiences, showing how these characteristics structure every element of family life and work habits—human productivity. He then closed the chapter with this verse about how doing the wrong things, or doing things wrongly, creates injustice and eventually results in God's judgment.

Wrong provides for or produces more wrong. These wrongs, if left uncorrected add up, and will eventually result in God's judgment, which comes without partiality for persons or human traditions. This last verse was not only shocking to Jewish and Pagan sensibilities, but is shocking to Christian sensibilities as well because it suggests that God's judgment can bleed into the church.

Christ's church, His resurrected body (Colossians 1:24), regeneration in Christ, provides the only way to avoid God's judgment through forgiveness of sin and righteous living. There are the two sides of the gospel coin. The gospel is not just about forgiveness on the one side, but it is also about new life in Christ, the putting on of the various characteristics Paul listed on the other. The forgiveness side is a matter of justification and is a done deal, completed by God's grace through Christ in the heavenlies. Christ sealed the deal with His blood on the cross in history. Justification is by grace alone.

The Lord also guaranteed that all of His people would be swept up in the cascade of regeneration through the dispensation of the Holy Spirit. This is the sanctification side of the gospel coin. It is *through* faith, not *by* faith. "For by grace you have been saved through faith. And this is not your own doing; it is the gift of God" (Ephesians 2:8).

But, while justification happens outside of time and is the action of God, sanctification happens in time and is the action of the Holy Spirit. And because sanctification happens in time, in history, it is a more messy process because there is a time related leeching or porosity or overlapping of the categories that distinguish the new life from the old.

There is never a clean break between the old self and the new self from a trinitarian perspective because of the overlap of identity between the particular and the universal (between the individual and the social elements of human identity). During the transitional time period there is a Romans 7 struggle between the old and the new identities. The reality of that struggle exposes the church, exposes God's people who are in the process of sanctification, to various expressions of God's judgment against sin. It is a judgment against the accumulation of sin in history.

Not only were the ancient Israelites liable to God's judgment for their various failures to engage God historically and faithfully, as were and are all of the various religions (human traditions) of the world, but Christ's church itself, just as the Temple before it, is not immune from the judgment of God. Therefore, said Paul, it is incumbent upon Christ's people to get the gospel right, which means right belief, right practice and right expression.

Paul's vision revealed to him the reality of the ancient struggle for sovereignty between God and humanity. It wasn't merely a struggle between the Jews and the Gentiles, but between God and humanity. Paul noted that "not all who are descended from Israel belong to Israel" (Romans 9:6), and similarly (and conversely) all

Gentiles do not belong to Satan, based on the extension of that Romans 9:6 principle and the New Man/Old Man struggle of Romans 7. Remember also that those who are being saved have been called "before the foundations of the world" (Ephesians 1:4). They were and are being saved out of other religions (and out of no religion) into Christ. "There is neither Jew nor Greek, there is neither slave nor free, there is no male and female, for you are all one in Christ Jesus" (Galatians 3:28).

The categories of human divisions are being done away with in Christ. In Christ the Old has died and the New is born. These categories (Jew, Greek, slave, free, male, female, etc.) are destined to resolve into the realization of the unity of the trinitarian Godhead manifest in Christ, in history, in the world. *In Christ* the old categories are obsolete.

Jerusalem had been destroyed twice, generations before Paul came on the scene, and various Jews had been carried off into the Gentile nations generations before Paul. Some of them had been faithful, some had not. But the result had been intermarriage and interbreeding throughout the Middle East. The Samaritans were one such a racially mixed group.

Today, not only are the geographic borders between nations increasingly fluid, but the genetic differences between the so-called races or nationalities continue to mix. Also add to this the mixing and confusion of the various national and historic cultures that has come about with the advent of modern science and technology because of modern communication and travel. This mixing, this confusion of these old categories is not a bad thing if it resolves in Christ. Inasmuch as it fails to resolve in Christ, our world is liable to God's impending judgment. That is what Paul was saying to the Colossian church of his time. And it is still applicable to the church in our time, as well.

Paul's vision was not about Jews and Christians. Rather, Christ put an end to all human classifications by stepping into history and claiming the whole world and all of humanity for the God of Scripture. This vision would take time to unfold, of course. And it continues to unfold even today. Christ is not finished with the world. However, people—individuals and groups—have been hanging on to their previous identities (old identities, the Old Man) more tenaciously than Paul thought they would. Consequently, the establishment of the kingdom has tarried beyond Paul's expectation.[71]

The transition from the old to the new self had been relatively fast and clean for Paul. Of course, he had his struggles and difficulties, which he shared freely (Romans 7). Nonetheless, Paul's vision of the end (*telios*), purpose or final goal of a united humanity under God in Christ has turned out to be a much larger vision than anyone has yet expected. It remains a distant goal, but has not faded as the preeminent goal of Jesus Christ. That is the work of the kingdom that lies before us.

CȜ℘

Because God is not bound by time, He is not concerned about time, about how long it will take. He is aiming for perfection, but knows where we human beings are coming from. So, He is patient and graceful beyond our wildest imaginations in order to get it right. Each person participates in God's plan in one way or another. Ultimately, people are either in or out of God's kingdom. God's covenant is like marriage, and people are either married or they are not. Yet being married is a process of give and take, of highs and lows, of joys and sorrows. *Christos Singularis!*

---

71 This may have surprised Paul, but it did not surprise God. See Matthew 25:1-ff and 2 Peter 3:9.

20

CLARITY IN CHRIST

*Masters, give to your slaves what is just and equal,
knowing that you also have a Master in Heaven. Continue
in prayer and watch in it with thanksgiving, praying
together about us also, that God may open to us a door of
the Word, to speak the mystery of Christ, for which I also
have been bound, that I may make it clear, as I ought to
speak. Walk in wisdom toward those on the outside,
redeeming the time.* —Colossians 4:1-5 (ESV)

Work is so important that Paul continued to address it. Of course, he was speaking about more than mere work, but by addressing masters and slaves he focused on the various issues and relationships associated with slavery. I am suggesting that today we can best understand Paul's comments by applying them to work because for the most part that was the purpose of slavery. So, rather than dismiss Paul's concerns about slavery because we think that slavery has been abandoned in the Twenty-First Century, it is more productive to apply Paul's comments about slavery to work relationships, to employers and employees.

Paul's concern was that masters (employers) treat their slaves (employees) justly and fairly. Obviously, Paul was not limiting such treatment to only masters and slaves, but would extend this call for justice and fairness to all human relationships. Nonetheless, his focus here was on work relationships, probably because the relationship between masters and slaves (employers and employees) are so easy to abuse because of the perceived difference in values and status. Social equals are more likely to make the effort to be just and fair with each other because of their status parity. CEOs of different companies are more likely to treat each other as equals than a CEO and a janitor.

Why should a CEO treat a janitor with justice and fairness when everything about them proclaims inequality? They are not equally educated, not equally connected, not equally gifted, nor equally paid. It appears that they likely have very little in common. Everything in society accents their differences, the superiority of one and the inferiority of the other. Similarly, what do masters and slaves have in common? Only their humanity, and that is exactly why Paul directed masters to treat their slaves fairly and justly. The point Paul was making was their common humanity.

The primary reason for this emphasis is given in the last phrase of the verse, "knowing that you also have a Master in heaven" (v. 1). The Roman Centurion understood what it means to be under authority (Matthew 8:9). Paul pointed out their common humanity, their equality under Christ. Both master and slave on earth are under Christ in heaven. Both are called to be servants—slaves—in Christ (Matthew 20:27). In Christ masters are slaves and slaves are free (1 Corinthians 7:22). Christians are to treat others as we would have others treat us (Luke 6:31)—all others, not just some.

PRAYER

"Continue steadfastly in prayer, being watchful in it with thanksgiving" (v. 2). Some commentators think that this verse is connected with the previous verse and some don't. Some think that it is a general admonition to pray among believers, and no argument can be made against such a position. Believers should pray together regularly, watchfully and thankfully. Yet verse 2 does follow verse 1, so there is also reason to assume that they are connected. Indeed, masters and slaves (employers and employees) should pray together if they are both believers because praying together will bring them both closer to the Lord and to one another.

The opportunity to pray can be offered. But if it is refused, if one of the parties does not want to engage in prayer with the other, the believer should pray privately for the unbeliever anyway. The believer should not impose upon the unbeliever, but should simply lift the unbeliever up as a prayer concern in private, apart from the unbeliever, if the unbeliever is not interested.

Praying with or for those we have contact with is a good thing. Christians should pray for God's blessings to be with those we have contact with, and especially those we work with. We need to pray that God's blessings will lead people to Christ. If however, someone is actively engaged in unrepentant sin, then our prayers must be that God will chastise such a person (Deuteronomy 28:15), but only enough to make them open and receptive to the gospel of Jesus Christ, enough to see the wisdom of God's way.

I am not suggesting that Christians themselves make an effort to personally chastise unbelievers for unbelief—heaven forbid! There is plenty of pain and chastisement in the world without adding to it as some kind of mistaken and wrong-headed method of evangelism or as an effort to establish or purify God's kingdom. Just as vengeance belongs to the Lord, so the Lord will judge His people (Hebrews 10:30). We must always take care to engage in judgment according to Christ's policies (Acts 10:42).[72]

While it is true that Christians are to engage in discipleship and discipline, and that discipleship relationships involve chastisement (*paideia*),[73] correction (*epanorthōsis*) and encouragement (*parakaleō*), such things should not be engaged apart from personal commitment to God's covenant by all those involved. They should also be engaged under the authority of a church and by those trained and commissioned for it. We cannot shove Christian practices and values down the throats of unwilling people (1 Corinthians 5:4-5). Such efforts tend to backfire and end up doing more harm than good.

LOVE

Of course, we can and we must love our neighbors as we love ourselves (Matthew 19:19), including our enemies and those who persecute us (Mark 5:44). How does that love manifest? In Christ we are free to do good works, to show our love, first for the brethren but also for those outside the fellowship (John 13:35, Galatians 5:13). In order to practice Christian love, we must understand it. Christian love is not unconditional, not mere *agapē*, not mere charity, though charity is involved. Christian love is not mere friendship (*phileō*) or mutual care and concern, though these things are also involved.

Christian love is always more than brotherly love or romantic

---

72 Christians can and should encourage one another and feel free to discuss Christian issues. Discipline, however, must be exercised only within the bounds of church membership and by those who are charged with such responsibility (elders). If Christians have an issue that requires resolution, and they cannot resolve it themselves, then they should seek the counsel of their elders.

73 For more on this see: *Varsy Arsy—Proclaiming the Gospel in Second Corinthians*, Phillip A. Ross, Pilgrim Platform, Marietta, Ohio, p. 128.

love or even commitment and service to humanity. Christian love necessarily involves Christ. Christian love is, first and foremost, love of Christ, which is love of God and of God's Holy Spirit. Christian love is trinitarian love. It is love of God, love of Christ and love of God's activities and involvement in the world through the Person of the Holy Spirit. The trinitarian character of Christian love insures that it is always actively manifest in the world through the works and actions of God's people through regeneration. But it also demands that the first and highest object of our love is Jesus Christ.

This is where Humanism fails. Humanism can never produce more than self-love, whether individual or corporate, which is nothing more than pride. Why is Humanism always a function of self-love? Because it ignores and denies Jesus Christ. Because it amounts to humanity loving humanity, whereas Christianity is humanity loving God in response to God's love for humanity. Humanism does not and cannot give glory to God apart from God's judgment against it.

This is why pride is so emphasized in our contemporary humanistic world. In contrast, Christian love always means more than promoting human welfare. Of course, it is good to promote human welfare, and Christian love always includes it and never neglects it. In contrast, Christian love is always centered first and foremost in the glory of God. Christian love is engaged, not for the self-directed purposes of human welfare, but in sacrificial service to the glory of God.

The sacrifice involved in Christian love engages the personal willingness to risk one's own life and limb for the cause of Christ. It is a function of giving, not getting.[74] Terrorist bombers who blow themselves up in the service of Allah are themselves filled with their own self-importance and the pride of personal self-fulfillment through the exercise of lust, greed and gluttony in the hope to receive Allah's supposed heavenly rewards for their sacrifice. But they know nothing of the meaning of Christian sacrifice. It's easy to die for a cause, but it is much more difficult and much more rewarding in this life and the next to live for Christ's cause.

NOBILITY

There is no other cause more noble, where nobility is defined

---

74 See *Marking God's Word—Understand Jesus*, Phillip A. Ross, Pilgrim Platform, 2007, second edition, p. 162-ff, "Take Up Your Cross."

and exercised as a function of Christian love. Genuine nobility is not the self-importance and pomposity found in the history of human nobility, of kings and empires. The historic noble classes of every time and every continent have gotten the idea of nobility wrong. Genuine nobility—Christian nobility because there really is no other—is the nobility of sacrifice and service as Jesus Himself understood and practiced it.

Genuine nobility was never a function of birth or blood. That was the error that the Old Testament Jews had made. God closed the door on that misunderstanding by destroying the Temple and scattering Israel in A.D. 70. Genuine nobility is always a function of God's grace manifest first and foremost in Jesus Christ and through Christ or in Christ to the world. Christian nobility is not a matter of inheritance by blood, but of inheritance by God's grace. Paul had been encouraging the idea of the nobility of work by teaching people how to work for Christ in all that they do. Nobility is the privilege of working for Christ, *in Christ*. Here Paul taught the nobility of continuing "steadfastly in prayer, (and) being watchful in it with thanksgiving" (v. 2).

"At the same time," said Paul, "pray also for us, that God may open to us a door for the word, to declare the mystery of Christ, on account of which I am in prison—that I may make it clear, which is how I ought to speak" (vs. 3-4). Paul's allusion to prison was a double entendre. He was likely in prison at some point before, after or during the time he wrote this letter. Nonetheless, the Greek word (*deō*) is a verb that literally means to bind.

Paul was not simply saying that he was in prison because of his commitment to Christ, though that was true. He was also saying that in Christ he was bound to speak the mystery of Christ, and he wanted prayer to enable him to speak it clearly. He was a bond slave to Christ (Romans 1:1, 6:22). Sure, Paul was in prison, but he wasn't in prison because of what Rome had done to him. He was in prison because of what Christ had done to him. Of this he was certain. He did not lament being a slave to Christ, he rejoiced in it.

MYSTERY

Paul was praying for a "door of utterance" (v. 3—Authorized Version). The English Standard Version translates it as "door for the word" because the Greek word is *logos* and is usually translated as *word*. Paul wanted an opportunity, not for himself, but for the

Word of God. Of course the Word of God does not manifest apart from human means. So, he knew that the purpose of such an opportunity would be for him "to declare the mystery of Christ" (v. 3) as an agent of God's Word.

The Gnostics and too many Christians have completely misunderstood what Paul meant by mystery (*mustērion*), mostly because they have approached it with the categories of Greek philosophy. Vine says that the word *mystery* points to "that which, being outside the range of unassisted natural apprehension, can be made known only by divine revelation."[75] The word Paul used is a variation of *muō*, which means to shut the mouth. This is where they get the idea that it is a secret. The idea that Paul was communicating was not that this mystery is a secret, but that it cannot be merely spoken, that it transcends language and the human intellect. It cannot be conveyed from one individual sinner to another by merely speaking, writing or any other means. Its source is God alone—the trinitarian God of Christianity.

To say that its source is the trinitarian God of Christianity means that all of the various aspects of the Trinity are involved in such a way that neither the individual Persons, nor the wholeness or unity of the Godhead are violated. Some of the analogical categories of the Trinity are: Father, Son, Holy Spirit; universal, particular, actual; spiritual, individual, social. Each of these categories or dimensions are trinitarian because they are inhabited by the Holy Spirit, and the Holy Spirit is never alone. The Trinity never sacrifices particularity for universality, or universality for particularity, but establishes the completeness or wholeness of each at the same time.

The mystery, for which the Gnostics thought that initiation was required, but for which God alone is the source, is regeneration by the power and presence of the Holy Spirit. While grace comes by faith, faith comes by hearing or regeneration, the gift of ears to hear. Regeneration, a work of the Holy Spirit, provides the faith oriented perspective that assumes or presupposes the reality and effectiveness of God in Christ, a reality and effectiveness that changes the life of the believer. The believer's own changed life then becomes the proof of the existence of God that cannot be denied. If the changed life is real, God is real.

---

75 *Vine's Complete Expository Dictionary Of Old And New Testament Words* , E-Sword PC Version, W. E. Vine, Merrill F. Unger, William White, Jr. Thomas Nelson Publishers.

However, regeneration is not like an inoculation. Nor is it magic. Rather, it is mysterious because it opens people up to see more than they can understand, more than they can communicate to others. Paul had spoken much about the veil that kept the Old Testament Jews from seeing the truth of God (2 Corinthians 3). Apart from Christ the Old Testament Jews could not see (discern, perceive, tolerate) the purpose of God's law. It had been veiled because of the horrific consequences of Adam's sin.

DEATH

Adam's sin brought alienation from God, an alienation that will ultimately result in the death of Adam's kind, not in a merely physical sense but in a spiritual or covenantal sense, a trinitarian sense. Adam's death sentence (Genesis 2:17) concerned not the immediate death of the individual but the ultimate death of Adam's humanity, his race or kind. Restitution would require a new kind, a new generation (or a regeneration), a new humanity, a new Spirit, a new covenant. There are various ways to understand and explain this idea of a new humanity.

For instance, Christ's paternal lineage (part of His DNA) came from outside of humanity. Christ is not paternally related to Adam (to humanity), but directly to God Himself (John 1:13) as God's Son. Christ removed the veil by providing the way of salvation, apart from which no one can tolerate the awful specter of the potential destruction of humanity (2 Corinthians 3:14) that, if uncorrected, would result from Adam's sin. This was also part of the great mystery to which Paul alluded.

Paul wanted prayer to help him "make it clear" (v. 4), to make the mystery understandable. Yes, understanding it would require regeneration. Yes, understanding it would require biblical study. Yes, understanding it would require some explanation. Yes, it would require the inspiration of the Holy Spirit. Paul couldn't regenerate anyone, nor could he make people study the Bible. But he could share his own perspective, his own understanding as a person who had been regenerated and who had spent his entire life studying Scripture. He could make it easier for those who followed him by pointing out various biblical landmarks.

He wanted to speak as he "ought to speak" (v. 4), with clarity. *Ought* implies a moral imperative. Paul was morally bound to speak clearly, plainly, and not to intentionally hide or obscure anything. However, this mystery of God is a big topic. It's a large idea that had been in process for thousands of years before Paul came on the scene. So, there was a lot to consider. Add the trinitarian aspects and implications of the Godhead, and clarity grows exponentially in complexity.

The clarification of something complex cannot be resolved into something simple. Rather, the clarification of something complex is resolved only by minds that can grasp the actual complexity. Not all complexity can be reduced to simplicity. The problem with boiling ideas down is that it leaves only the bones. The flesh, meat, core or crux of the idea is often boiled away.

Analogously, nuclear physics is not for everyone. This is not to say that nuclear physicists are better than anyone else, they are not. It is only to say that people are gifted differently, and that those who exercise their God-given gifts in Christ are in unity through the exercise of those gifts. Christian unity is not a matter of everyone thinking, believing or doing the same things or the same kinds of things. Rather, Christian unity is a matter of various people thinking, believing and doing various things in the conscious service of Jesus Christ. Christ Himself is our unity. Unity is not uniformity of thought, belief or action (1 Corinthians 12:15).

Subscription to a common statement of faith does not create or guarantee Christian unity. Nor does subscription to a common organizational constitution. While Christian unity may involve such subscriptions, the reality of Christian unity requires the actual exercise of common commitment to Christ, primarily the kind of commitment to Christ that will not be broken by the vicissitudes of life and will never abandon the cause of mutual reconciliation in Christ —never, come what may.

The mystery of Christ, which is related to Christian unity, was not unclear to Paul. The vision that God had given him in a moment would take a lifetime to explain—and more! We are still trying to explain it today, some two thousand years later. Nonetheless, it was clear to Paul and I'm sure that he thought or hoped that he could make it clear to others. And he has!

Yet there are people today, and have been throughout history, who don't want to see what Paul saw, who refuse to see it because they hate God (Matthew 6:24), because the reality of God threatens their autonomy (Psalm 2). Such people made every effort to obscure Paul's words and work in Colossae, in Corinth, in Rome, in Ephesus, etc. Everywhere Paul went there were people trying to besmirch his character and smear his testimony in order to undermine his doctrine.

This is the real mystery! This is the source of confusion, the real source of biblical fog and darkness. Jude reported that before the ink was dry on the New Testament, such people had "crept in (to the churches) unnoticed who long ago were designated for this condemnation, ungodly people, who pervert the grace of our God into sensuality and deny our only Master and Lord, Jesus Christ" (Jude 1:4). Such people are still with us!

Paul asked for prayer that an opportunity would come for the Word of God to declare the mystery of Christ through him, through his testimony, that he would speak it clearly as he ought, as he was morally obligated to do. Paul's prayers were answered. He did make the gospel clear. But what we find in his letters is that his efforts to make it clear have been contaminated by the fog of unregenerate analysis. Paul was everywhere and always struggling against false apostles (2 Corinthians 11:13, Revelation 2:2).

The false apostles who railed against Paul were unregenerate, and even degenerate. Nonetheless, these were also people who needed to be reached for Christ. Only God could regenerate them. Paul couldn't. Yet, something needed to be done to counteract the corrosive effects of their denial of the doctrines of Christ that Paul had been preaching.

What could be done? Paul provided an answer. "Walk in wisdom toward outsiders, making the best use of the time" (v. 5). The Authorized Version translated it, "redeeming the time." Redeeming is a much better translation of the Greek (*exagorazō*), which literally means to buy up or ransom, and figuratively to rescue from loss.

DIVISIONS

The first thing to notice about verse 5 is that Paul acknowledged a single division of humanity. Paul had written to the Galatians that Christ had come to put an end to all of our human traditions and divisions. "There is neither Jew nor Greek, there is neither slave nor free, there is no male and female, for you are all one in Christ Jesus" (Galatians 3:28). Christians are one in Christ because they have abandoned all other human classifications and divisions. However, those who have not abandoned those old classifications and divisions are still bound by them. They *will not* let go of them.

Consequently, Christian unity divides humanity into two classifications: believers and unbelievers. Where believers are united in Christ, unbelievers are not, but not because of anything that God or Christianity has done to them. Rather, their exclusion from the people of God is a consequence of their own refusal to acknowledge the truth of their own common humanity in Christ, primarily through ignorance or denial of the reality of the Trinity. Unbelievers are personally responsible for their own unbelief because they willingly refuse to believe.

Nonetheless, Paul would not abandon the hope of reconciliation with the whole world, including unbelievers—especially unbelievers. Not that Paul was trying to unite believers and unbelievers, but that he was trying to help unbelievers become believers, which would then unite them with Christ and with Christ's church. Thus Paul commanded believers to "walk in wisdom toward outsiders" (v. 5). By *walk* Paul meant for Christians to walk the walk, to live the life that Christ had called them to, to deport themselves in a manor worthy of the name Christian, to make every effort to be the people of God, to be full of love, wisdom, faithfulness and charity. Note that Paul did not dismiss or overlook the faithlessness of the unbelievers. He did not dismiss the category of outsiders. He maintained the line of division between believers and unbelievers, but commanded believers to behave in such a way that their lives would invite unbelievers to cross the line.

I'm not suggesting that Paul meant that Christians should not talk about the gospel. Paul never stopped talking about it. But he knew that his talk and his discussions were for believers, for those inside the camp. He knew that those outside the camp would not be swayed by mere talk, but that such talk would need to be inspired and accompanied by the Holy Spirit. He knew that the critical faculties of unbelievers hold believers to a higher standard—and quite rightly so. Believers do have a higher standard.

Christ has set a higher value on simple honesty and integrity than on getting all the doctrines and duties of religion right, because honesty and integrity provide the only possible foundation for the doctrines and duties of faithfulness. If those who profess Christianity are themselves destitute of the practice of truth and honesty, they have nothing of any value to offer unbelievers (or believers, for that matter)—and everyone knows it.

So, when professing Christians are engaged in sin—sexual

immorality, impurity, passion, evil desire, covetousness, idolatry, anger, wrath, malice, slander, obscene talk, quarreling, jealousy, hostility, slander, gossip, conceit, or disorder; not to mention the denial of ultimate truth, the engagement of false images, lying, disregard of authority, murder, theft, extortion, bullying, etc.—they are displaying their own lack of faith, honesty and integrity. Everyone knows that Christians engaged in such things cannot be trusted, and will be much worse off in God's judgment court than unbelievers will be. Paul acknowledged that everyone knows it, but that unbelievers "by their unrighteousness suppress the truth" (Romans 1:18).

The foundation for resistance and the ultimate destruction of such sin—Christian and otherwise—is simple honesty and integrity in all relationships, not just among Christians but universally. First and foremost, honesty and integrity must be exercised in one's relationship with Jesus Christ, and then with other people, all other people. If Christian faithfulness doesn't begin here, it doesn't begin at all.

TIME

Paul also commanded Christians to redeem the time (v. 5). There are two Greek words for time. *Chronos* is sequential time, the kind of time that can be measured with a watch or calendar. In contrast, *kairos* is a fixed or definite period, a season, and suggests an opportune or seasonable period of time. *Chronos* is clock time, undirected time, time without purpose. Whereas *kairos* is directed time. *Kairos* lends itself to historical movement and moments. *Kairos* is purposeful time. The word that Paul used here was *kairos*.

Paul was interested in, not only redeeming the time, but in redeeming the purpose of time, the purpose of history. Paul called the Colossians and all Christians to make use of the purpose of history, to engage wisdom with regard to outsiders—unbelievers. Wisdom is the accumulation of knowledge, and accumulated knowledge produces history. Paul calls Christians to use biblical wisdom, to use the accumulation of knowledge in the light of Christ with regard to their own walk, their own lives, to use biblical wisdom to understand their own place in history. Paul called people to see the historical role of Christianity in world history, and to identify their own place in that history by confessing the truth of Christ and the truth of regeneration in Christ. The distinction between believers and unbelievers pertains to the role of Christianity in history and the role of Christ in one's own life.

CG&O

The role we play is dependent upon our identity, our character. Christian character is always intimately bound up with Christ. He is our role model, our prototype. However, we do not play His role, nor does He play ours. Every role is unique in Christ. No two are ever the same. The better we master our role by being more like Christ, the more authentic, unique, whole and complete we each and all become. *Christos Singularis!*

21

FALSE DICHOTOMY

*Let your speech be always with grace, having been
seasoned with salt, that you may know how you ought to
answer each one. Tychicus, the beloved brother and faithful
minister and fellow-servant in the Lord, will make known
to you all things about me. I sent him to you for this very
purpose, that he might know the things about you, and that
he might comfort your hearts, along with Onesimus, a
faithful and beloved brother, who is one of you. They shall
make known to you all things here. Aristarchus my fellow
prisoner greets you, and Mark, the cousin of Barnabas
(regarding whom you received commandments; if he comes
to you, receive him), and greetings from Jesus, who is
called Justus, those being of the circumcision. These alone
are my fellow-workers for the kingdom of God, who
became a comfort to me.* —Colossians 4:6-11 (ESV)

Here Paul provides instructions about talking, about speech.
Interestingly, the Greek word is *logos*, but unlike John 1:1
the object is not God's speech or God's Word, but ours—human speech. Nonetheless, more than the words are in view.

When Paul said, "Let your speech always be gracious" (v. 6). And
logos indicates, not the mere words, but the logic, structure and perspective behind the words. Human speech always arises out of a context or perspective, and the context or perspective determines the
meaning of the speech. Context refers to the surroundings, circumstances, environment, background, or settings that determine, specify, or clarify meaning. Words are defined with other words in a web
of interrelated meanings. And the specific meanings often depend
upon or issue from a particular situation. The situation is often
assumed because it is shared, or thought to be common to those

involved.

If our speech is to be gracious and salty, our perspective or worldview must also be gracious and salty. Christian talk should be engaging, stimulating and interesting, but not provocative in a worldly way. Rather, in a way that honors God by showing that God is engaging, stimulating and interesting.

By directing our speech Paul intends to direct our person, our character, our identity. We ourselves must be gracious and salty. Christians are to reflect the character of Jesus Christ in engaging, stimulating and interesting ways—but not simply for the sake of stimulation. Rather, our purpose is to illuminate the goodness, truth, and beauty of God.

Most people have a pretty good idea about what it means to be gracious. Mostly Paul means to be under God's grace or filled with God's grace or divinely directed or influenced by God. That influence fills God's people with the saltiness of the fruit of the spirit—love, joy, peace, patience, kindness, goodness, faithfulness, gentleness, and self-control (Galatians 5:22-23) because all "grace and truth came through Jesus Christ" (John 1:17).

Thus, our speech, our perspective, our character, is to be "seasoned with salt" (v. 6). The Greek word (*halas*) literally means salt, but according to Strong's the figurative meaning is prudence. Prudence protects and preserves us from worldly rot. Prudence seasons life. It makes living taste better. The same word for salt was used by Jesus, "You are the salt of the earth, but if salt has lost its taste, how shall its saltiness be restored? It is no longer good for anything except to be thrown out and trampled under people's feet" (Matthew 5:13).

When salt looses its taste, its saltiness, it no longer preserves, protects or seasons. Salt, as Paul used it here, is to be understood figuratively, not literally. The reference is to prudence, which means being cautious, deliberate, consulting, sagacious, and discerning. Salt that has lost its taste is none of these things. Christians who are not prudent are useless and will be cast under foot—ignored and walked on. They will live tasteless lives and be overwhelmed by worldly rot.

BALANCE

Christians are to be filled with and guided by both grace and prudence—charity and caution, kindness and discernment. These two characteristics, graciousness and saltiness, work together to maintain an important balance. Too much grace gets people taken advantage of, and too much prudence keeps them from doing anything. The balance keeps people "wise as serpents and innocent as doves" (Matthew 10:16) in the midst of a sinful world filled with wolves.

The purpose of being guided by grace and prudence is to know how to answer people, how to respond to people. Christianity is all about responding to people, about our interaction with others, about relationships, about love. If we respond too graciously, people will take advantage of us. If we respond too prudently, we will avoid interaction with others. Neither extreme serves the purposes of Christ. So, we are to be prudently gracious, or graciously prudent in all things, neither overly kind nor overly careful.

Paul began closing this letter in verse 7. His closing includes various greetings and acknowledgments by name, adding a personal touch to the letter. This was not merely a kindness, but also served to verify the authenticity of the letter as Paul revealed his knowledge of various people in the Colossian community.

Tychicus, who, with Onesimus, carried this letter to Colossae, would tell them about Paul's activities and affairs. The people needed to know *what* Paul was doing with regard to the wider mission of Christ. But they also needed to know *how* Paul was doing. They needed to hear a third hand account of Paul's faithfulness. Hearing it from Paul was good, but collaborating testimony from a third party would add credibility to Paul's witness. Tychicus would confirm what Paul had been talking about and would add important details and further explanations where questions or concerns would arise.

EXAMPLE

Tychicus was not simply a messenger, but he was a witness, an example who would show them how to be a Christian. He would demonstrate how Christians think and act. They would see in Tychicus the fruit of Paul's ministry, and would be able to imitate Tychicus, as Paul imitated Christ (1 Corinthians 4:16). Paul called him "a beloved brother and faithful minister and fellow servant in the Lord" (v. 7).

In this simple description Paul laid out the essential elements of Christian leadership—brotherliness, faithfulness and service.

Being a leader always means being an example, and being an example always means doing what followers do. It does not mean special preference for the leader, but always means modeling the behavior of the ideal follower. Good leaders do not set themselves apart from others. They do not seek special favors or treatment, but are in unity with those they lead.

The Greek root of *beloved* is *agapē* or unconditional love, but it is not the mere feeling of love. It is also the action and response of love, which is charity. Being regarded as a beloved brother made him family, with all the kindness and commitment that is involved in family relationships—at least that is the ideal. Family relationships always involve responsibility, fellowship and accountability because they are eternal relationships. Friendships can be seasonal, but family relationships are forever. We never stop being a mother, father, brother, sister, aunt, uncle, etc.

Tychicus was also a faithful minister. Being a minister is important. To minister or attend to is to serve. The Greek word is *diakonos*, and we usually associate it with a particular church office. But it isn't always associated with an official office. Scripture uses the word in two ways. One way refers to a particular office, as when Paul spoke of leadership qualifications in 1 Timothy. There Paul was talking about the qualifications for a particular church office.

The word is also used as a verb to indicate the more general activity of Christian service, to which all Christians are called. Paul mentioned Phoebe in this regard (Romans 16:1). Where some individuals are called to serve in the official capacity of the office of Deacon within a specific church, all Christians are called to service, to be engaged in the practical, mundane activities of Christian service to Christ, to the church, to one another and to the world.

Service is the heart of Christianity, and was so indicated when Paul called Tychicus a "fellow servant" (v. 7). Paul did not say that Tychicus was his personal servant, nor a servant of the church, as if his job was to do the bidding of church members. Rather, Tychicus was a fellow servant along with Paul. Paul described himself as a servant or slave of Christ (Romans 1:1). Christ was their common master.

It's not that Christians are merely to be servants to other Christians, but that Christians are fellow servants of Christ. Servants don't simply serve each other, though they help one another and are all blessed by the well-being of the household. But their primary duty is always to serve their master first and foremost (Matthew 23:8).

However, in the case of Christianity, because of the trinitarian nature of the body of Christ, because Christ dwells in the church and in individuals, Christians do serve one another secondarily. That is, our first priority is to serve Christ, and inasmuch as Christ is manifest in and as the body of Christ, Christians also serve fellow Christians. It is important to keep our focus on Christ, so that God's purposes are served and not simply human desires. Jesus spoke of this when He spoke of serving the least of His people in Matthew 25:34-40.

Evangelism

Thirdly, then, Christian service should ideally overflow the boundaries of the church and spill into the neighboring areas. We need to serve God's purposes in the church and God's purposes in the world. Such overflow of service, the activity of Christian love, is also called evangelism. Evangelism is not simply or even primarily a matter of talking to other people about the love of Christ or the gospel of grace. Rather, the leading element of evangelism should be Christian love and service overflowing from the church, from the fellowship, and spilling out into the wider neighborhood. Church members should be so engaged in Christian service—*agapē*, ministries of teaching, healing, counseling, caring, feeding, etc.—that unchurched neighbors are simply swept up in the process.

This was how the early church operated. We often forget that the early church was a church on the run, first fleeing persecution by the Temple officials (Paul led that charge prior to his conversion), then fleeing the destruction of Jerusalem in A.D. 70, and later fleeing Roman persecution. Josephus claims that 1,100,000 people were killed during the siege of Jerusalem, and 97,000 were captured and enslaved. There are no reports about how many people escaped, who fled before, during or after Jerusalem fell. Prior to the siege, Paul encouraged Christians to leave the city. And many did. Nonetheless, with the fall of Jerusalem and the destruction of the Temple, Jews and Christians were involved in a major population migration.

People fled for their lives, they left Jerusalem, and later Rome, for other lands. As a consequence of that migration the early church ministered to the needs of the people and told the story of Jesus, who had predicted the fall of the Temple (Matthew 24:1-2) and the persecution of the church (John 15:20). Those Christians connected the fall of Jerusalem with the coming of Christ. In the midst of that mass migration over many decades—even centuries—the church was established throughout the known world by ministering to those in need, by identifying itself as the body of Christ, and by sharing the stories of Jesus and His people.

This was a church engaged in the birth and development of a culture, a future, that was yet to come. It was not a church reflecting on the losses of the past. The church was focused on the future in the midst of turmoil because Christ's vision for humanity, a vision captured by John on Patmos (Revelation), pulled believers into the culminating purpose of history itself. John's vision, his vision of the purpose (*telios*) of Christ, was the establishment of the kingdom of God on earth (Revelation 21:2). The Spirit of Jesus Christ, who had gone ahead as the leader of His people, was pulling history into the future.

Paul sent Tychicus to Colossae "for this very purpose, that you may know how we are and that he may encourage your hearts" (v. 8). Of course, Tychicus brought this letter to Colossae prior to the destruction of Jerusalem. Paul and others had been aware of the build up of Roman legions and of the preparations for siege. Paul was aware of the political situation as it developed. He could read the signs of the times (Matthew 16:3).

WHO KNOWS

In Verse 8 we find a translation difficulty. The English Standard Version reads, "that you may know how we are." But the English Majority Text (the Greek source of the Authorized Version) reads "that he may know your circumstances." In the older versions Paul wanted Tychicus to learn about their circumstances, and in the newer versions Paul wanted Tychicus to tell them about his circumstances, which he had already recounted in verse 7. I suspect that both are true because communication flows in both directions. Tychicus was the mediator, who would tell them about Paul and hear about them as well.

Tychicus would not simply tell them about Paul's activities and affairs, he would also inquire about their activities and affairs. Communication is a two-way street. Christianity is not simply a matter of sitting in church or hearing the gospel. It is also a matter of response, of interaction with the gospel and with other people.

The work of the pastor, evangelist, missionary or whoever is not sufficient. The gospel message must produce fruit in the lives of those who hear it. The fruit is a matter of both character and behavior, of grace and faith. It produces both a worldview or perspective and various kinds of actions or activities. The gospel of God's grace does produce knowledge, but if that knowledge does not in turn produce various beliefs and behaviors, it is fruitless knowledge. God's Word does not return void because it produces a prosperous effect in the world among those who hear it (Isaiah 55:11). That effect often "speaks" louder than the mere words of the gospel.

Tychicus was also instructed to encourage their hearts. This encouragement (*parakaleō*) was composed of calling, inviting and invoking them to faithfulness. This comfort and encouragement is the work of the Holy Spirit, the Paraclete, in the life of the believer. The primary source of Christian comfort and encouragement issues from regeneration because regeneration brings the Holy Spirit "on line," if you will. This encouragement included imploring, begging, instruction, consolation, comfort, exhortation and prayer. And while the Greek word *kardia* does mean heart, it is not limited to emotions but implies the very center of our human being—our thoughts and desires. The point is that this kind of gospel encouragement was deep, not superficial. It was considered to be of central importance by everyone involved.

USEFUL

Verse 9 introduces Onesimus. Paul had entrusted this letter to the Colossians to the joint care of Tychicus and Onesimus. Onesimus had been a slave who had belonged to Philemon, a wealthy citizen of Colossae and a prominent member of the church there. Onesimus had been a heathen who had defrauded his master, Philemon, by running away from Colossae. He ended up in Rome and came into contact with Paul, who was in Roman custody. Paul had been able to receive visitors and manage his own household because he had proven himself to be trustworthy and responsible to his captors. Somehow Paul came in contact with Onesimus.

While in Rome Onesimus was converted under Paul's tutelage. Onesimus confessed his sin, called upon Christ and sought reparations with his former master, who was also a Christian. Paul then facilitated those reparations between Onesimus and Philemon by sending this letter to Colossae with Tychicus and Onesimus. He also included a personal letter to Philemon, pleading for Philemon's understanding and asking him to treat Onesimus as a fellow believer. Paul went on to say that Tychicus and Onesimus would let the Colossian church know what had happened in Rome. They would tell the Colossians about Paul's imprisonment and Onesimus' conversion in their report about Paul's activities.

Onesimus had returned to the city where it was well known that he had been neither a Christian nor even an honest slave. He voluntarily returned to the master he had run away from. By doing so Onesimus provided his own testimony regarding his changed life as a witness that the gospel was true, that Christ was who He said He was, and that regeneration was real. Onesimus witnessed with his life by willingly returning to his own slavery to face the consequences of his dishonesty in order to demonstrate the reality of his own changed life.

One of the potential consequences was his own execution for the desertion of his post. Onesimus would also need to reimburse his master for the loss of income that resulted from his absence. Thus, Paul wrote to Philemon, "If he has wronged you at all, or owes you anything, charge that to my account" (Philemon 1:18). The potential cost of Onesimus' return was indeed great for both Onesimus and Paul. But this kind of costly evangelism is also effective.

Paul sent Onesimus as a missionary, but he was not sent to a foreign land where he didn't know anyone. He was sent home as a changed man, where everyone had previously known him as a liar and a Pagan and a slave. Paul sent him to those who had known him before his conversion because they would not be able to deny the power of God in Christ through Onesimus. They would see how God had changed Onesimus. They would see his willingness to do what was right even when it cost him dearly.

This kind of witnessing is much more powerful than witnessing to people you don't know and who don't know you. However, if you are going to witness to people who knew you before your conversion, your conversion must be real or it will backfire. It's easy to fool people who don't know you. But it is much more difficult to fool your own family and friends who grew up with you, who knew you when you were a jerk.

Paul mentioned Aristarchus in verse 10. Aristarchus was also mentioned along with Gaius as having been seized by the Ephesians during the riot stirred up by angry silversmiths (Acts 19:29) because of Paul's criticism of their work. Paul accused them of producing idols, which God had forbidden.[76] From that time forward Aristarchus seems to have traveled with Paul. Aristarchus must have been known to the Colossians as well, otherwise mentioning him by name would have been meaningless. Aristarchus may have been a converted silversmith and/or a well-known Pagan whose life had also been changed by Paul. Whatever the case, I suspect that Aristarchus' testimony and changed life were probably similar to that of Onesimus in the sense of having a genuinely changed life.

Paul also mentioned Mark and Barnabas, who also must have been known by the Colossians, and who may have ministered among them. Apparently the Colossians had received instructions from Mark. The last phrase of verse 9 may suggest that Mark was known by reputation. So, Paul asked them to welcome Mark if he showed up.

CIRCUMCISION

Paul's phrase "men of the circumcision" (v. 11) is curious, both interesting and important. He had used the word *Jew* (*Ioudaios*) elsewhere (Colossians 3:11). So why not use it here? It seems that by using this phrase Paul was making a point about something. Justus was Jewish, and the phrase "men of the circumcision" probably indicated his association with those known as the circumcision party. Perhaps Justus was one of those who thought that Christians should become Jews, and be circumcised (Galatians 2:12-ff) as was the Jewish custom.

That was a controversy in which Paul had been involved. Perhaps Justus himself had converted to Judaism or was a Jew of the *diaspora* who had returned to Judaism and thought that all Christians should convert to Judaism. Whatever the case, Paul seems to have identified Justus in this way.

If this is the case—and I think it is—then Paul's admission that the men of the circumcision had "been a comfort to" (v. 9) him may be an important statement about Christian toleration and diversity. Yes, Paul opposed the circumcision party, but I suspect that his opposition did not include breaking fellowship with them—not at this point anyway. This is an important issue.

---

76 See *Acts of Faith—Kingdom Advancement*, Phillip A. Ross, Pilgrim Platform, Marietta, Ohio, 2007, p. 208-ff.

Paul was adamantly opposed to requiring circumcision of Christians, or the host of ceremonies associated with Old Testament faithfulness. "Look," said Paul to the Galatians,

> *if you accept circumcision, Christ will be of no advantage*
> *to you. I testify again to every man who accepts circum-*
> *cision that he is obligated to keep the whole law. You are*
> *severed from Christ, you who would be justified by the*
> *law; you have fallen away from grace. For through the*
> *Spirit, by faith, we ourselves eagerly wait for the hope of*
> *righteousness. For in Christ Jesus neither circumcision*
> *nor uncircumcision counts for anything, but only faith*
> *working through love (Galatians 5:2-6).*

To require circumcision would mean returning to the inferior teaching of the law and abandoning the superior teaching of the Spirit, of grace through faith. And since grace has come through Christ, it would mean the abandonment of Christ, as well. This is a serious issue.

Of this verse (Galatians 5:2) Calvin said,

> *But what is the meaning of this, that Christ will profit*
> *nothing to all who are circumcised? Did Christ profit*
> *nothing to Abraham? Nay, it was in order that Christ*
> *might profit him that he received circumcision. If we say*
> *that it was in force till the coming of Christ, what reply*
> *shall we make to the case of Timothy?*[77] *We must observe,*
> *that Paul's reasoning is directed not so properly against*
> *the outward rite or ceremony, as against the wicked doc-*
> *trine of the false apostles, who pretended that it was a ne-*
> *cessary part of the worship of God, and at the same time*
> *made it a ground of confidence as a meritorious work.*
> *These diabolical contrivances made Christ to profit noth-*
> *ing; not that the false apostles denied Christ, or wished*
> *him to be entirely set aside, but that they made such a di-*
> *vision between his grace and the works of the law as to*
> *leave not more than the half of salvation due to Christ.*
> *The apostle contends that Christ cannot be divided in this*
> *way, and that he 'profiteth nothing,' unless he is wholly*
> *embraced.*[78]

Calvin said that the false apostles made a false division in the

---

77   After arguing against the need for Christians to be circumcised, Paul circumcised Timothy to make him more acceptable to the Jews (Acts 16:3).

78   *Calvin's Commentaries*, Volume XXI, Baker Book House, 1993, p147.

gospel by requiring circumcision and the host of Old Testament ceremonies and practices that were used by the Jews to identify themselves as being faithful to God. These particular false apostles argued that Christianity is a subset of Judaism, such that Christians needed to embrace both Judaism and its ceremonies in order to embrace Christ, that Christ made no sense apart from Judaism.

Paul, on the other hand, argued that Judaism is a subset of Christianity, and that Christianity is the larger concern, a concern for the whole world and not just for the Jewish people. This larger concern had always been part of God's original plan for the salvation of humanity set forth in God's original decree. Paul argued that Judaism made no sense apart from Christ. For Paul, then, circumcision and Judaism's ceremonies were nothing in the light of Christ.

"For in Christ Jesus neither circumcision nor uncircumcision counts for anything, but only faith working through love" (Galatians 5:6). The issue is not circumcision versus uncircumcision, nor ceremonies versus no ceremonies. The issue is not law versus grace. Rather, the issue is that this kind of thinking creates a false dichotomy between circumcision and uncircumcision, between grace and law, between faith and works. Did the Old Testament illuminate the work of Christ? Or did the work of Christ illuminate the Old Testament? Calvin argued that Paul said that such a question posed a false dichotomy, a false division and that Paul would not recognize such a division.

So, it seems that in the light of this concern Paul's remark that Justus and the men of the circumcision had been a comfort to him suggests at the very least that Paul and these men of the circumcision refused to break fellowship over this issue.

The Greek word translated *comfort* (*parēgoria*) here literally means to passionately proclaim one's argument or position in an assembly, not for the purpose of division but for the purpose of unity, and to do in such a way as to bring consolation and comfort. Strong's uses the word *harangue* in its definition, which is correct but archaic. Webster's 1828 dictionary defines harangue as "1. A speech addressed to an assembly or an army; a popular oration; a public address. This word seems to imply loudness or declamation, and is therefore appropriated generally to an address made to a popular assembly or to an army, and not to a sermon, or to an argument at the bar of a court, or to a speech in a deliberative council, unless in contempt." And Paul was not expressing contempt. In the midst of the harangue of the men of the circumcision Paul found consolation and comfort. Consolation and comfort are not anathema. Consolation and comfort suggest continuing fellowship.

Paul, unlike the false apostles, seems to have maintained fellowship with men from both the circumcision camp and the uncircumcision camp. Paul refused to choose between law and grace. Paul knew that the law was of no avail, unless it was perfectly obeyed—and no one could do that, save Christ alone.

Nonetheless, the men of the circumcision argued that some conformity to the law, to the Old Testament, was necessary, but they also argued for the centrality of faith in Christ. Paul acknowledged that salvation was by grace alone, and that they knew that salvation had come through Christ. Yet they continued to struggle with the law, with circumcision and ceremonies. Paul knew that struggle too, which is seen in Romans 7. He knew that the context of Christ was what we call the Old Testament. Christ's advent changed things. It changed some things regarding the Old Testament, but not everything. Neither Christ nor Paul advocated the abandonment of the Old Testament.[79]

Fine, said Paul. *Let's not break fellowship over this issue and continue to work this out together—in Christ.* These men were a comfort to Paul. He found them to be faithful—not perfect, perhaps not ideal, but faithful. And being faithful they would grow in Christ.

This is huge! This has been a central concern within the Christian community for thousands of years. The relationship between law and grace, works and faith, seems to have always been a central concern of Christianity. It was a major concern of the Reformation, and Christians have been arguing about it for a very long time. Perhaps engaging the argument, rather than ending it some day, is part of what it means to be faithful. Perhaps the discussion itself plays an important role in Christian fellowship, orthodoxy and maturity. Indeed, I believe it does, and that discussion and argument of the major concerns of faithfulness and orthodoxy are necessary for Christian maturity.

Thus, to forbid discussion of unorthodox concerns among church members is detrimental to sanctification. Christ has no fear that false belief will win His people to the "dark side." He knows full well that the light of His revelation must penetrate and dispel all darkness. Indeed, it is the absence of discussion that allows the

---

79 See *Rock Mountain Creed—Jesus' Sermon on the Mount,* Phillip A. Ross, Pilgrim Platform, Marietta, Ohio, 2011.

darkness to remain dark.

Indeed, wrestling with the deep issues is a necessary part of faithfulness. This issue, the relationship between law and grace, between faith and works, has never been resolved in such a way that all Christians have agreed. It wasn't then and it isn't now. And yet Paul refused to break fellowship over it. The truth is that unless Christian fellowship is maintained among those who differ over this issue (and others), the issue itself cannot be resolved. Resolution of the issue requires ongoing discussion within the bounds of common commitment to Christ because new Christians are always in the churches.

This is not to suggest that churches or church leaders should ever embrace unorthodox teaching. Clearly, no one should, but not everyone knows better. The heart of Christianity is instruction and education. It does, however, mandate that local churches and their leaders must be well-informed in the areas of Christian theology and history, and that they must be willing to both take a particular theological position and be willing to adjust and/or abandon that position when presented with a better, more biblical and faithful position. It means that Christian leaders must never pronounce or suggest that some view is anathema without solid support from their own churches, associations and denominations.

The trinitarian character of Jesus Christ and of His churches means that there cannot be Lone Ranger Christians who operate without support and authorization from their church bodies. The beliefs and doctrines of Christianity must be held in common. The individual and corporate character of the churches must function in harmony. And apart from formal declaration of anathema, all baptized Christians should be welcome in all Christian churches. Indeed, anyone who claims to be a Christian has put themselves under the covenant of God in Jesus Christ, and put the burden of proof upon themselves.

Formal church membership is simply the corporate acknowledgment of the reality and jurisdiction of God's covenant upon members. While elders are to work productively to keep false believers from false belief, it is the work of the Holy Spirit to enforce God's covenant in Christ. Thus, the Holy Spirit both works from within believers through their regeneration, and works without unbelievers through their damnation. And both areas of the Spirit's work serve the glory of God in Christ.

Yes, of course, such a position of grace, mercy and toleration will bring struggle and strife to the churches, but that struggle and strife is the engine of both enthusiasm for the faith and sanctification in the faith. And the curtailment of theological struggle and strife sucks the life and vitality out of congregations.

So, maintaining fellowship serves its final resolution, if there is a final resolution. And if there isn't, it serves the discussion and contributes to sanctification and maturity. If the point of the argument is not its final resolution but our ongoing sanctification, fellowship must be maintained in the midst of differences. In fact, it may be that the differences are the engines of sanctification that drive us deeper into Scripture.

The ultimate solution to this conundrum is likely to be trinitarian. The *solas* of the Refomation stand together, not alone. *Sola Scriptura* (Scripture Alone), *Solus Christus* (Christ Alone), *Sola Gratia* (Grace Alone), *Sola Fide* (Faith Alone) and *Soli Deo Gloria* (God's Glory Alone). How can they stand alone together? Because they stand in the singularity of God. *Christos Singularis!*

22

CLOSING

Epaphras, who is one of you, a servant of Christ Jesus, greets you, always struggling on your behalf in his prayers, that you may stand mature and fully assured in all the will of God. For I bear him witness that he has worked hard for you and for those in Laodicea and in Hierapolis. Luke the beloved physician greets you, as does Demas. Give my greetings to the brothers at Laodicea, and to Nympha and the church in her house. And when this letter has been read among you, have it also read in the church of the Laodiceans; and see that you also read the letter from Laodicea. And say to Archippus, "See that you fulfill the ministry that you have received in the Lord." I, Paul, write this greeting with my own hand. Remember my chains. Grace be with you. —*Colossians 4:12-18 (ESV)*

Epaphras was the founder of the Colossian church (Colossians 1:7), and probably many of the other churches in the Lycus valley. Paul referred to him as "our beloved fellow-servant," who was "a faithful minister of Christ" (Colossians 1:7), and "a servant of Christ Jesus" (v. 12). Clearly, Epaphras was one of the more significant saints of the earliest church who labored with Paul for the gospel. Epaphras may have been originally from Colossae ("one of you"), and perhaps that was why he was "always struggling on your (their) behalf in his prayers" (v. 12).

Paul's commendation of Epaphras' prayers set the bar for faithful pastors, who are to be engaged in prayer on behalf of their people. The marginal or optional translation of the word *struggle* (*agōnizomai*) is striving or agonizing. What was the content of his prayers? "That you (they) may stand mature and fully assured in all the will of

God" (v. 12). This tells us that a pastor's concern is to be for the maturity and assurance of his people as they engage the will of God —all of it, not just some of it.

There is a sequence or process that is described here. Prayer leads to maturity. Maturity leads to assurance "in all the will of God" (v. 12). And this assurance leads to personal conformity to the very will of God. Although this particular verse says that Epaphras was praying for the Colossians, we can extrapolate a general application that the method for Christian development leads from prayer to maturity to assurance to the engagement of the will of God, from prayer to service. Indeed, all Christians are to embark on this journey, not just those who are interested in Christian leadership, because all Christians are called to leadership of one kind or another. At the very least, all parents are called to be Christian leaders for their children.

FERVENT

It all begins with prayer, and that prayer needs to be both fervent and laborious. The Greek word (*agōnizomai*) is used several times and it will be worthwhile to explore what it means:

- to strive, "Strive to enter through the narrow door" (Luke 13:24),
- to fight, "My kingdom is not of this world. If my kingdom were of this world, my servants would have been fighting, that I might not be delivered over to the Jews" (John 18:36), "Fight the good fight of the faith" (1 Timothy 6:12), and "I have fought the good fight, I have finished the race, I have kept the faith" (2 Timothy 4:7),
- to exercise self control, "Every athlete exercises self-control in all things" (1 Corinthians 9:25),
- to struggle, "For this I toil, struggling with all his energy that he powerfully works within me" (Colossians 1:29).

This kind of prayer is not simply what we usually think of as prayer, but is what Paul referred to when he said to "pray without ceasing" (1 Thessalonians 5:17). Of this verse Albert Barnes wrote,

> *we are to maintain an uninterrupted and constant spirit of prayer. We are to be in such a frame of mind as to be ready to pray publicly if requested; and when alone, to improve any moment of leisure which we may have when we feel ourselves strongly inclined to pray. That Christian is in a*

bad state of mind who has suffered himself, by attention to worldly cares, or by light conversation, or by gaiety and vanity, or by reading an improper book, or by eating or drinking too much, or by late hours at night among the thoughtless and the vain, to be brought into such a condition that he cannot engage in prayer with proper feelings. There has been evil done to the soul if it is not prepared for communion with God at all times, and if it would not find pleasure in approaching his holy throne."[80]

To pray without ceasing cannot mean that we are to be on our knees twenty-four hours a day. Nor can it mean that we are to be exclusively engaged in prayer every moment. Rather, it means that we must develop a habit of prayer or communication with God such that we are continually online with Him, such that we are in continual conversation with Him. Everyone has an internal dialog that we call thinking. That voice in our heads runs pretty much all the time. Sometimes we talk out loud about our thoughts, but we are always thinking. At night it kicks into dream mode, but it's always running.

Sometimes we don't remember our dreams or even what we have been thinking about. But Paul here calls us to engage this process consciously and continuously, to think intentionally about God, to converse with God with that inner voice all the time. This is the only way that we can pray without ceasing. We must continually engage God as our inner conversation partner, and lift things up in prayer, not just when we are vocally or privately praying but all the time. At times our prayer will be a harangue toward God like that of the persistent widow (Luke 18:1-8). This is what we are to strive for, to fight for, to exercise self-control for, to struggle for. We are to be fervently engaged in this kind of prayer, emotionally occupied with God. It is to be a top priority, something that is never forgotten or left behind. This is what is sometimes called conscience.

This is where the practice of faithfulness begins. But it doesn't end here. It doesn't end with prayer. It begins with prayer. Prayer requires a relationship with the Lord and leads to maturity (*teleios*), to perfection, fullness, wholeness. This kind of prayer leads to wholeness and completeness because it connects us to God, and God is our wholeness, our completeness. Only in God, in Christ, are we complete human beings. God fills the emptiness of our anxiety. God gives direction to our purposelessness. God gives

---

80 *Notes on the Bible*, Albert Barnes, 1 Thessalonians 5:17, www.eSword.net.

reason (justification) to our existence.

People are not whole, not complete, not mature or perfect apart from God. In the same way that a husband or wife makes us complete through covenantal participation and emotional connection, so God makes us complete through covenantal participation in the body of Christ (the church) and through spiritual connection—first with Christ (or in Christ) and then with God's people.

GREAT LIE

One of the great lies of this age is that people are individuals apart from Christ.[81] We are not, not entirely! We think we are until we come to Christ, until we find our deeper identity in Christ through the trinitarian character of God. Apart from Christ there is a very high cost for people to continue to think of themselves as individuals. That cost is death. What do I mean?

The most basic requirement of human life requires the ability of self-replication or reproduction. Individuals are not self-replicating. Individuals cannot reproduce. Reproduction requires a male and a female. There can be no individuals without the larger reality of humanity as a social organism. This is the conundrum that God's Trinity alone satisfies. I am always a we because there is no I apart from we. If people stopped reproducing humanity would die out as a species. God has provided the means, structure and order for the process of human reproduction, for human life on this earth.

God's order is called the family, and it rests upon a covenant—a promise, an agreement, a commitment. People often mistakenly think that this covenant is or must be between one man and one woman because reproduction requires one man and one woman, but there is more to it than that. We call it a marriage covenant, but there is more to it than what most people usually think.

God gave this covenant to Adam and Eve in the garden (Genesis 1:28). At first, Adam had no "helper fit for him" (Genesis 2:20). He was incomplete, he was not *teleios*, not whole, not self-sufficient. Apart from Eve humanity would have died out with Adam. Adam, as an individual, was not able to reproduce. In order for humanity to live in time, on this earth, reproduction is necessary. Again, apart from reproduction, humanity will die out as a biblical kind. Thus, one unit of humanity is composed of a male and a

---

81 For more on this theme see *Arsy Varsy—Reclaiming the Gospel in First Corinthians*, by Phillip A. Ross, Pilgrim Platform, Marietta, Ohio, 2009, "Compartmentalization," p. 107.

female. That is the most basic element of the human kind because it is self-replicating. People can and do deny this, but the denial of God's truth does not make it any less true.

There is another essential element involved in reproduction, in families. God is the creator and author of life itself, including human life. People can copulate, but only God can create life. People can stop life, end life, thwart life, frustrate life, interfere with life, abort life and prevent life. But we cannot create life. Because God is the creator and author of life, and the creator and author of marriage and families, God is always necessarily involved in marriage and family life, even when people ignore or deny His presence. God orders it.

He provides the context in which life—marriage and families—can exist. He provides the context or circumstance for human life to flourish, which is to say that God is the foundation upon which the marriage covenant rests, and that apart from that foundation human life will be less than *teleios*, less than perfect, less than whole, less than complete, less than God intends. Indeed, apart from God, who is the Creator and Sustainer of life, death prevails (Proverbs 8:36).

The point is that God is a covenant partner in all marriage. He is always the superior partner. The central human covenant is not marriage between one man and one woman, but is between one man, one woman and the One God who is the creator and author of life itself.[82] The covenant is trinitarian (Colossians 2:10). It provides for human individuality, human corporality, and human eternality (or human sustainability). It is not that God's covenant with man is simply *like* a marriage covenant, but that God's covenant with man, with humanity, is bound to the process and the fruit of human reproduction. Human reproduction requires one man, one woman and the One God who is creator and author of life itself. Out of these three comes one. The three are one in unity, in Christ. The three are one.

Epaphras prayed that all Christians "may stand mature (*teleios*) and fully assured in all the will of God" (v. 12). Through prayer Christ's church, Christ's people, are able to stand mature, to stand in God's covenant. From the practice of so standing, we are

---

82 The central covenant is between God and man in Christ. The New Covenant through Jesus Christ is intended to be between God and humanity. See the James Jordan footnote, p. 11. Marriage is the central human to human covenant, and reflects the fact that all covenants exist in the context of Christ's covenant.

able to be fully assured (Colossians 2:2). The Greek word (*plēroō*), translated here as *fully assured*, is used ninety times in the New Testament, and it means:

- to be fulfilled, "All this took place to fulfill (to fully assure) what the Lord had spoken by the prophet" (Matthew 1:22),
- to be filled, "And the child grew and became strong, filled (fully assured) with wisdom. And the favor of God was upon him" (Luke 2:40),
- to be finished, "After he had finished (fully assured) all his sayings in the hearing of the people, he entered Capernaum" (Luke 7:1),
- to accomplish, "who appeared in glory and spoke of his departure, which he was about to accomplish (fully assure) at Jerusalem" (Luke 9:31),
- to be fully come, "for my time has not yet fully come (is not yet fully assured)" (John 7:8),
- etc.

You get the idea. This full assurance is the purpose, fulfillment and consummation of our covenant with God.

We're not done with this verse yet, "That you may stand mature and fully assured in all the will of God" (v. 12) It is not simply maturity or assurance, but the maturity and assurance that *comes from engagement with the will of God*. The way that we know the will of God is through this kind of prayer that Paul was talking about.

The kind of prayer that strives to enter through the narrow gate, the kind of prayer that fights the good fight of faith, that exercises self-control, that struggles "with all his energy that he powerfully works within" (Colossians 1:29) us. Engage this and the will of God will be made manifest in you because this is the will of God.

Epaphras knew what Paul knew. He knew the will of God because he stood mature and fully assured in the will of God through prayer. Paul said, "For I bear him witness that he has worked hard for you and for those in Laodicea and in Hierapolis" (v. 13). Epaphras was a model Christian because he modeled or imitated Paul (1 Corinthians 4:16). If Paul was an evangelist, and Paul is our model, then we are to be evangelists, we are to engage the evangel—the gospel—as Paul engaged it.

GREETINGS

Paul was near the end of this letter, and needed to express love and greetings from others who had asked him to do so. "Luke the beloved physician greets you, as does Demas" (v. 14). He also wanted to express his love and concern for others he knew that they had contact with. "Give my greetings to the brothers at Laodicea, and to Nympha and the church in her house" (v. 15). By mentioning two other churches, he insured that those churches would know about this letter. Paul was well aware that the churches he dealt with had common problems and that it would benefit all the churches to read and study his letters. This was not a function of pride for Paul, but was more the simple realization of his position, leadership, ability and stature among the churches.

Nympha should be translated *Nymphas*. John Gill noted the correction. He said that those unskilful in the Greek language, have taken the word to suggest a woman. But it is a contraction of Nymphios, or Nymphidios, or Nymphodoro .[83]

Notice also that Nymphas (Authorized Version) hosted a church in his house. Calvin comments,

> *When he speaks of the Church which was in the house of Nymphas, let us bear in mind, that, in the instance of one household, a rule is laid down as to what it becomes all Christian households to be—that they be so many little Churches. Let every one, therefore, know that this charge is laid upon him—that he is to train up his house in the fear of the Lord, to keep it under a holy discipline, and, in fine (lastly—ed.), to form in it the likeness of a Church.*[84]

Clearly Calvin was not arguing against local churches. No one spoke more highly of the church than Calvin. The point is not to abandon churches, but to make them more common by doing in the home what was also to be done in the church. According to Calvin home life should be practice for church life or social life. What was learned at home would be practiced in the church and in society at large. The home was where character and morals were inculcated.

"And when this letter has been read among you, have it also read in the church of the Laodiceans; and see that you also read the letter from Laodicea" (v. 16). Here we see the beginning of the New Testament. Paul recommended that this letter be read at the Laodicean church, and by implication at others. Because there were

83 *John Gill's Exposition of the Entire Bible*, Colossians 4:15, eSword.net.
84 *Calvin's Commentaries*, XXI, Baker House, Grand Rapids, Michigan, 1993, p. 230.

common problems and situations in the churches, and especially in neighboring churches where the social context was similar Paul's advice and counsel would have wide application.

In the same way, he wanted the Colossians to read a letter that he had received from Laodicea. This letter has been lost. Vincent reported that the extant *Epistle to the Laodicaeans* is a late and obvious forgery that pretends to be Paul's letter to Laodicea.[85] Paul was more likely talking about a letter that he had received from Laodicea. Nothing is known about it. Nonetheless, the churches did find that Paul's letters and a few others were quite helpful, and they began collecting them and making copies for other churches who undoubtedly requested them. Again, this was the beginning of the collection of literature that is known as the New Testament.

"And say to Archippus, 'See that you fulfill the ministry that you have received in the Lord'" (v. 17). Speculation suggests that Archippus was Philemon's son, and that he held some office in the church. The Greek indicates that he may have been a Deacon. Paul's language then suggests that Archippus was not as motivated as Paul thought he ought to be. Or perhaps someone had reported this lack of motivation to Paul. You know how church people complain.

At any rate, Paul tried to chastise, encourage and/or inspire Archippus to take a greater interest in and responsibility for his ministry. Paul knew that once God grabs a person, He doesn't let go. The thing to notice here is how public Paul's counsel was. This letter was to be read by and spread among the churches in the area, and Archippus had been named as a potential shirker of his responsibility. Paul was not afraid to name names in public as a way to encourage better behavior.

BONDAGE & GRACE

Finally Paul wrote, "I, Paul, write this greeting with my own hand. Remember my chains. Grace be with you" (v. 18). Certainly Paul could write. He was highly educated, and a competent scholar of his day. But did he actually "write" his letters to the churches. Language like we have here in verse 18 and similar language in Paul's other letters (First Corinthians, Galatians, Second Thessalonians and Philemon) suggest that he didn't actually do the writing

---

85 *Vincent's Word Studies in the New Testament,* Marvin R. Vincent, Hendrickson Publishers, 1985.

himself. Romans 16:22 even includes a greeting from the secretary who actually did that writing.

We should think of Paul's letters as being published rather than being written. When Paul sent a letter to a church it was for public consumption. I imagine that Paul, being a scholar and a student of the Bible and of culture as well, read and wrote a lot (2 Timothy 4:13). That's what scholars do. Nonetheless, when it came time to send a letter he probably had a scribe who was skilled in calligraphy do the actual writing or publishing for public use.

Whatever else that Paul wrote, other than the few letters collected in the New Testament, has been lost or destroyed. Paul was hated by many people. He suffered much persecution and difficulty. He often fled for his life from one town to another. Undoubtedly, whatever had been captured by his enemies was undoubtedly destroyed. So, it's not surprising that we have only a few letters that have been assiduously preserved and protected by the churches.

This last verse is Paul's signature, written in his own hand as a method of authentication. Paul's final words of this letter were about bondage and grace. He probably had Onesimus in mind. Why Onesimus? First, taking this letter to Colossae was a mission trip for Onesimus. We might even say that one of the purposes of this letter was to provide Onesimus with an opportunity to testify to the truth of the gospel by demonstrating Paul's message in the flesh. Onesimus was returning to his slave master as a new man in Christ —born again, regenerated—and willing to make amends for his errors and former ways, and to do so publicly as a mission and a ministry.

Not only was Onesimus a slave who found freedom in Christ, but Paul was also in bondage, in prison in Rome. Paul's situation was not much different from that of Onesimus. They were both men who had been prisoners to sin, who had been freed in Christ only to be in bondage again because of their freedom in Christ.

Paul had the highest regard for Onesimus. Interestingly, Paul and Onesimus shared bondage and grace. They both had known the bondage of slavery to sin, and joy of freedom in grace through faith in Christ. "Remember my chains. Grace be with you. Amen" (v. 18).

Paul had bondage on his mind because he wrote from Rome where he was a prisoner. He sent a runaway slave home to his master in order to testify to the power of God's grace. Bondage and grace filled Paul's final thoughts. I can imagine Paul thinking as he wrote these last two thoughts, in spite of his bondage, in spite of his gospel bonds, his "bonds in Christ (that were) manifest in all the palace, and in all other places" (Philippians 1:13), in spite of all of that, God's grace prevailed. It prevailed for him, and it prevailed for Onesimus. Grace trumped bondage—that's the message of the gospel in a nutshell. God's grace unlocks human bondage. God's grace conquers bondage to sin.

Christos Singularis!

APPENDIX

Look at this photo from across the room to see an optical illusion.

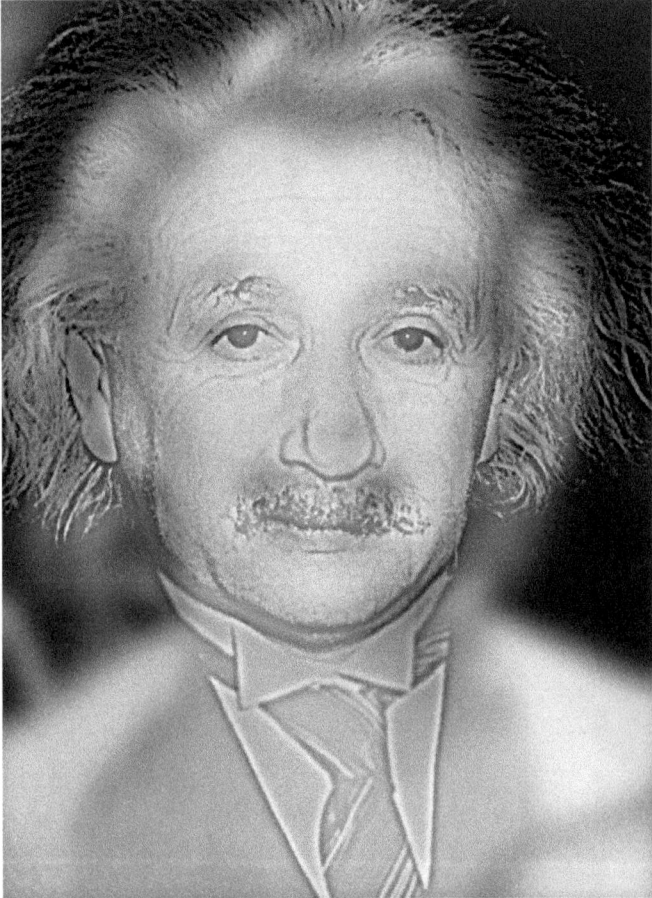

Scripture Index

Alphabetical Index

BOOKS BY PHILLIP A. ROSS

IT'S ABOUT TIME!—THE TIME IS NOW

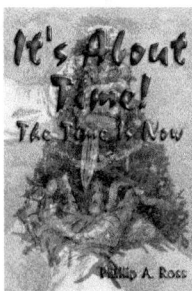

40 pages. 2008.

This book is about thinking about God, the gospel, and Jesus Christ. We all need to make more time to do that. It is for the Mid-Ohio River Valley, but it is also for every valley where people live. It comes to a valley perspective from a valley perspective. This booklet is not about a mountaintop experience nor is it from a mountaintop perspective. Rather, it is from the "street," down in the valley where people actually live. It is not sad or morose, but it is serious—and it's about sin, yours and mine. It is an invitation to think more deeply about the things that we deeply care about, the things we believe. It's about Jesus.

These essays were originally written in 1998 as a short sermon series during Advent. They are not the usual Advent presentation of well-worn platitudes and biblical pablum. Unlike too many of my peers, I can't stomach that kind of stuff. To me, warm milk not only tastes bad, but it makes me sleepy.

This booklet is about the time in which we live. Hopefully, you will find it to be timely in your own life, as well. Time is a funny thing. We all live in it. Most of us are slaves to it, driven by appointments and schedules that must be kept. Asking people to think about time is like asking a fish to think about water—with one important difference. As far as we know, fish can't think at all, at least not in the way that we define thinking. I will ask you to think about time, about how much time you have, how much you need, and what you do with it.

ENGAGEMENT—ESTABLISHING RELATIONSHIP IN CHRIST

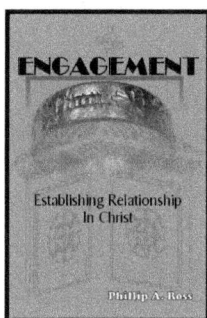

104 pages, 1996, 2008.

The material in this book is not my usual fare, but was an attempt to put my best understanding of Scripture and salvation in Christ into a succinct format for a church that did not know me. It is not a expositional book study, but is more of a topical study intended to speak to the needs of contemporary people by uncovering various biblical truths and at the same time revealing various contemporary misunderstandings about the Bible and salvation.

As you will come to understand, it created quite a stir among those who heard it. But it did not generate church renewal or revival, at least not in the way that anyone would notice, not in what are considered to be the measures of renewal and revival. Rather, many hearers found it quite disturbing, and I then found myself in defensive mode as it seems to have raised more questions that it answered.

What you will see here is a synopsis of the historic, Protestant, Reformed position. If it seems unusual it is more likely because this theological position has been all but abandoned by the vast majority of contemporary Christians and their churches over the past 20, 50 or 100 years, depending on where you live and what circles you fellowship in.

THE BIG TEN—A STUDY OF THE TEN COMMANDMENTS

105 pages, 2001, 2008.

We live in an age of increasing lawlessness. It is not simply that there is a void of law, far from it. Quite the opposite is actually true. There is an overwhelming preponderance of laws, the size, scope and complexity of which world has never before seen. The body of law for any modern country, and in particular the United States—the most litigious society in history—is phenomenal.

So, how can I say that we live in an age of increasing lawlessness?

What is in view here is not human law, but God's law. Just to speak the phrase brings a chill upon many a backbone. People don't like to talk about God's law. To do so is to be branded a fundament- alist, legalist, theonomist and/or extremist, all in the most vile sense of the words. For the most part contemporary Christians believe that they have arrived at a time in history that is beyond the application of any Old Testament laws, and in many cases, a time that is beyond all biblical law. People have converted the gospel of grace to mean a gospel without law—without obligation or respons- ibility.

The good news that is preached in too many pulpits today is lawlessness, couched in terms of a gospel of positive thinking, of upbeat moralisms intended to make life better, richer, fuller, more meaningful, and happier. In order to justify the human distaste for biblical law, people—Christians among them—no longer speak of God's law or the human obligation to it, not even in Bible study or worship.

However, the Bible is not a divided witness. It is a whole, a unity. God's Word, God's testimony is completely true.

THE WISDOM OF JESUS CHRIST IN THE BOOK OF PROVERBS

414 pages, 2006.

This study of Proverbs is an attempt to uncover the biblical message of Proverbs verse by verse in the light of Jesus Christ. We can- not pretend to be other than Christians who live on the redemption side of the Cross, while Proverbs was written on the anticipation side of the Cross. Nonetheless, the Christian faith is founded on the eternal consistency of God. God does not change. The God of Solomon, the author (and editor) of Proverbs, is the same God spoken of in the New Testament. In fact, the God of Solomon is Jesus Christ by the power of the Holy Spirit. Thus, the present work acknowledges this fact of faith and applies it by read- ing Proverbs in the light of Jesus Christ.

MARKING GOD'S WORD—UNDERSTANDING JESUS

324 pages, 2006.

Contemporary Western churches are a wreck, regardless of denominational affiliation or lack thereof. Mainline churches have been in serious decline for 50 years. The so-called contemporary churches are simply picking up transfer growth from other churches. Saying that there is a problem is one thing, but clearly defining the problem is something else. That something else is the subject of Marking God's Word. Clearly, there is much confusion in and out of the church about Christianity. Is confusion about the gospel of Jesus Christ new to the Modern and/or Postmodern world? That is the question that has haunted this treatment of Mark. *Marking God's Word* will help you see the gospel with new eyes, from a perspective that is obscured by sin and selfishness. Yet, this is not a new perspective. Rather, it is an old perspective that has a long and noble history of reformation and revival. Come, see Christ again, for the first time.

ACTS OF FAITH—KINGDOM ADVANCEMENT

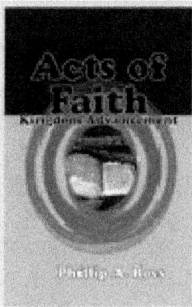

326 pages, 2007.

Acts of the Apostles continues the story of Jesus after His death. The story of the misunderstanding of the gospel among those who person-ally knew Jesus continues in the ministry of Paul. Paul, who was knocked off his high horse and thrown to the ground against his will and born again by the power of the Holy Spirit, came to see that he had been completely blind, and had his eyes miraculously opened. Paul – formerly the chief enemy of Christ, who became the chief disciple—took up the ministry and perspective of Jesus and began preaching the message of Christ to anyone who would listen. But Paul had the same difficulties that Jesus had—people thought he was crazy, that he didn't know what he was talking about, that he had gotten the gospel mes-sage wrong. Paul was hounded to death by the enemies of Christ, just as Jesus had been. Again, what is discovered in Acts of Faith is not a new perspective on Paul, but a very old one—the forgotten perspective of God's remnant.

INFORMAL CHRISTIANITY—REFINING CHRIST'S CHURCH

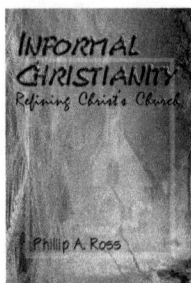

136 pages, 2007.

Informal Christianity reviews the personal and informal realities involved in a personal relationship with Jesus Christ that provide the foundation of Christianity. Where the internal and subjective realities of regeneration are absent from the lives of church members, churches find themselves on a foundation of sand. Such churches turn away from the heart of Christianity—doctrine and theology—to focus on peripheral concerns of administration and maintenance. Christians and churches that do not enthusiastically embrace biblical doctrine and theology as the life-blood of faithfulness, tend to spend their time and energy polishing the outside of the cup (Matthew 23:25). Such efforts concern themselves with church growth—noses and nickels—rather than Christian maturity (Ephesians 4:13).

Informal Christianity aims to drive a nail through the heart of such trivial indulgence on the part of those who fail to live up to the potential of their Christian calling because such a failure amounts to the denial of the power and presence of the Holy Spirit in their own lives. Yes, the flesh is weak, no one is disputing that. But "the spirit indeed is willing" (Matthew 26:41). Christians "receive power when the Holy Spirit has come upon" (Act 1:8) them. Such power is the "strength that God supplies" (1 Peter 4:11). To wallow in administrative trivialities is to deny the power of God (Mark 12:24) and to deny one's citizenship in the Kingdom of God.

While great effort is being poured into the administrative expansion of churches (church growth), the very heart of personal faithfulness is being ignored, denied, denigrated and trivialized by the very principles that have been adopted to generate such growth. The proper priorities and first things (Matthew 6:33) are giving way to the "wisdom of men" (1 Corinthians 2:5). Informal Christianity cuts through the trees that have become veritable logs in the eyes of contemporary Christians to reveal again the forest of faithfulness in which the life of Christianity dwells.

PRACTICALLY CHRISTIAN—APPLYING JAMES TODAY

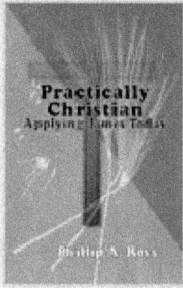

135 pages, 2006.

Practically Christian offers a fresh and insightful application of the ancient Christian epistle of James to the contemporary American Evangelical world. Against the Antinomian backdrop of a Christianity shaped by the Church Growth Movement, Practically Christian puts teeth into Christianity, pressing for a practical realism in order to re-store some theological balance and sanity to the practice of the faith.

"Practically Christian offers a fresh and insightful application of the ancient Christian epistle to the contemporary American evangelical world. Against the Antinomian backdrop of a Christianity shaped by the church growth movement, Ross puts teeth into Christianity, pressing for a practical realism in order to restore some theological balance and sanity. His book is by no means dull reading or trite, but is replete with fresh anecdotes illustrating the salient points he is conveying. I found his exposition of James 1:2-4 to be especially instructive and profound, and on that basis alone the book was worth reading. Ross's commitment to Reformed doctrine is quite obvious throughout. Many parts of the book I wish I had written myself!" —David C. Brand, Pastor and author

ARSY VARSY—RECLAIMING THE GOSPEL

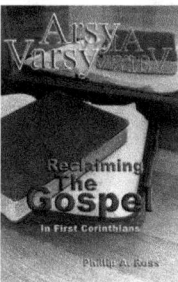

399 pages, 2008.

"Corinth was a city of wealth and culture, seated at the crossroads of the Roman Empire, where all the trade and commerce of the empire passed through. It was a city of beauty, a resort city, located in a very beautiful area, but it was also a city of prostitution and of passion. It was devoted to trade and commerce, but also to the worship of the goddess of sex" (*The Corinthian Crisis*, by Ray Steadman).

Paul had a problem with the Christians at Corinth. They were a large, successful church. They were growing leaps and bounds. They thought they were doing great. But not Paul. Paul found that they had substituted the wisdom of the world (the philosophy and culture of the Greeks) for the wisdom of Christ (the philosophy and culture of the Bible). This volume contrasts the folly of Greek (and ultimately modern American) worldly wisdom with the gospel of Christ. Stones are turned over and small-minded creatures that thrive in the dark scatter in the light of Christ.

Ross brings Paul's struggle to light with clarity and passion that leaves the worldly no where to hide in this panoptic treatment to First Corinthians.

VARSY ARSY—PROCLAIMING THE GOSPEL IN SECOND CORINTHIANS

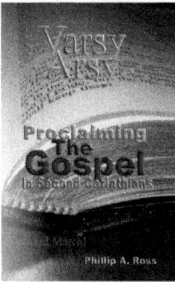

356 pages, 2009.

Paul continued the same thrust of his criticism and correction in his Second Letter to the Corinthians, apparently because the same problems continued to dog the church. Paul's Second Letter is more personal as he ramped up the tone and clarity of his criticism. At one point he thought that he may have overstepped the bounds of propriety and apologized for his curtness—but not for his correction. Personal attacks against Paul, against him personally and the style and content of his ministry, had continued. So, Paul addressed them with clarity and severity.

The Jews and the Greeks provided substantial difficulties for Paul's ministry. But worse than those who had blatantly refused to conform to the light of Christ were those who disguised themselves as apostles of Christ, those who thought that they were helping the cause of Christianity by redefining it to fit into their own ill-conceived ideas. Apparently, the errant Corinthian leaders had been involved in these kinds of creative adaptations of the gospel. As much as Jesus had opposed the Pharisees, Paul opposed the false apostles. Both were guilty of perverting the doctrines and wisdom of Scripture.

Before we think that this idea is impossible because it is so outrageous, we need to realize that this *modus operandi* is not at all unusual. Satan's methodology has always been to counterfeit the truth because he has no truth or light himself. Satan goes the extra mile to make his wisdom look like Christ's wisdom—and many people are fooled by it (Matthew 24:24, 2 John 1:7), "as the serpent deceived Eve by his cunning" (2 Corinthians 11:3). It's the same old same old, a different instance of the same thing.

Against this backdrop, Paul clarified and reclaimed the true gospel, bringing to light many of the common errors that continue to haunt the church in our own day.

THE WORK AT ZION—A RECKONING

Two-volume set, 772 pages, 1996.

The Work at Zion is the journal of a spiritual conversion that turned a ministry upside down. This collection of sermons details a preacher's rediscovery of classic, historical, Protestant Christianity in the midst of apathy and apostasy. The logical conclusion of modern Christianity is brought to a head and set in stark contrast to God's Word.

Sin is always the key to receiving Jesus. When people do not believe themselves to be sinners, they perceive no need for Jesus. The modern secular world has done everything it can to eradicate sin from modern awareness. Secular psychologists and educators insist that sin is outdated, that the doctrine of the Fall overly emphasizes the negative, to the detriment of personal self-esteem... But this modern, secular theory runs directly counter to the teaching and testimony of scripture. Scripture shows us that the confession of personal sinfulness is a prerequisite for salvation in Christ.

Books may be purchased through the various Internet bookstores, www.pilgrim-platform.org or through your local bookstore.